गुरु

GURU

THE UNIVERSAL TEACHER

गुरु

GURU

THE UNIVERSAL TEACHER

SWAMI B.P. PURI

FOREWORD BY
SWAMI B.B. BODHAYAN

MANDALA
PUBLISHING
San Rafael, California

MANDALA
PUBLISHING

PO Box 3088
San Rafael, CA 94912
www.mandalaearth.com
info@mandala.org

Find us on Facebook: www.facebook.com/mandalaearth
Follow us on Twitter: @mandalaearth

Library of Congress Cataloging-in-Publication Data available.

ISBN: 978-1-68383-132-7

Special thanks to Kaisori Bellach, Pandita Geary, Paul Sherbow, and Swami B.S. Narayan.

Readers interested in the subject matter should visit the Gopinath Gaudiya Math website at www.gopinathgaudiyamath.com or write to:

Ishodyan, Sri Mayapur
District Nadia, West Bengal
India, Pin: 741313

ROOTS of PEACE REPLANTED PAPER

Mandala Publishing, in association with Roots of Peace, will plant two trees for each tree used in the manufacturing of this book. Roots of Peace is an internationally renowned humanitarian organization dedicated to eradicating land mines worldwide and converting war-torn lands into productive farms and wildlife habitats. Roots of Peace will plant two million fruit and nut trees in Afghanistan and provide farmers there with the skills and support necessary for sustainable land use.

Manufactured in Hong Kong

10 9 8 7 6 5 4 3 2 1

vande 'haṁ śrī-guroḥ śrī-yuta-pada-kamalaṁ śrī-gurūn vaiṣṇavāṁś ca
śrī-rūpaṁ sāgrajātaṁ saha-gaṇa-raghunāthānvitaṁ taṁ sa-jīvam
sādvaitaṁ sāvadhūtaṁ parijana-sahitaṁ kṛṣṇa-caitanya-devaṁ
śrī-rādhā-kṛṣṇa-pādān saha-gaṇa-lalitā-śrī-viśākhānvitāṁś ca

I offer my most respectful obeisances unto the lotus feet of my divine preceptor and my instructing gurus. I offer my most respectful obeisances unto all the Vaishnavas and unto the Six Goswamis, including Srila Rupa Goswami, Srila Sanatana Goswami, Raghunatha Das Goswami, Jiva Goswami, and their associates. I offer my respectful obeisances unto Sri Advaita Acarya Prabhu, Sri Nityananda Prabhu, Sri Caitanya Mahaprabhu, and all His devotees, headed by Srivasa Thakur. I then offer my respectful obeisances unto the lotus feet of Lord Krishna, Srimati Radharani, and all the gopis, headed by Lalita and Vishakha.

One who can protect me from the death that is this material life, is guru. One who can protect me from the fear of death, is guru. One by going to whom I do not have to go to anyone else, by listening to whom I do not have to listen to anyone else, is guru. The reservoir of grace whom the Surpreme Lord, the personification of the supreme good, has made responsible for looking after my welfare, is my guru. One by whose grace I can get rid of my controlling ego, is guru. One who brings the revealed truth to us, who by showering us with such truth can make us humbler than a blade of grass and more tolerant than a tree, is guru. One who makes us respectful to others without having any desire for respect from others, who can manifest transcendental kirtan in our mouths by transferring his own potency, of the Lord, is guru. Only the lotus feet of sri guru can free us from the shackles of illusion.

One who gives me the transcendental knowledge that all the people of the world are respectable and worshipable by me, that the whole world is meant for service to guru and everyone is my guru, that I am a servitor of Krishna, and that service to Krishna is my only duty, is sri guru.

—*Srila Bhaktisiddhanta Saraswati Thakur Prabhupada*

Acaryadeva is not a sectarian concern, for when we speak of the fundamental principle of *gurudeva,* or *acaryadeva,* we speak of something that is of universal application. There does not arise any question of discriminating my *guru* from yours or anyone else's. There is only one *guru,* who appears in an infinity of forms to teach you, me and all others.

—*Srila A.C. Bhaktivedanta Swami Prabhupada*

Wandering throughout the universe, by the mercy of Krishna, the living entity who is fortunate meets a bona fide spiritual master. By the mercy of the spiritual master, he gets the seed of the bhakti-lata. By worshiping Krishna and rendering service to the spiritual master, one is liberated from the illusory world of maya, and attains the lotus feet of the Lord.

—*Sri Chaitanya Mahaprabhu* (CC 2.19.151)

To understand transcendental knowledge, you must approach a self-realized soul, accept him as your spiritual master, and take initiation from him. Inquire submissively and render service unto him. Self-realized souls can impart knowledge unto you, for they have seen the truth.

—*Lord Krishna* (Bhagavad Gita 4.34)

Do not practice the craft of being guru for the purpose of injuring others through malice. Do not adopt the trade of a guru in order to get immersed in the slough of this world. But if you can, indeed, be My guileless servant; you will be endowed with my power—then you need not fear.

—*Srila Bhaktisiddhanta Saraswati Thakur Prabhupada*

A spiritual master may be one of three kinds. The first-class guru extends one foot from the spiritual world into the material world and takes souls from here to there. The guru in the intermediate stage is situated here, but he has extended one foot there and he is taking souls to the spiritual world. The lowest class of guru has both feet here, but he clearly sees the highest plane and is trying to take the souls from here to that plane. In this way, we may roughly conceive of three kinds of guru.

—*Srila B. R. Sridhar Dev Goswami*

The key to success in spiritual life is unflinching devotion to both the spiritual master and Krishna. To those great souls who have full faith in both Krishna and the spiritual master, the inner meaning of the scriptures is fully revealed.

—*Svetasvatara Upanisad* (6.23)

Who-so-ever you meet, instruct them regarding Krishna, by My command, be guru; deliver this land. In this you will not be obstructed by the current of the world. You will have my company again at this place.

—*Srila Bhaktisiddhanta Saraswati Thakur Prabhupada*

A sober person who can tolerate the urge to speak, the mind's demands, the actions of anger and the urges of the tongue, belly and genitals is qualified to make disciples all over the world.

—*Śrī Upadeśāmṛta* (1)

To receive the knowledge of the higher world, we have to completely surrender ourselves to a saint who has descended from that world, and hear from him.

—*Srila Bhaktisiddhanta Saraswati Thakur Prabhupada*

Contents

Srila Bhakti Bibudha Bodhayan Maharaj
President Acharya, Sri Gopinath Gaudiya Math

Foreword

It gives me great pleasure to learn that Mandala Publishing has decided to publish this book, *Guru: The Universal Teacher*, on the holy day of Sri Gaura Purnima, 2017. This is a very special book that brings together various articles written by my spiritual teacher, His Divine Grace Srila Bhakti Pramode Puri Goswami Thakur, the Founder President (*acharya*) of Sri Gopinath Gaudiya Math.

The word *guru* originated in India, originally known as Bharatavarsha, and is used by people from various different cultural backgrounds. The literal meaning of *guru* is teacher, however, in Vedic spiritual traditions, *guru* refers to the personification of one who gives initiation to the followers within that particular tradition. According to Vedic culture, a person's guru is the most important person to help progress in devotional practices and is considered nondifferent from the Supreme Personality of Godhead, Sri Krishna. In fact, for the ardent disciple, one's guru is even more powerful than Sri Krishna Himself. The reason for this is that if the object of our services, Sri Krishna, is displeased with our service, then the guru is qualified and able to win Sri Krishna's favor on our behalf. However, if the guru is displeased with our services, then Sri Krishna will not accept any service from us until we are excused or forgiven by our guru. Such is the exalted position and importance of the guru.

Ultimately, Sri Krishna is the guru of all living entities, including even the gods and goddesses. However, in order to teach us the importance of the guru and how to serve the guru, He accepted Sandipani Muni as His spiritual master. During His stay at Gurudeva's ashram, Sri Krishna performed *guru-seva* with great tolerance.

In Indian culture, when greeting a spiritually exalted person, we use the word *deva* after the person's name. The suffix *deva* offers respect to the individual as one would to God. Guru is the most valuable personification to a disciple and as such, in order to greet the guru in such a respectful manner, disciples use the title Gurudeva.

The Vedic word *tattva* means absolute or eternal truth. As the Vedic scriptures stipulate, the Supreme Personality of Godhead, Sri Krishna, is the personification of eternal, absolute truth. Here, we can say that *guru* means "spiritual teacher," and *tattva* means "the Supreme Personality of Godhead, Sri Krishna." Thus, we can conclude that the spiritual teacher and Sri Krishna are both equal to one another.

In the Brahma-Madhva-Gaudiya-Saraswata tradition (*sampradāya*), the most important personification of guru is His Divine Grace Srila Bhakti Siddhanta Saraswati Goswami Thakur Prabhupada. He has said that, whenever a guru thinks that he is nondifferent from Sri Krishna and that his disciples should worship him, that he should not be considered to be a guru. In such a case, we can replace the second letter in the word *guru* with an "a," transforming the word into "*garu*." Here *garu* means "cow." In India people worship the *garu* (cow) as Sri Krishna's dearest animal. Occasionally, Indians also use the word *garu* to address people with lesser intelligence. The actual meaning of Srila Bhakti Siddhanta Prabhupada's words is that those who truly represent *guru-tattva* abide by the following instructions of Sri Rupa Goswami:

vāco vegaṁ manasah krodha-vegaṁ
jihvā-vegam udaropastha-vegam
etān vegān yo viṣaheta dhīrah
sarvām apīmāṁ pṛthivīṁ sa śiṣyāt

> The inner meaning of this verse is–only that personification who is able to control the six urges of speech, mind, anger, tongue, stomach, and sensual emotion, is eligible to accept disciples all over the world. (*Upadeśāmṛta* 1)

The correct manner to channel these urges is:

1. Speech—one should speak with humility; both the tone and dialog should not be harmful to anyone. Also, we should always chant the glories of the Supreme Lord and His devotees, instead of engaging in mundane gossip.
2. Mind—one should control one's thoughts by always engaging the mind in the services of the Supreme Personality of Godhead, Sri Krishna.
3. Anger—one should control the harmful emotion of anger. Anger should only be used when people are disobeying the Supreme Lord and His devotees in order to rectify their forgetful nature.
4. Tongue—one should only utilize the tongue to taste the Lord's remnants; no mundane restaurant food that cannot be offered should be taken. One should also not discriminate among the different types or tastes of the Lord's remnants.
5. Stomach—one should not be greedy and overindulge in filling the stomach.
6. Sensual emotion—one should not be promiscuous; it is best to practice sense control and be celibate with full love for Sri Krishna's services.

Nowadays, due to the lack of understanding regarding the true nature and qualities of Gurudeva, people are easily misguided or misdirected by many pretenders who pose as a guru but have no control over the above-mentioned urges. A pretender guru is an individual who is not recognized by previous teachers of an authorized lineage and is greedy to accept disciples in order to obtain a life-long income from them to maintain his own livelihood or the subtlest of material desires, to be renowned as a holy person (*pratiṣṭha*).

In fact, Gurudeva's duty is to only act for the benefit of the disciple's soul—not to get involved in the disciple's mundane problems. However, if in the name of Sri Krishna's services, the guru intentionally gets involved in his disciple's mundane problems and spends large amounts of time and energy engaging with his disciples in sentimental discourses for his own personal mundane interest, then we must know that this is not the quality of a real Gurudeva.

The word *guru* also means "heavy." In the Sanskrit language, which is often referred to as the heavenly language, the word *guru* has two syllables, namely: "gu," which indicates "darkness of ignorance" and "ru," which indicates "light of bliss." Therefore, the inner meaning of guru is as follows: he who is eligible to take disciples out of the darkness of their ignorance and bring them to the light of bliss. Such a personification is qualified to receive the title "Gurudeva." Here darkness refers to illusion (maya) and light means the Supreme Personality of Godhead, Sri Krishna.

As per the instruction of Sri Krishna Chaitanya Mahaprabhu, who is another form of Sri Krishna and appears in this Kali Yuga (age of hypocrisy), the real Gurudeva should display the following qualities in his daily life:

tṛṇād api sunīcena
taror iva sahiṣṇunā
amāninā mānadena
kīrtanīyaḥ sadā hariḥ

> One should chant the Holy Name of the Lord in a humble state of mind, thinking oneself to be lower than the straw in the street; one should be more tolerant than a tree, devoid of all sense of false prestige, and should offer all respect to others. In such a state of mind one can chant the holy name of the Lord constantly with purity. (*Śikṣāṣṭakam* 3)

Currently, due to the influence of Kali Yuga, we find that the gurus from different institutions, and sometimes even within the same institution or tradition (*sampradāya*), criticize each other. We may also find multiple institutions within the same tradition. If one institution's Gurudeva is criticizing the Gurudeva of another institution, it should be noted that such a guru is not representing Gurudeva in reality. A real Gurudeva should be completely free from the influence of Kali Yuga.

My grand-spiritual master, His Divine Grace Srila Bhakti Siddhanta Saraswati Goswami Thakur Prabhupada, was born in Purushottama Dham and by his endeavor, the Sri Brahma-Madhva-Gaudiya *sampradāya's* loving message has been spreading all over the world. Anyone that criticizes Srila Bhakti Siddhanta Prabhupada or attempts to discredit his authenticity is certainly not an authorized follower of this lineage.

sampradāya-vihīnā ye mantrās te niṣphalā matāḥ
ataḥ kalau bhaviṣyanti catvāraḥ sampradāyinaḥ
śrī-brahma-rudra-sanakāḥ vaiṣṇavāḥ kṣiti-pāvanāḥ
catvāras te kalau bhāvyā hy utkale puruṣottamāt

Any mantra that does not come in disciplic succession is considered to be fruitless. Therefore, in the age of Kali, four divine individuals will found disciplic schools. These four Vaishnavas are pioneers of the Sri, Brahma, Rudra, and Sanaka *sampradāyas*. All of them will preach out of the city of Purushottam in Orissa. (*Padma Purāṇa* 1.5-6)

rāmānujaṁ śrīḥ svīcakre madhvācāryaṁ caturmukhaḥ
śrī-viṣṇu-svāminaṁ rudro nimbādityaṁ catuḥsanaḥ

Lakshmi Devi accepted Ramanuja as her representative, Lord Brahma took Madhvacharya, Rudra took Vishnuswami, and the four Kumars, Sanandan, Sanatan, Sanaka, and Sanat Kumar, accepted Nimbaditya as their representative in establishing their disciplic lines. (*Padma Purāṇa* 1.7)

I sincerely hope that the content of this book, *Guru: The Universal Teacher*, will allow the reader to understand the real meaning of *guru*. Actually, a guru is not just one individual but the embodiment of all the members of the lineage (*parampara*). As soon as an aspiring student is able to realize the real meaning of *guru-tattva*, all quarrels between the disciples of different gurus, with the issue of their Gurudeva's glory, will cease and they will become peaceful and blissful.

It is my humble request to the readers of this book to kindly excuse us if we have made any typographical, grammatical, or other errors herein and to try and perform their spiritual practice with proper understanding of *guru-tattva* as described in this book.

An unworthy servant of servants in the Gaudiya lineage,

Swami B.B. Bodhayan
President Acharya, Sri Gopinath Gaudiya Math

Srila Bhakti Pramode Puri Goswami Thakur
Founder Acharya, Sri Gopinath Gaudiya Math

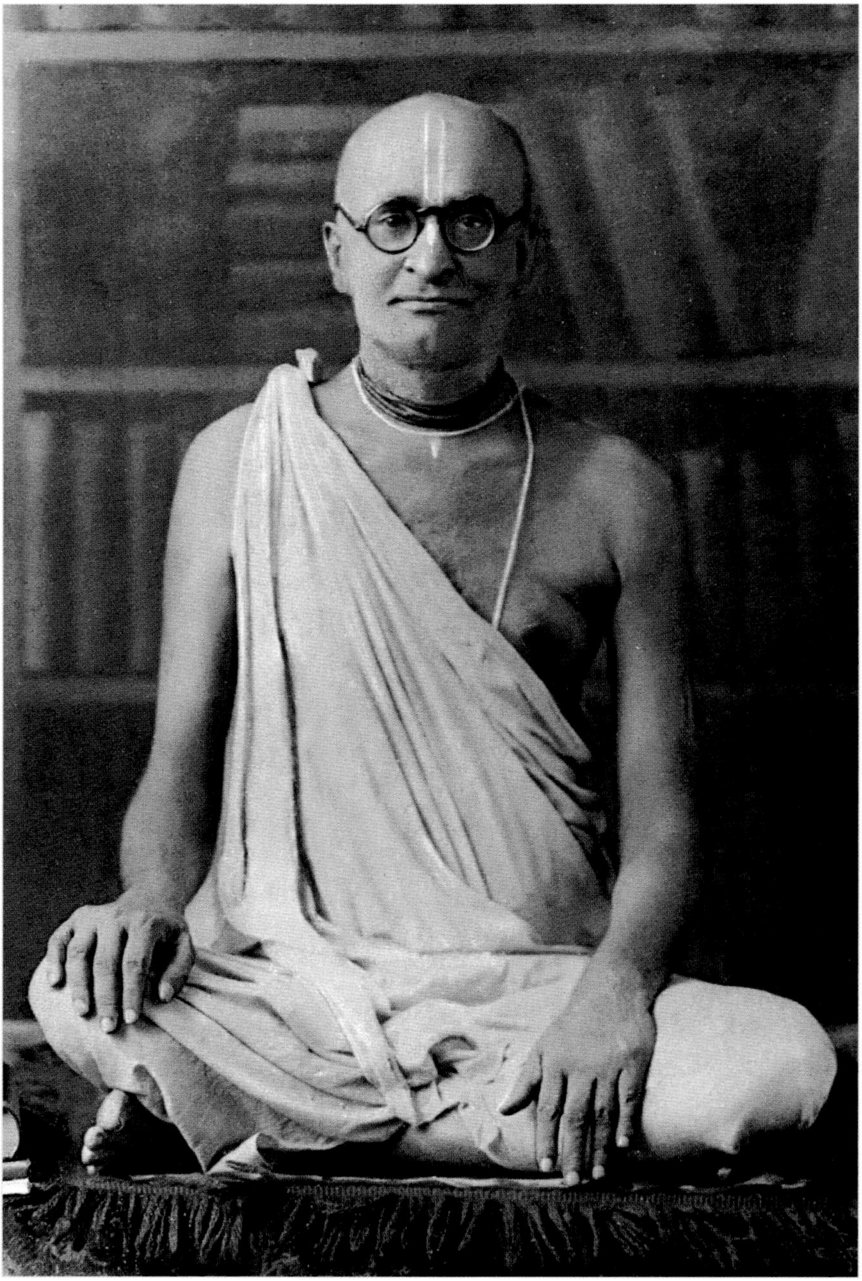

Srila Bhaktisiddhanta Saraswati Thakur Prabhupada

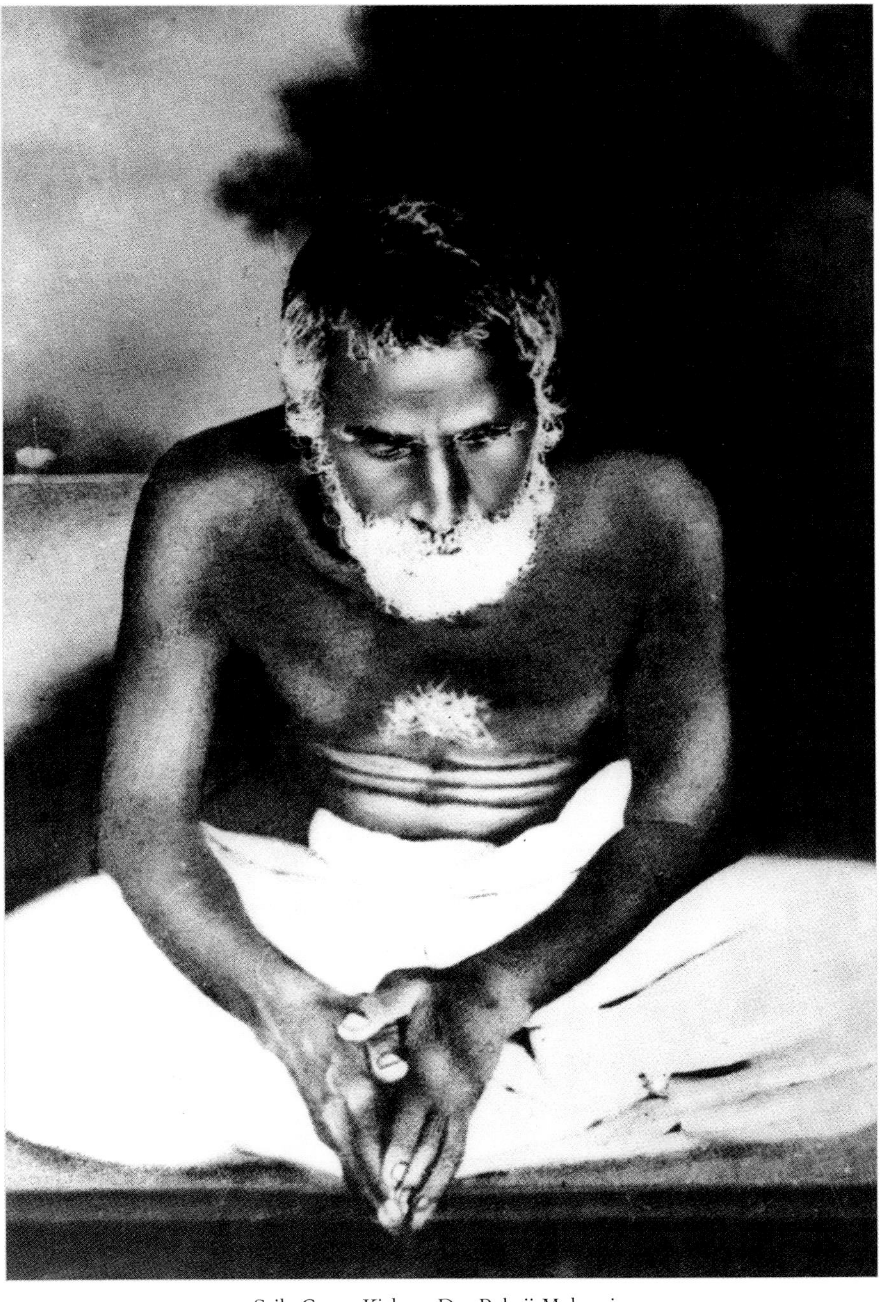

Srila Gaura Kishora Das Babaji Maharaj

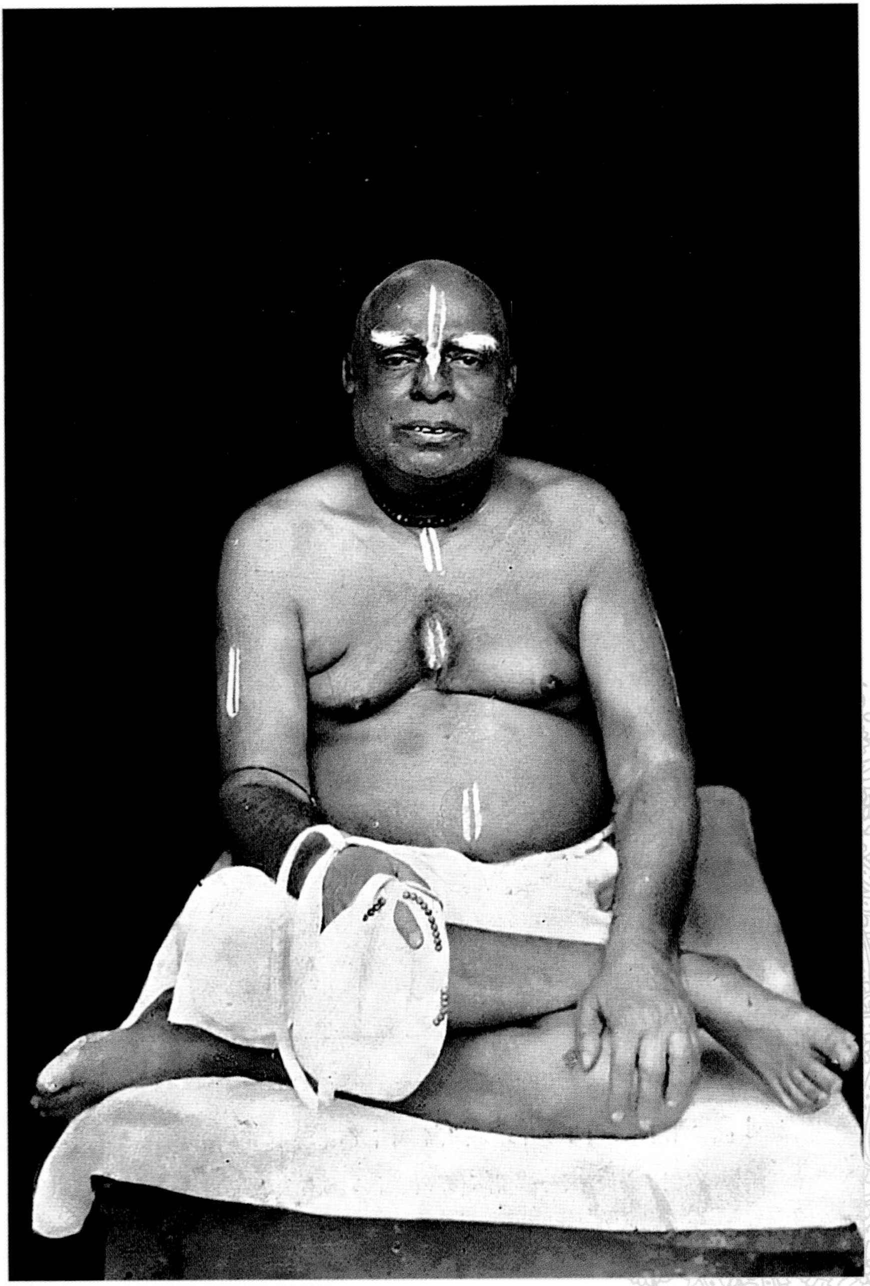

Srila Sachidananda Bhaktivinoda Thakur

guru | \'gur-(ˌ)ü, 'gü-(ˌ)rü *also* gə-'rü\
noun (pl. gurus)

- A spiritual teacher; one who plants the seed, or mantra, into the heart of the disciple.
- One who imparts spiritual teachings.
- One who has completely surrendered to their guru.
- One who inspires advancement in devotional life.
- One who is the personification of humility, tolerance, compassion, and dedication.
- One whose heart is full of pure love for the Supreme Lord.

ORIGIN from Sanskrit *guru 'weighty, grave'* (compare with Latin *gravis*), hence *'elder, teacher.'*

guru: gu "darkness," ru "that which counteracts"; spiritual master.

SYNONYMS

- *Guru and mystic*: spiritual teacher, teacher, tutor, sage, mentor, spiritual leader, leader, master; Swami, Maharaj, maharishi.
- *Guru*: expert, authority, pundit, leading light, master, specialist.

ANTONYMS

Disciple

CHAPTER 1

The Glories of Sri Guru

Krishna Das Kaviraj Goswami starts his *Caitanya-caritāmṛta* with a discussion of *guru-tattva*. He tells us that Krishna, the source of all incarnations, the avatāri and ultimate object of all service, the *viṣaya-vigraha*, appears as His own servant, the *āśraya-vigraha*, in order to show His mercy to the devotees. This is the guru, who mercifully reveals Krishna to his disciples. Since the guru is the *āśraya-vigraha*, he never claims to be the object of service; nor does he think of himself in this way. Rather, he presents himself as the eternal servant of the servant of the servants of Krishna or Sri Chaitanya, just as Mahaprabhu presented Himself while dancing in front of Lord Jagannatha's chariot in Puri:

nāhaṁ vipro na ca narapatir nāpi vaiśyo na śūdro
nāhaṁ varṇī na ca gṛhapatir no vanastho yatir vā
kintu prodyan-nikhila-paramānanda-pūrṇāmṛtābdher
gopī-bhartuḥ pada-kamalayor dāsa-dāsānudāsaḥ

I am not a *brāhmaṇa*, nor a *kṣatriya*, nor a *vaiśya*, nor a *śūdra*. Neither am I a *brahmacārī*, a householder, a retired man, or a renunciant monk. My real identity is that I am the most insignificant servant of the servant of the servant of the lotus feet of Krishna, the lover of the *gopīs* and overflowing ocean of supreme

> and immortal joy. (*Caitanya-caritāmṛta* 2.13.80, quoted in *Padyāvalī* 74)

Nevertheless, even though the spiritual master identifies himself as Krishna's servant, the disciple who wishes to receive the spiritual master's blessings will look on him with transcendental intelligence as a direct manifestation of Krishna or Sri Chaitanya. Since the spiritual master is Krishna's most beloved associate, he is not different from Him. Krishna gave this very instruction to Uddhava in *Śrīmad Bhāgavatam* 11.17.27.

ācāryaṁ māṁ vijānīyān
nāvamanyeta karhicit
na martya buddhyāsūyeta
sarva deva mayo guruḥ

> O Uddhava! You should consider the guru to be My very self—that is, the embodiment of love for Me and therefore nondifferent from Me. You should therefore never disrespect him by envying him or thinking him to be an ordinary man, for he is the sum total of all the demigods.

Krishna follows this verse by speaking two others (ŚB 11.17.28 and 29) that give essential information about how an exemplary disciple should serve the spiritual master:

sāyaṁ prātar upānīya
bhaikṣyaṁ tasmai nivedayet
yac cānyad apy anujñātam
upayuñjīta saṁyataḥ

> In the morning and evening one should go begging and bring whatever one gathers to the spiritual master. One should then take permission before one himself eats.

śuśrūṣamāṇa ācāryaṁ
sadopāsīta nīca-vat
yāna-śayyāsana-sthānair
nāti-dūre kṛtāñjaliḥ

While engaged in serving the spiritual master one should take the attitude of a humble servant. When the guru is walking, the servant should humbly walk behind. When the guru lies down to sleep, the servant should also lie down nearby, and when the guru has awakened, the servant should sit near him, massaging his lotus feet and rendering other, similar services. When the guru is sitting down on his asana, the servant should stand nearby with folded hands, awaiting the guru's order. In this way one should always worship the spiritual master.

Raghunatha Das Goswami writes in his *Manaḥ-śikṣā* that we should think of the guru as the dearest companion of the Lord (*mukunda-preṣṭhatve smara*). Sri Jiva Prabhu makes a similar statement in the *Bhakti-sandarbha* (213), "Pure devotees, however, think of both the spiritual master and Lord Shiva as nondifferent from the Lord due to their being most dear to the Lord" (*śuddha-bhaktās tv eke śrī-guroḥ śrī-śivasya ca bhagavatā sahābheda-dṛṣṭiṁ tat-priyatamatvenaiva manyante*).

Srila Vishwanatha Chakravarti takes up the same theme in the seventh verse of his *Gurv-aṣṭakam*:

sākṣād-dharitvena samasta-śāstrair
uktas tathā bhāvyata eva sadbhiḥ
kintu prabhor yaḥ priya eva tasya
vande guroḥ śrī-caraṇāravindam

I worship the lotus feet of my spiritual master, who is said by all scriptures to be Lord Hari himself, and

> is indeed thought of that way by all the saints. But this identity is due to his being very dear to the Lord.

Another way to think of the guru: as the direct manifestation of Srimati Radharani. Similarly, one can see him as Srimati Radharani's personal companion. My own dear spiritual master, Srila Bhaktisiddhanta Saraswati Thakur, identified himself as the servant of the beloved of Srimati Radharani, or Sri Varshabhanavi-dayita Das. He also revealed to his intimate associates that he was in fact Nayanamani Manjari, the companion of Sri Rupa Manjari in *kṛṣṇa-līlā*. Therefore, we pray to our spiritual master in his identity as Srimati Radharani's handmaiden:

tvaṁ gopikā vṛṣa-raves tanayāntike'si
sevādhikāriṇi guro nija-pāda-padme
dāsyaṁ pradāya kuru māṁ vraja-kānane śrī-
rādhāṅghri-sevana-rase sukhinīṁ sukhābdhe

> O Sri Guru! You remain constantly by the lotus feet of the daughter of Vrishabhanu, where you have been given the right to render service. Please give me the joy of swimming in the ocean of service to Srimati Radharani.

There is also a *prāṇam-mantra* to the guru in his *sakhī* form:

rādhā-sammukha-saṁsaktiṁ
sakhī-saṅga-nivāsinīm
tvām ahaṁ satataṁ vande
mādhavāśraya-vigrahām[1]

> I worship you, my spiritual master, in your form as a *gopī* living among the other *sakhīs,* always in the company of Srimati Radharani. You are the repository of love for Madhava.

[1] Some versions of this mantra have *guru-rūpāṁ parāṁ sakhīm* in the last quarter: "I worship you, my guru, in the form of the topmost *sakhī*."

One of the nine Yogendras, Kavi, spoke to King Nimi as follows:

> The Supreme Lord has created a process whereby even the most ignorant and foolish people can attain Him. This process is known as *bhāgavata-dharma*. Anyone who has faith in this process will never be bewildered. Even if he runs with his eyes closed, he will neither slip nor fall.
>
> Those who are averse to the Lord's service fall into the grips of His illusory energy and forget their eternal identity. This leads to identification with the material body and further disruption of the intelligence. As a consequence, one becomes absorbed in everything but Krishna, everything that is the nonself. And the result of this is fear.
>
> Therefore an intelligent and discerning individual will make the spiritual master his personal Deity (*guru-daivatātmā*) and recognize him as his dearmost friend. Following him with this attitude, the disciple should embark on the path of exclusive devotion to the Supreme Lord. Such worship primarily takes the form of loudly glorifying the names of the Lord that are related to his birth and activities without any care for or attachment to what people might think. (ŚB 11.2.34–37)

In the following chapter of *Śrīmad-Bhāgavatam*, Prabuddha, the next of the nine masters of yoga, continues the discourse on *bhāgavata-dharma*. He begins, in 11.3.22, by saying that one must take initiation from a spiritual master who is situated in full knowledge of the scriptural form of the Lord, who has had direct experience of the Lord, and who is free from anger, lust, greed, and other base qualities, and then study *bhāgavata-dharma* under him:

tatra bhāgavatān dharmān
śikṣed gurv-ātma-daivataḥ
amāyayānuvṛttyā yais
tuṣyed ātmātma-do hariḥ

> Knowing the spiritual master to be one's ever well-wisher, dearest friend, and the manifestation of the supremely worshipable Lord Hari, one should serve him constantly, with sincerity, and with this attitude learn from him *bhāgavata-dharma*, or the various religious activities that will please Krishna, the giver of the soul.

Our most worshipable spiritual master, Srila Bhaktisiddhanta Saraswati Thakur, writes in his *Vivṛti* commentary on this verse:

> Once one has taken shelter of the spiritual master, the *jīva* should serve him, taking the attitude that the guru is not a part of this illusory manifestation or mundane creation but one who has taken full shelter of Krishna and is therefore nondifferent from Him. The word *guru* means "heavy" or "important." If under the influence of the illusory energy, one takes the guru as *laghu,* "light," and furthermore tries to use him to serve his own circumstantial ends, then he will attain results of a transient nature. This attitude is contrary to the concept of obedience, and so Rupa Goswami has advised us of our duty to serve the spiritual master with a sense of faith and trust. We should serve Krishna with full awareness of His transcendental nature as well as awareness of the transcendenal nature of His servants. By so doing, Krishna will be pleased with us, and as a result of His pleasure, our eagerness to serve His servant, the guru, will steadily increase, which in turn will lead to Krishna's ever greater satisfaction. With this we will come to realize the truth of the famous verses from the *Upaniṣads*:

yasya deve parā bhaktir
yathā deve tathā gurau
tasyaite kathitā hy arthāḥ
prakāśante mahātmanaḥ

> Only unto those great souls who have implicit faith in both the Lord and the spiritual master, who is His manifestation and not different from Him, are all the imports of Vedic knowledge automatically revealed. (*Śvetāśvatara Upaniṣad* 6.23)

> *bhidyate hṛdaya-granthiś*
> *chidyante sarva-saṁśayāḥ*
> *kṣīyante cāsya karmāṇi*
> *tasmin dṛṣṭe parāvare*

> When one has a vision of the Supreme Truth, the knots binding his heart are untied, his doubts are removed, and his bondage to the results of his past deeds is eradicated. (*Muṇḍaka Upaniṣad* 2.2.9)[2]

But before the *jīva* can realize the purport of these two verses in his life, he must first follow the instructions Srila Rupa Goswami gives in the *Bhakti-rasāmṛta-sindhu* (1.2.74):

> *guru-padāśrayas tasmāt*
> *kṛṣṇa-dīkṣādi-śikṣaṇam*
> *viśrambhena guroḥ sevā*
> *sādhu-vartmānuvartanam*

> First take shelter of a spiritual master. Take initiation and instruction from him. Serve the spiritual master in a spirit of trust and affection and follow the path taken by the saintly devotees.

When one has accomplished these four acts, he is considered a beginner on the path of devotional practice and can begin to hear *Śrīmad Bhāgavatam*, the revealed text of the Vaishnavas. At this point he can start to become truly free of the fear that comes from absorption in what is "not Krishna." As stated in *Śrīmad Bhāgavatam* (11.2.37):

---

[2] See also *Śrīmad-Bhāgavatam* 1.2.20 and 11.20.30.

bhayaṁ dvitīyābhiniveśataḥ syād
īśād apetasya viparyayo 'smṛtiḥ
tan-māyayāto budha ābhajet tam
bhaktyaikayeśa-guru-devatātmā

> When the living entity is distanced from the Supreme Lord, he is attracted by the material energy, which is separate from the Lord. As a consequence, he is overpowered by fear, his conception of life is reversed, and he becomes forgetful of his constitutional position. All this takes place by the Lord's illusory energy. Therefore, one who is actually intelligent worships the Lord by the process of unalloyed devotional service, making his spiritual master his worshipful Deity and the source of life.

Śrīmad-Bhāgavatam (1.7.7) also states:

yasyāṁ vai śrūyamāṇāyāṁ
kṛṣṇe parama-pūruṣe
bhaktir utpadyate puṁsaḥ
śoka-moha-bhayāpahā

> By hearing this *Śrīmad Bhāgavatam,* one is blessed with devotion to Krishna, the Supreme Person. This devotion puts an end to all mourning, bewilderment, and fear.

Realizing the purport of these verses means that one has truly become a consecrated servant of Krishna. In other words, one does not accept anything other than service to Krishna as the direct or indirect result of his actions. This is the meaning of *bhāgavata-dharma*. Although *bhāgavata-dharma* takes countless forms when it appears in this world, those who take it up are no longer bound by the path of works and ritual (karma), knowledge or philosophical speculation (*jñāna*), or the impulse to act whimsically.

The kind of genuine spiritual master who both practices and preaches *bhāgavata-dharma* is rare in this world. Sri Chaitanya Mahaprabhu both taught and exemplified the pure path of devotion, which is based on a correct understanding of spiritual truth. In the course of time, however, the path of *bhāgavata-dharma* was gradually diluted by various false teachings, which distorted the world's perception of it. Seeing this, Mahaprabhu mercifully sent two powerful individuals in two successive generations: Srila Bhaktivinoda Thakur and His next manifestation in my spiritual master, Srila Bhaktisiddhanta Saraswati Thakur. The very presence of these two great souls on this earth made it holy. They both set out on a mission to deliver the conditioned souls by preaching *bhāgavata-dharma*.

The corpus of texts authored by Mahaprabhu's dear associates, the Six Goswamis, contains the essence of all the Vedic scriptures, from the Vedas and Vedanta to the epics and *Purāṇas*. Srila Bhaktivinoda Thakur and Srila Prabhupada Bhaktisiddhanta Saraswati extracted the essence of the Goswamis' writings and presented them in Sanskrit, Bengali, Hindi, English, and Urdu. They produced monthly, fortnightly, and even daily publications in each of these languages. Bhaktisiddhanta Saraswati built temples and preaching centers in various places throughout India where the Lord in His Deity form could be worshiped and served. In these centers, he established morning and evening programs of kirtan, readings from scripture, and lectures to establish the glories of the Holy Name and devotional service. And both of these great souls adopted various innovative means to fulfill Chaitanya Mahaprabhu's desire on this earth. Our most beloved and worshipable Srila Prabhupada curated exhibitions that taught the principles found in the *Bhāgavatam* as well as the various stories told therein. He was ready to use slides and film and other then modern technologies to spread the message of Chaitanya Mahaprabhu. In this way, he gave his life's breath to bringing wayward souls to the path of devotional service.

Despite all these efforts, Srila Prabhupada was often disturbed by the conditioned souls' seemingly unbreakable preference for activities and beliefs opposed to bhakti. Being full of compassion, he felt pain at seeing the suffering this led those souls to. Unfortunately, the actions of some so-called gurus are such that, in order to induce people to become their disciples, they tacitly approve their disciples' undisciplined, wayward life of sin. Passing this approval off as compassion and liberality, such so-called gurus are even accepted by some as the dominant spiritual leaders of their time. But these so-called spiritual leaders' failure to establish moral discipline in those who are serving as Gaudiya Vaishnava exemplars in society gradually leads to a general laxity. By ignoring scriptural injunctions and permitting waywardness, a guru does not help those he is supposed to be guiding but only deprives them of true happiness, success, and ultimate spiritual attainment.

The Supreme Lord appears as the guru principle in two forms: as the inner guide, or *antaryāmī*, and as the great devotee, or *mahānta*. Uddhava states this clearly near the conclusion of the teachings Krishna gave him. He says in *Śrīmad-Bhāgavatam* (11.29.6):

naivopayanty apacitiṁ kavayas taveśa
brahmāyuṣāpi kṛtam ṛddha-mudaḥ smarantaḥ
yo 'ntar bahis tanubhṛtām aśubhaṁ vidhunvann
ācārya-caittya-vapuṣaḥ svagatiṁ vyanakti

> Even if they should think on them with increasing amazement for eons on end, the wise could not reach the end of Your glories, O Lord, for in the form of the intelligence within and the teacher without You destroy all inauspiciousness and reveal the way to attain You.

Srila Vishwanatha Chakravarti explains:

> Uddhava speaks this verse in response to an expected objection from Krishna: "If I give everything My devotees want, including lesser, material goals, then My gifts cannot be called completely unconditioned; they are conditional, like those who ask for them." Uddhava answers this objection: "You cannot say this, because the very devotional acts Your devotees are engaged in come from You. Your desire to see them achieve the highest benefit is without reservation—such that Your devotees could serve You for thousands of lifetimes without being able to repay their debt to You. The wise (those who have attained knowledge of Brahman) could worship You for a lifetime of Brahma without being able to repay even a drop of the infinite blessings You have given them. The more they think of these blessings, the greater their amazement and joy, which means that these blessings simply increase and the possibility of removing the debt incurred thus becomes less."

What is the nature of these blessings? "O Krishna! You appear externally as the *ācārya*"—that is, both the *mantra-guru* and the *śikṣā-guru*, "and You give Your mercy through the mantra and the instructions on how to advance in spiritual practice." Krishna says in the Bhagavad Gita (10.10) that to those who are fully committed to Him He gives the intelligence by which they can come to Him. As the indwelling guide, Krishna gives direction and inspiration to His devotees, leading them to the ultimate goal of eternal, personal association with Him.

As the *chaitya-guru* Krishna removes all understandings that lead away from bhakti and awakens the inclination for pure devotion. If He did not, the *jīva* would spend countless millions of lives simply wandering from one form of life to another without any hope of escape. In the Bhagavad Gita, Krishna also speaks of *vyavasāyātmikā buddhi*, the intelligence that gives resolute determination; in fact, the true symptom of intelligence is the ability to control the lower self by one's resolve. As the *antaryāmī*, Krishna also gives the spiritual strength to follow through with appropriate action.

At the same time, the advanced devotee gives the seeker shelter at his feet, setting the standard of exemplary devotional behavior and teaching the ways and means of pleasing the Lord through devotional service. Following and satisfying such a spiritual master satisfies the Lord. Unless one finds shelter at the lotus feet of an advanced devotee, one cannot expect to enjoy this great good fortune. The *karmīs*, *jñānīs*, and yogis have their own gurus, through whom they achieve sense enjoyment, liberation, or mystic perfection. But hidden in all their practices are gross and subtle desires for the satisfaction of their own senses. This means that the real goal of life, satisfying Krishna's senses, which is the definition of divine love, cannot be attained. Any actions not performed for the satisfaction of the Lord naturally increase one's bondage to the material world and so are contemptible.

On the path of knowledge, even though the gross desires for sense gratification are not present, the desire for liberation possesses the *jñānīs* and is even more dangerous than the desire for sense gratification that possesses the *karmīs*. Even though such *jñānīs* may appear on occasion to adopt devotional practices, they ultimately aim at effacing the distinctions between knowledge, the knower, and the known—that is to say, between devotion, the devotee, and God. The cultivation of knowledge itself is not reprehensible if it retains an awareness of these distinctions. However, impersonal gnosis concludes that the individual soul merges into God's existence and does not recognize the inconceivable eternal difference-in-oneness that is the true relationship between the living beings and God. There are statements in the *Upaniṣads* such as *so'haṁ*, *ahaṁ brahmāsmi* and *tat tvam asi śvetaketo* that lead these philosophers to a misunderstanding that they are in every respect equal to Brahman, or God. Naturally, this has disastrous consequences for the life of devotion. Devotees thus avoid such speculations. *Śrī Caitanya-caritāmṛta* (2.6.268) states:

sāyujya śunite bhakter ghṛṇā lajjā bhaya
naraka vāñchaye tabu sāyujya nā laya

> The devotee feels disgust, shame, and fear when he hears talk of merging into Narayana. He will go to hell before accepting the liberation of undifferentiated oneness with God (*sāyujyā*).

Those who deny the existence of attributes in the ultimate truth seek this undifferentiated kind of liberation. Devotees of Vishnu are willing to accept four kinds of liberation: *sārṣṭi* (having the same opulences as the Lord), *sārūpya* (having the same form as the Lord), *sāmīpya* (living in proximity to the Lord), and *sālokya* (living in the same abode as the Lord). Krishna's exclusive devotees, however, seek nothing but service and are indifferent to the various kinds of satisfaction that come from liberation.

This is stated in the *Bhāgavatam* in a number of places. For example, Krishna tells Uddhava in *Śrīmad Bhāgavatam* 11.20.31–34:

> Those who wholeheartedly engage in My devotion generally do not gain any benefit from the cultivation of philosophical knowledge or from renunciation. For the devoted yogi who has surrendered his thoughts to Me, neither knowledge nor renunciation are considered to be the sources of true good in this world. Through the practice of devotional service to Me, My devotee easily attains all the benefits gained through ritual practices, penance, philosophy, renunciation, yogic discipline, charity, or performance of prescribed duties. However, being saintly, patient, and single-minded, My devotees care nothing for such rewards. Even so, I still bestow these on them, even up to and including liberation and freedom from rebirth.

The *Bhāgavatam* states that the fifth and ultimate goal of life is divine love, *prema*. More commonly, people seek the four mundane goals—the expert performance of worldly duties (dharma), the financial and other rewards that come from such success (*artha*), sense pleasures (*kāma*), and liberation (*mokṣa*, or *mukti*). People seeking the first three goals are generally called *karmīs*, and those seeking the fourth by merging into Brahman are called *jñānīs*. Those who pray for the liberation of union with Paramatma are called yogis.

The special characteristic of *Śrīmad Bhāgavatam* is found in its prefatory statement, *dharmaḥ projjhita-kaitavo'tra*: "This book is free of any fraudulent concepts of religion." Krishna Das Kaviraj discusses the meaning of the word *kaitava* ("fraudulent") in *Śri Caitanya-caritāmṛta* 1.1.90–91:

> *ajñāna tamera nāma kahiye kaitava*
> *dharma artha kāma vāñchā ādi e saba*
> *tāra madhye mokṣa vāñchā kaitava pradhāna*
> *jāhā haite kṛṣṇa bhakti haya antardhāna*

> I give the name "fraudulent" to the darkness of ignorance, which consists of desires for the four goals of human life. Of such desires, however, the desire for liberation is the biggest fraud of all, for it obliterates all devotion to Krishna.

Krishna Das refers to Sridhar Swami, who says that the prefix *pra* added to the verb *ujjh* indicates that the rejection of false religion extends as far as and includes the desire for liberation (*praśabdena mokṣābhisandhir api nirasta iti*). In another context, Kaviraj Goswami refers to the same word, *kaitava*, and defines it in the *Caitanya-caritāmṛta* (2.24.94):

> *duḥsaṅga kahiye kaitava ātma-vañcanā*
> *kṛṣṇa kṛṣṇa-bhakti vinu anya kāmanā*

> By bad association, I mean the kind of self-deception that is also called *kaitava*. This refers to any desire other than that leading to Krishna and devotion to Krishna.

In other words, bad company refers to anyone who is possessed by a desire other than for Krishna and to Krishna. Such persons consciously or unconsciously cheat themselves and others. This is, as Kaviraj Goswami says, "the darkness of ignorance."

So although the four customary goals of human life are all characteristic of ignorance of one's constitutional position as a servant of God, the fourth, *mokṣa,* is considered especially symptomatic of ignorance. Even though those seeking liberation generally masquerade as highly intellectual and learned philosophers, at heart they avoid the essence of spiritual life, namely, their eternal identity as servant of Krishna. The principal function of the spiritual master is therefore to smear the unguent of divine knowledge over the eyes of those who have sunk into this blindness of their constitutional position.

When the disciple takes initiation, he learns from the guru four branches of spiritual knowledge:

1. *Sva-tattva*: the true nature of the self as worshiper of the Lord.
2. *Para-tattva*: the nature of the Supreme Truth as the Supreme Person, Krishna.
3. *Sādhya-sādhana-tattva*: spiritual practices and their goal.
4. *Virodhi-tattva*: the things that are inimical to attaining spiritual perfection.

On becoming conversant with these four aspects of spiritual knowledge, one becomes free from most obstacles and fixes the mind on Krishna, devotion to Krishna, and the search for divine love for Krishna.

The great devotee Uddhava addressed his beloved Krishna:

> O Lord! Those who are expert in distinguishing the essential from the nonessential are described as swans. Such persons take shelter of Your lotus feet, for this refuge is the source of all joy. Others, such as the *jñānīs, karmīs,* and yogis, identify with their

religious goals and practices and thus do not take shelter of Your lotus feet. O Lord of the universe, O lotus-eyed one! They are all under the spell of Your maya to the point of being rendered almost completely unconscious.

O Acyuta, unfailing friend of all creatures! In Your incarnation as Ramachandra, all the demigods headed by Brahma came to bow their crowned heads at Your feet, but You chose to make friendship with creatures like the monkeys rather than with gods or even men, because the monkeys had taken shelter of You. Therefore it is not shocking that You should accept subordination to Your exclusive devotees like Nanda, the *gopīs,* Vali, and others.

In other words, You are controlled by the love of Your devotees. Those who worship You become the recipients of Your protective affection. There is nothing strange about this, for those who love You exclusively, without mixing their devotion with other practices like karma or *jñāna,* make You their own. When You appeared as Rama, You established a loving friendship with the apes and monkeys. In Vrindavan also You engaged in loving exchanges with the cows and other creatures of the forest. You stole butter and other milk products and gave them to the monkeys. Had any of these creatures performed religious rituals or studied philosophy that made You serve them affectionately in this way? On the other hand, can anyone who has become a great scholar in the monistic philosophy claim to have ever won Your affection? Can we point to any example of this? Therefore, since we are Your servants and surrendered to Your lotus feet, we have no interest in the culture of knowledge as a means to liberation.

taṁ tvākhilātma-dayiteśvaram āśritānāṁ
sarvārtha-daṁ sva-kṛta-vid visṛjeta ko nu
ko vā bhajet kim api vismṛtaye'nu bhūtyai
kiṁ vā bhaven na tava pāda-rajo-juṣāṁ naḥ

> It is also notable that You showed unlimited affection and mercy to those born in the families of the enemies of the gods like Prahlada when they took shelter of You. Those who know this never turn to the deluded belief that sense pleasures or liberation are worthy values to strive for, nor can they ever leave Your lotus feet, which are the abode of fearlessness and eternal joy.

In the *Chāndogya Upaniṣad* it is said that only one who has a teacher, or *ācārya*, knows the Vedas (*ācāryavān puruṣo veda*). This means that only one who has taken shelter of a spiritual master through initiation can know the Supreme Person.

What is meant by the Sanskrit word *ācārya*? The *Manu-saṁhitā* (2.40) states:

upanīya tu yaḥ śiṣyaṁ
vedam adhyāpayed dvijaḥ
sa-kalpaṁ sa-rahasyaṁ ca
tam ācāryaṁ pracakṣate

> The *brāhmana* who gives his disciple the sacred thread and then teaches him the Veda along with the rituals (*kalpa*) and their esoteric significance (*rahasya*) is called an *ācārya*.

The above definition is a general one and applies to the Vedic system of brahminical *upanayana*, which is only given to *brāhmaṇas* who are going to undertake the study of the Vedas. Nevertheless, the same general principle applies to all spiritual paths. Thus the title *ācārya* is given to the teacher who takes disciples through initiation and then guides them to an understanding of a spiritual path.

The *Vāyu Purāna* also gives a relevant definition of the word *ācārya*:

ācinoti yaḥ śāstrārtham
ācāre sthāpayaty api
svayam ācarate yasmād
ācāryas tena kīrtitaḥ

> The *ācārya* is one who has studied and understood the meaning of the scripture, who then inculcates this meaning into the behavior of others while himself practicing what he preaches.

Ācāra means "conduct." Just as Sri Chaitanya Mahaprabhu exemplified the teachings He promoted, so any *ācārya* does the same. An *ācārya* is more than a teacher of words. Rather, he is interested in forming his students' character in the spirit of the scriptural texts and with the goal of leading them to Krishna's lotus feet.

Some *brāhmaṇas* who study the Vedas thoroughly object to the fact that Krishna's name cannot be found anywhere in these revealed texts, which are the basis of all *sanātana-dharma*. If such a person concludes that Krishna is not real or the Vedas are not true, he is wrong in either case and cannot be accepted as a genuine *ācārya*, for his study of scripture has led to a mistaken conclusion. Krishna states in the Bhagavad Gita (15.15):

vedaiś ca sarvair aham eva vedyo
vedānta-kṛd veda-vid eva cāham

> I am what is to be known from all the Vedas. I am the author of the Vedanta and I am also the knower of the Veda.

The Vedas talk of the *puruṣottama*, the Supreme Person. That person is Krishna. In His incarnation as Dvaipayana Vyasa, He composed the

Vedanta, the systematic understanding of the essential teachings found in the *Upaniṣads*, which are the most important part of the Vedic literature when in comes to understanding the nature of the Supreme Truth. Krishna's knowledge of the Vedas is established in the Bhagavad Gita. He concludes His teachings in texts 18.65–66 by stating that He is revealing "the most confidential (*guhyatama*) knowledge." What is that knowledge?

man-manā bhava mad-bhakto
mad-yājī māṁ namaskuru
mām evaiṣyasi satyaṁ te
pratijāne priyo'si me

sarva-dharmān parityajya
mām ekaṁ śaraṇaṁ vraja
ahaṁ tvāṁ sarva-pāpebhyo
mokṣayiṣyāmi mā śucaḥ

> Think of Me always. Become My devotee. Sacrifice to Me and offer your obeisance to Me. Do this and you will come to Me. I promise you that this is the truth, for you are very dear to Me. Give up all other duties and simply surrender to Me. I shall deliver you from all sin, have no fear.

Therefore Srila Kaviraj Goswami states in *Caitanya-caritāmṛta* 2.20.124–25:

veda śāstra kahe sambandha abhidheya prayojana
kṛṣṇa prāpya sambandha bhakti prāptyera sādhana
abhidheya nāma bhakti prema prayojana
puruṣārtha śiromaṇi prema mahā-dhana

> The Vedic knowledge is subdivided into three parts known as *sambandha* ("relationship"), *abhidheya* ("signification"), and *prayojana* ("the aim or end"). Knowledge of Krishna as the goal of spiritual life is called

> *sambandha*. Knowledge that devotion is the means to attain Him is called *abhidheya*. The ultimate goal of life, *prayojana*, is love of Krishna, or *prema*. This *prema* is the greatest treasure of spiritual life and is foremost among all the objectives of human life.

Thus, one who studies all the scriptures comes to the conclusion that devotional service to Krishna is their essence; he who teaches this conclusion by precept and example is called an *ācārya*. The *Caitanya-caritāmṛta* (1.1.13) says this of Advaita Acharya: "He was known as *ācārya* because He glorified devotional service to Krishna" (*ācāryaṁ bhakti-śaṁsanāt*).

Another popular etymological definition of the word *guru* is found in the scriptures:

> *gu-śabdas tv andhakāraḥ syāt*
> *ru-śabdas tan-nirodhakaḥ*
> *andhakāra-nirodhitvāt*
> *gurur ity abhidhīyate*

> The word *gu* means "darkness," and *ru* means "that which counteracts." The guru is thus known because he counteracts or eliminates the darkness of ignorance.

The teacher who illuminates the consciousness of a disciple who takes refuge in him by giving that disciple transcendental knowledge is appropriately called *guru*.

The spiritual master holds the Supreme Lord in his heart. This is the most important reason for his "weightiness," or greatness. He does not have a restricted vision based on distinctions between "us and them." He is most liberal—an incarnation of the Vedic dictum, *vasudhaiva kuṭumbakam*: "The world is his family." The spiritual master never has the superficial understanding—or "lightness"—that leads to the kinds of prejudices that are based on bodily consciousness.

According to the fourth chapter of the *Hari-bhakti-vilāsa* (4.342, 344), worshiping the spiritual master, or *guru-pūjā*, is an essential aspect of Deity worship:

pūjayiṣyaṁs tataḥ kṛṣṇam
ādau sannihitaṁ gurum
praṇamya pūjayed bhaktyā
dattvā kiṁcid upāyanam

> When one prepares to worship Krishna, one should first worship the spiritual master, who is next to the Deity. He should pay obeisances and then worship him with devotion, making some offerings.

prathamaṁ tu guruṁ pūjya
tataś caiva mamārcanam
kurvan siddhim avāpnoti
hy anyathā niṣphalaṁ bhavet

> The Lord Himself says, "One who first worships the guru before worshiping Me attains perfection. Otherwise, his devotional service will be fruitless."

The chapter continues (4.355–57) with several other statements exalting the benefits of serving the spiritual master:

> Service to the guru is the superlative religious activity. There is no religion purer or more glorious than this. Lust and anger and other things that have undesirable effects on the soul can all be overcome by devotion to the spiritual master.

> O King! Those who honor the guru even more than they honor their own parents will become guests in the world of Brahman.

And verse 4.351–52 state:

> *gurur brahmā gurur viṣṇur*
> *gurur devo maheśvaraḥ*
> *gurur eva paraṁ brahma*
> *tasmāt sampūjayet sadā*

> The guru is Brahma. The guru is Visnu. The guru is Shiva. The guru certainly is the *Param-brahma*. Therefore worship him always.

> *yo mantraḥ sa guruḥ sākṣāt*
> *yo guruḥ sa hariḥ smṛtaḥ*
> *gurur yasya bhavet tuṣṭas*
> *tasya tuṣṭo hariḥ svayam*

> The mantra is the guru himself. The guru is Krishna Himself. When the guru is satisfied with his disciple, then Krishna will be satisfied with that disciple.

> *harau ruṣṭe gurus trātā*
> *gurau ruṣṭe na kaścana*
> *tasmāt sarva-prayatnena*
> *gurum eva prasādayet*

But, according to verse 4.360:

> If Krishna is angry with someone, the guru can save him. If the guru is angry with that same person, however, he cannot be helped. Therefore be careful to satisfy the guru.

Śrīmad Bhāgavatam 7.15.26 states:

yasya sākṣād bhagavati
jñāna-dīpa-prade gurau
martyāsad-dhīḥ śrutaṁ tasya
sarvaṁ kuñjara-śaucavat

> If one thinks his guru, who has lit the lamp of spiritual knowledge within him, is an ordinary human being, then everything he has learned is like the bathing of an elephant, which sprays itself with dust after going into the water.

Krishna tells Uddhava in *Śrīmad Bhāgavatam* 11.19.43, "My friend, I am your well-wisher, the guru." In his commentary on this verse, Sridhar Swami quotes from the *Purāṇas*:

eka eva paro bandhur
viṣame samupasthite
guruḥ sakala-dharmātmā
yatrākiñcana-go hariḥ

> Your one true friend when there is danger is the guru, who is the essence of all religion to the disciple and in whom Krishna, the savior of the poor, is always present.

There is something special about the relationship between the spiritual master and the disciple. Even when the disciple does not specifically ask questions, because the guru has the disciple's well-being at heart, the guru still speaks (*anāpṛṣṭam api brūyur guravo dīna-vatsalāḥ*).

Ultimately, the best gift one can give to one's guru is to transmit the knowledge he has given one—to pass it on.[3]

[3] *tasmiś ca jñāne yaḥ sandeśaḥ saṁvādaḥ ācāryānukūlaṁ vacaḥ, tad-ājñānuṣṭhānaṁ vā sa eva dakṣiṇā, tat-santoṣa-karatvāt, jñāna-paryāyakatvāc ca* (ŚB 11.19.39).

CHAPTER 2

The Necessity for Sri Guru

This earth consists of seven continents, of which Jambudwip, Asia, is the most auspicious. According to the *Śrīmad Bhāgavatam*,[1] Jambudwip has nine divisions: Ajanabh, Kimpurusha, Harivarsha, Ilavrita, Ramyaka, Hiranmaya, Kuru, Bhadrashwa, and Ketumala. Of these, Ajanabh was named Bharata, or Bharatavarsha, as it was the land assigned by Ṛṣabhadeva's son Bharata. It was in this Bharatavarsha that the Supreme Lord, Sri Krishna, appeared at the end of the Dvāpara age to reveal His exceptional, humanlike pastimes.

By the Lord's grace, some have had the good fortune to take birth in this holy land, which serves as the threshold of the spiritual world. To be born here in a human body is the culmination of untold births and rebirths, for it allows us to undertake the quest for the ultimate perfection of spiritual life. Unfortunately, a human life is short and the window of opportunity small. *Śrīmad Bhāgavatam* therefore advises us not to waste a moment but to take up this challenge without delay. No one knows when death will strike, so there is an urgency to make good our eternal obligation to realize our relationship with God. We have only the time we have been given in order to accomplish this task—just these fleeting and undependable few hours that can be taken away from us at any moment. It is the duty of every human being not to misuse the time that they have been given but to take advantage of every second in trying to serve the Lord.

---

[1] ŚB 5.2.19.

This is the purport of the *Śrīmad Bhāgavatam* verse (11.9.29), which was spoken by Dattatreya Avadhuta:[2]

labdhvā sudurlabham idaṁ bahu-sambhavānte
mānuṣyam artha-dam anityam apīha dhīraḥ
tūrṇaṁ yateta na pated anumṛtyu yāvan
niḥśreyasāya viṣayaḥ khalu sarvataḥ syāt

> After many, many births, one is finally born in a most rare and valuable human body, which provides an opportunity to attain the supreme goal but is nevertheless temporary. Therefore, the wise individual should immediately take up the effort to find the thing that provides the supreme good in all times and circumstances, and not give up that effort up to the very moment of his death.

Yadu, the son of the celebrated King Yayati, encountered the *avadhūta* as the *avadhūta* was joyfully wandering around without a care in the world despite his complete renunciation and poverty. When the king asked him how he managed to remain so happy despite his poverty, the *avadhūta* told the king of his twenty-four teachers.[3] These twenty-four gurus were his *śikṣā-gurus*. (The scriptures allow for many instructors, but only one initiating, or *dīkṣā-guru*.)

Sri Krishna told the story of the meeting between the *avadhūta* and King Yayati to Uddhava just before He left this world because He wanted to prepare Uddhava for the separation he would suffer when He was gone.

Then again, a little further on in the Eleventh Canto (chapter 20, verse 17), Krishna tells Uddhava:

---

[2] The name is mentioned in Vishwanatha's comment on 11.9.32.

[3] See the chapter, "Guru Is Everywhere."

> *nṛ-deham ādyaṁ sulabhaṁ sudurlabhaṁ*
> *plavaṁ sukalpaṁ guru-karṇa-dhāram*
> *mayānukūlena nabhasvateritaṁ*
> *pumān bhavābdhiṁ na taret sa ātma-hā*

> This human body is the root of all benefits. It seems so easily obtained, yet it is in fact extremely rare. It is like a boat especially designed for crossing the ocean of material existence. If one has a spiritual master to guide him like the boat's helmsman and is given the favorable winds of My mercy, but still fails to cross over, then he is willfully committing suicide.

Srila Prabhupada writes in his *Vivṛti* commentary on this verse:

> The human body is the human being's only chance to attain personal auspiciousness. One only comes to the human form of life after many births. The spiritual master who is expert in the path of *bhajana* does the work of the helmsman. The Lord's mercy functions as the wind that powers the boat across the ocean of material life, where we suffer and enjoy the results of our past deeds. Someone who has not even come to the realization that this human body is a boat, a vehicle meant to take him to the other side of this ocean, who has not been able to recognize the spiritual master who will guide him, nor been able to understand how the mercy of the Lord is pushing him to that destination, is destroying a great opportunity whose return is far from guaranteed. Is it not appropriate, then, to say he is committing suicide?

This is why the scriptures and the Vaishnava saints repeat over and over again that we must have a sense of urgency about the purpose of life: To take shelter of a spiritual master without delay and take up the path of devotion to Krishna. *Śrīmad Bhāgavatam* 11.10.5 states:

mad-abhijñaṁ guruṁ śāntam
upāsīta mad-ātmak

> One should worship a spiritual master who is peaceful, who knows My nature well, and who has made Me the center of his life.

Sanatana Goswami Prabhu remarks that *mad-abhijña*, which is translated as "knows My nature well," means that the qualified guru has personal and direct experience of Krishna's glories. Foremost among these is the Lord's affectionate and protective attitude toward His devotees (*mām abhito bhakta-vātsalyādi-māhātmyānubhava-pūrvakaṁ jānātīti tathā tam*). The words *mad-ātmakaḥ* ("who has made Me the center of his life") mean that as a result of this experience, he has given his soul, or his entire inner life, over to Krishna (*mayi ātmā cittaṁ yasya tam*).

The *Muṇḍaka Upaniṣad* (1.2.11) states:

tad-vijñānārthaṁ sa gurum evābhigacchet
samit-pāṇiḥ śrotriyaṁ brahma-niṣṭham

> In order to realize that [the extent of the guru's self-surrender], one should take fuel for the sacrificial fire in hand and approach a spiritual master who is learned and fixed in Brahman.

In Vedic times, when the principal religious practice was the fire sacrifice, one desiring knowledge of the Vedas would approach a spiritual master with an offering of wood for the sacred fire. In later times, when the performance of fire sacrifice became less central to the culture of spiritual life, the words *samit-pāṇiḥ* ("taking fuel for the sacrificial fire in hand") were explained in a figurative way. Indeed, the Gaudiya

Vaishnava *ācāryas* understand Bhagavad Gita 4.34, which describes the appropriate way to approach a spiritual master to receive instruction:

tad viddhi praṇipātena
paripraśnena sevayā
upadekṣyanti te jñānaṁ
jñāninas tattva-darśinaḥ

> To learn the truth, go humbly to a saint (*praṇipātena*), ask submissive questions of him (*paripraśnena*), and render service (*sevayā*) to him. The self-realized can impart knowledge for they have seen things as they are.

Baladeva Vidyabhushana defines *praṇipāta* as the physical offering of obeisance by falling on the ground before the spiritual master; *paripraśna* refers to asking questions about things like the Lord's nature, attributes, and powers; and *sevā* means serving at the guru's bidding with the attitude of a menial servant. Vishwanatha says that the fuel for the sacrificial fire consists of questions like, "Where have I come from? How have I become entangled in this material condition? How can I become freed from it?"

The *Kaṭha Upaniṣad* (2.3.14) states, *uttiṣṭhata jāgrata prāpya varān nibodhata*: "Arise! Awake! Take the benefits this human life has to offer and become enlightened." This verse indicates the necessity of taking a spiritual master and becoming initiated in the mantra by him, for it is an exhortation to awaken to one's spiritual identity, which can only be achieved by taking shelter of the most qualified teacher one can find and becoming initiated by him.

The *Śvetāśvatara Upaniṣad* (6.23) says:

yasya deve parā bhaktir
yathā deve tathā gurau

tasyaite kathitā hy arthāḥ
prakāśante mahātmanaḥ

> Only unto those great souls who have the highest devotion both for the Lord and, in equal measure, for the spiritual master, who is His manifestation and not different from Him, are all the imports of Vedic knowledge automatically revealed.

Unless one has this highest devotion (*parā bhakti*) for the spiritual master, one cannot hope to have the meaning of the scriptures revealed.

In His teachings to Rupa Goswami, Mahaprabhu says:

brahmāṇḍa bhramite kona bhāgyavān jīva
guru-kṛṣṇa-prasāde pāya bhakti-latā-bīja

> In the course of traversing the universal creation of Brahma, by the grace of guru and Krishna, some fortunate soul may receive the seed of the creeper of devotional service. (*Caitanya-caritāmṛta* 2.19.151)

As soon as the devotee has received this seed, he takes on the role of a gardener, carefully planting the seed in his heart and then watering it with acts of devotion, such as hearing and chanting. By the spiritual master's grace, the seed sprouts and starts to grow, becoming a luxuriant vine that grows up toward the universal coverings, crossing the Viraja River, and passing through the Brahmaloka until it reaches the spiritual sky. From there it continues to grow until it reaches Goloka Vrindavan, where it winds around the desire tree of Krishna's lotus feet. The gardener goes on caring for the creeper throughout, watering it with hearing and chanting about Krishna. The luxuriant creeper growing around the desire tree of Krishna gives abundant fruits of divine love, which the gardener enjoys with great pleasure.

While one is engaged in the practices of devotional service, one must take special care not to commit offenses, for these act on one's devotional garden like an intoxicated elephant, doing untold damage. Besides this, committing offenses allows suckers to sprout from the creeper's main stem. These suckers are the innumerable desires for material enjoyment and liberation, and the performance of acts forbidden by shastra, deceit, duplicity, faultfinding, violence toward other living beings, focus on material gain, respect, fame, and so on. When watering the bhakti creeper these suckers are also nourished and curtail the growth of the main stem. So the gardener's first job is to prune these unwanted branches through obedience to the spiritual master and thus allow the main stem to grow all the way to Goloka Vrindavan. If one does this, one will attain the good fortune of tasting the fruits of the vine of devotion, divine love, which makes all the other goals of human life pale into insignificance.

Divine love arises out of pure devotion. Through faithful adherence to the spiritual master's directions, one will receive the blessings by which these are attained. Therefore, taking shelter of the spiritual master's lotus feet is an absolute necessity.

Forgetfulness of one's true identity is the source of all kinds of misfortune. The *jīva* is Krishna's eternal servant, and as soon as he forgets this, he becomes bound by the shackles of Maya's three *guṇas*. The only escape from this bondage is in taking shelter of a pure devotee spiritual master and serving Krishna. In the *Caitanya-caritāmṛta* (2.22.24–25), Krishna Das Kaviraj Goswami states:

kṛṣṇa nitya dāsa jīva tāhā bhuli gela
sei doṣe māyā tāra galāya bāndhila
tāte kṛṣṇa bhaje kare gurura sevana
māyā-jāla chuṭe pāya tabe kṛṣṇera caraṇa

The *jīva* is the eternal servant of Krishna, but has forgotten it. For this mistake, Maya has placed a rope around his neck. If he worships Krishna and

> serves the spiritual master, he can be freed from the illusory entanglements of material life and attain Krishna's lotus feet.

And in *Śrīmad Bhāgavatam* (10.87.33), the *śrutis* pray:

> *vijita-hṛṣīka-vāyubhir adānta-manas tura-gaṁ*
> *ya iha yatanti yantum ati-lolam upāya-khidaḥ*
> *vyasana-śatānvitāḥ samavahāya guroś caraṇaṁ*
> *vaṇija ivāja santy akṛta-karṇa-dharā jaladhau*

> O unborn Lord! Those who try to reign in the wild horse of the uncontrolled mind by conquering the senses and life airs become frustrated and confused about how to do so. They become filled with all kinds of anxieties if they refuse to take shelter of a spiritual master. They are like merchants sailing on the ocean on a captainless boat.

When Ramananda Ray expressed great humility because Mahaprabhu, a *brāhmaṇa* and sannyasi, was listening to him, a *śūdra* and householder, the Lord replied:

> *kibā vipra kibā nyāsī śūdra kene naya*
> *jei kṛṣṇa tattva vettā sei guru haya*

> A person who knows the truths of spiritual life is qualified to be guru, whether he is a *brāhmaṇa*, sannyasi, or *śūdra*. (CC 2.8.128)

In the *Amṛta-pravāha-bhāṣya*, Srila Bhaktivinoda Thakur discusses the above verse:

> The Lord is saying here, "I took birth as a *brāhmaṇa* and then was initiated as a renunciant. This means

> that by the accepted social norms I should not accept instruction in religious matters from someone in the lower castes. But no one should think in this way. Even though it is necessary for everyone to accept initiation in and instruction into the *varṇāśrama* system from a *brāhmaṇa* guru, when it comes to understanding Krishna, which is the ultimate goal and perfection of all living beings, the only qualification necessary for a teacher is that he knows the subject matter. All other considerations, especially those related to birth and social status, are secondary. The *Hari-bhakti-vilāsa* does indeed advise that where a qualified person in a higher caste is available, one should not take the mantra from someone in a lower caste. But such statements are directed to Vaishnavas who are compromised by social considerations—in other words, those for whom spiritual life is secondary to the mundane social order. For others, who have come to understand the glories of pure devotional service and wish to attain it, whether through the process of *vaidhi-* or *raganuga-bhakti,* they should approach the appropriate knower of the subject and accept him as preceptor, without consideration of caste or race."

The *Hari-bhakti-vilāsa* (10.165) quotes a verse from the *Magha-māhātmya* of the *Padma Purāṇa* that supports this opinion:

> *na śūdrā bhagavad-bhaktās*
> *te tu bhāgavattotamāḥ*
> *sarva-varṇeṣu te śūdrā*
> *ye na bhaktā janārdane*

> Devotees of the Lord are not considered to be *śūdra,* but the best of the bhagavatas. On the other hand,

> those in all the other castes are mere *śūdras* if they are not devoted to Janardana.

There are many such verses in shastra, like those cited in the *Amṛta-pravāha-bhāṣya*:

> *ṣaṭ-karma-nipuṇo vipro mantra-tantra-viśāradaḥ*
> *avaiṣṇavo gurur na syād vaiṣṇavaḥ śvapaco guruḥ*

> A *brāhmaṇa* expert in the six disciplines, with vast learning in the mantras and tantras, should not be considered a guru if he is not a Vaishnava. On the other hand, a Vaishnava, even if he is an outcaste, can be accepted as a guru.

> *mahā-kula-prasūto'pi sarva-yajñeṣu dīkṣitaḥ*
> *sahasra-śākhādhyāyī ca na guruḥ syād avaiṣṇavaḥ*

> A *brāhmaṇa* born in a noble family, who has been initiated in all the sacrifices and who has studied a thousand branches of knowledge, should not be considered a guru if he is not a Vaishnava.

> *vipra-kṣatriya-vaiśyāś ca guravaḥ śūdra-janmanām*
> *śūdrāś ca guravas teṣāṁ trayāṇāṁ bhagavat-priyāḥ*

> *Brāhmaṇas, kṣatriyas,* and *vaiśyas* are by nature the spiritual masters of those born as *śūdras*. *Śūdras* who are dear to the Lord, however, are spiritual masters to the other three castes.

The conclusion is that it is absolutely necessary to take shelter of a pure Vaishnava. King Nimi asked Prabuddha, "What is the easiest way to get free from the grip of Vishnu's unyielding Maya?" Prabuddha replied, "Even though everyone makes every effort to find happiness and avoid distress, we see that they nearly always get the opposite result. They use the money they have earned with great difficulty to accumulate a wife, children, relatives, pets, and all kinds of other temporal goods, all of which lead to the death of the soul, but none to real happiness. A person who wants to find the ultimate solution to life's problems approaches a spiritual master who is knowledgeable in the science of Krishna. *Śrīmad Bhāgavatam* (11.3.27) states:

tasmād guruṁ prapadyeta
jijñāsuḥ śreya uttamam
śābde pare ca niṣṇātaṁ
brahmaṇy upaśamāśrayam

> Therefore a person who wants to know where the ultimate happiness lies approaches a spiritual master who has experience of both the spiritual sound and the supreme spirit, whose desires for the temporary have been quietened, and who is thus free from the control of lust and greed.

The words *śabda brahma* refer to the divine revelation of the Vedas and other scriptural texts. Therefore one who is *niṣṇāta*, who has completely bathed in the scriptural revelation, is one who knows the spiritual truths; if he is not such a knower he will not be able to remove the disciple's doubts. On the other hand, if one takes the word *pare* to modify *brahmaṇi* rather than *śābde*, then *pare brahmaṇi niṣṇāta* means "someone who has direct experience of the transcendental, or that which lies beyond the perception of the material senses." If the spiritual master does not have this qualification, he will be unable to transmit transcendental understanding to the disciple.

How can we recognize if the guru has such qualifications? The evidence is in the word *upaśamāśrayaḥ*, "supremely peaceful": "one whose desires for the temporal have been quieted and who is thus free from the control of lust and greed." Sanatana Goswami defines the word *upaśamāśrayam* as "having taken shelter of bhakti yoga."

> The supreme spirit is Krishna. Tranquility (*śama*) means liberation, so *upaśama* means that which lies beyond liberation, i.e., loving devotion to Krishna. Taking shelter of loving devotion (*upaśamāśraya*) means to be engaged in devotional activities like hearing and chanting. One who has so taken shelter is the best of Vaishnavas.[4]

So the most essential quality of a Vaishnava guru is that he is always engaged in hearing and chanting about Krishna. No disciple can achieve the supreme good in his life without approaching a spiritual master of this sort (*gurūpasatti*).

ONE NEEDS A GURU TO INTERPRET SHASTRA

The *Śrīmad Bhāgavatam* was Srila Vyasadeva's final work. It was revealed to him when he was in the deepest trance. It is thus the most authoritative of all revealed texts describing the nature of the Supreme Lord. In *Śrīmad Bhāgavatam* we read that when Suta Goswami came before the sixty thousand sages in the forest of Naimisharanya, their leader, Shaunaka Rishi, greeted him and said, "Dear sinless Suta! You have studied the historical works, such as the *Mahābhārata* and the eighteen *Purāṇas*. Along with them, you have studied the twenty great law books (*dharma-śāstras*) written by seers such as Yajnavalkya. You have gone through these texts under the guidance of your gurus, who know both the formless Brahman and the Brahman with form and you have yourself taken on the role of a teacher and explained these works to your students.

vettha tvaṁ saumya tat sarvaṁ
tattvatas tad anugrahāt
brūyuḥ snigdhasya śiṣyasya
guravo guhyam apy uta

[4] *pare brahmaṇi śrī-kṛṣṇe śamo mokṣas tad-upari vartata iti upaśamo bhakti-yogas tad-āśrayaṁ sadā śravaṇa-kīrtanādi-paraṁ śrī-vaiṣṇava-varam ity arthaḥ (Dig-darśinī, Hari-bhakti-vilāsa* 1.32).

> O learned one! You know all that Vyasadeva knows and all that other wise men know by their grace, for spiritual masters speak in confidence to disciples they hold dear. (ŚB 1.1.8)

"Therefore, O best of sages, since you have this experience, please tell us the essence of all these scriptures. What is most auspicious for humanity? There are so many kinds of religious disciplines and duties, and so many scriptures describing them, each with many divisions and subdivisions and each claiming we should hear and study them. But we ask you, with your purified intelligence: what have you found to be the most beneficial conclusion of all? What is the essential and supreme truth? What will bring peace and satisfaction to the soul? We have heard that such peace and satisfaction come from turning toward Lord Hari and pleasing him, so please tell us how that can be accomplished, for of all topics worth hearing, that is the essence."

Altogether, the *ṛṣis*, headed by Shaunaka, asked six questions:

1. What is the most auspicious thing for all humanity?
2. What is that essential subject, which simply hearing will bring peace and satisfaction to both the *jīva* and the Supreme Soul?
3. Please describe Vasudeva's activities.
4. Please tell us the reason for Vasudeva's appearance in this world.
5. Please describe Vasudeva's glories.
6. Now that Lord Krishna has returned to His abode, where has religion taken refuge?

In *Śrīmad Bhāgavatam* 1.2.6, Suta immediately answered the first two questions at the beginning of his recital:

sa vai puṁsāṁ paro dharmo
yato bhaktir adhokṣaje

ahaituky apratihatā
yayātmā suprasīdati

> The supreme religious activity of the human being is that which results in devotion to the Supreme Lord, who is beyond the ken of our material senses. This devotion must be without motivation and uninterrupted—only then will it bring full contentment to the soul.

Unmotivated (*ahaitukī*) devotion means that the bhakta desires no material fruit, no material benefit, from his performance of devotional service. Uninterrupted (*apratihatā*) means that the *bhakta* allows for no obstacle in his performance of devotional service (or, as Vishwanatha says, *kenāpi nivārayitum aśakyā*, meaning "unable to be stopped by anyone"). Such devotion is further described as exclusive (*aikāntikī*), natural, or spontaneous (*svābhāvikī*), and independent (*nirapekṣā*). It is the ultimate religious activity of humankind. By the strength of such pure devotional service, all of one's self-destructive tendencies are calmed and one attains spiritual contentment.

Devotional service is principally characterized by hearing and chanting about Krishna. In its external forms, devotional service does not change drastically from the beginning practitioner to the perfected soul. Rather, devotional service in practice simply becomes *prema*, or love of God, when it matures. Thus the *Bhāgavatam* teaches the three aspects of spiritual knowledge: *sambandha*, or the understanding that Krishna is *svayaṁ-bhagavān*, the undifferentiated, nondual Supreme Truth and the son of the king of Vraja; *abhidheya*, or the active means by which one attains that Vrajendra-nandana in devotion; and *prayojana*, or the attainment of the ultimate goal of life, *prema*.

Normally, in order to attain any type of knowledge, including technical or professional knowledge, we need a teacher. How then can we think that when it comes to the most important knowledge—the nature, methods, and goals of spiritual perfection—we can dispense with a preceptor? The spiritual master who knows the supreme truth bestows divine knowledge on us. It does not matter what race he was born into, what his social status is, or whether he is a householder or a renunciant. The important thing is that he knows Krishna.

Regarding the need to take shelter of a spiritual master, the *Hari-bhakti-vilāsa* (1.28–29) states:

> By the mercy of Lord Krishna, when one hears the glories of devotional service through the association of His devotees and begins to feel a desire to practice it, one should approach a true spiritual master. For when one intensely feels the constant miseries of this world, and hears from the scriptures that such intolerable miseries will continue in the next life, the intelligent person desires deliverance.[5]

Sanatana Goswami comments:

> One may ask, since those who are attached to material sense gratification and its pleasures find even an awareness of such things difficult to achieve, how could they ever be expected to develop a desire for devotion? In answer to this, the author indicates that even those who want to cross over the ocean of misery and desire to practice devotion still depend on a *sad-guru*. Here it is said, "One who hears about the cycle of miseries from the scriptures" will come to believe in this Vedic teaching and will eventually perceive it directly, for such statements, being true,

---

[5] *kṛpayā kṛṣṇa-devasya tad-bhaktajana-saṅgataḥ*
bhakter māhātmyam ākarṇya tām icchan sad-guruṁ bhajet
atrānubhūyate nityaṁ duḥkha-śreṇī paratra ca
duḥsahā śrūyate śāstrāt titīrṣed api tāṁ sudhīḥ

> cannot be ignored. Thus he naturally desires to be freed from the endless cycle of misery. The word *api* here has the following force: if one desires liberation after hearing from sadhus and shastra but does not develop a desire for bhakti, which is glorious, then that is a great shame. If he does not consider these questions, he is like an animal without any rational capacity. Or, he is like an animal killer (*vyādha*), who simply goes through life accepting illusory miseries as inevitable.[6]

In support of these statements, Gopala Bhatta Goswami references *Śrīmad-Bhāgavatam* 11.9.29 (quoted in HBV 1.30):

labdhvā sudurlabham idaṁ bahu-sambhavānte
mānuṣyam arthadam anityam apīha dhīraḥ
tūrṇaṁ yateta na pated anumṛtyu yāvat
niḥśreyasāya viṣayaḥ khalu sarvataḥ syāt

> After many, many births, one finally has the good fortune to be born in a most rare and valuable human body, which even though it has only a brief duration, still provides an opportunity to attain the supreme goal of life. Therefore, the wise individual should without any delay take up the effort to find that which provides the supreme good in all times and circumstances, and not give up that effort even up to the very moment of his death.

---

[6] *nanu viṣaya-sukhāsaktānāṁ tādṛśa-jñānaṁ durghaṭam eveti kuto bhaktīcchāstu? satyaṁ, duḥkha-sāgara-taraṇecchayāpi bhaktiṁ vāñchan sad-gurum apekṣetaivety āśayena likhati—atreti. duḥkhasya śreṇī-paramparā śāstrāc chrūyata iti veda-vākye viśvāsāt sāpi pratyetavyaiva. na tv aviśvasanīyety arthaḥ. atas tāṁ duḥkha-śreṇīm api tarītum icchet, mā tādṛśa-māhātmyaṁ bhaktim icchatv ity aho bata śocyatety api-śabdārthaḥ. sudhīś cet, anyathā vicārābhāvena paśuvan nirbuddhir evety arthaḥ. yad vā, mithyā-duḥkhāvalī-sahanena vyādhādivat kudhīr evety arthaḥ.*

The point is that one can experience the pleasures of the senses even in the lower forms of life, but the higher purpose of life, spiritual realization, can only be attained in the human body.

Vishwanatha Chakravarti Thakur discusses the word *anumṛtyu*, which appears in the above verse, making the point that death is inevitable in every species of life. By underlining the fact that death is also inevitable for those in human bodies he conveys a sense of urgency. Since life is so tenuous, and death so inevitable and random, one should serve Govinda's lotus feet without delay. Nor can one appeal to the idea that he'll be reborn and can therefore serve Govinda later, because one will not necessarily get another chance at this rare human form of life. The guru is the connection to the transcendental reality. One must seek him out while we still have the chance.

In *Śrīmad Bhāgavatam* 11.20.17 (quoted in HBV 1.31), Krishna further explains the role of the spiritual master:

nṛ-deham ādyaṁ sulabhaṁ sudurlabhaṁ
plavaṁ su-kalpaṁ guru-karṇa-dhāram
mayānukūlena nabhasvateritaṁ
pumān bhavābdhiṁ na taret sa ātma-hā

> This human body is the root of all benefits. It seems so easily obtained, yet it is in fact extremely rare. It is like a boat especially designed for crossing the ocean of material existence. If one has a spiritual master to guide him as the boat's helmsman and is given the favorable winds of My mercy, but still he fails to cross over, then he is willfully committing suicide.

In his comment on this verse, Srila Vishwanatha Chakravarti Thakur exclaims: "In this verse, the Lord decries the person who rejects the spiritual master. Such a person is like a foolish pauper who throws a *cintamaṇi* gem into the mud."

After these verses, the *Hari-bhakti-vilāsa* begins a new section, called "Approaching the Spiritual Master" (*gurūpasattiḥ*). This section starts with a quote from the conversation between King Nimi and the nine great yogis. Nimi, king of Videha, asks Prabuddha, "O great sage, please explain to me how humankind can overcome this illusory world of Maya when they are filled with egoism and possessiveness and beset by uncontrolled senses."

Prabuddha replies, "In this world, we see that people are engaged in so many activities in the hope of eliminating distress and achieving happiness. However, the results of their activities deceive them and they never get the full happiness they are looking for."

There is a Bengali song that also says this:

sukhera lāgiyā e ghara bāṁdhinu
anale puṛiyā gelo
amiya sāyare sināna karite
amiya garala bhelo

> I built this house to be happy, but it burned down. It is as though I went for a bath in what I thought was an ocean of ambrosia and it turned out to be poison.

Of course, this song was sung in a different context—it describes Radharani's feelings of separation from Krishna. In Her pain She compares Her situation to that of a disappointed materialist. The song expresses a very elevated mood of love. Nevertheless, the verse is applicable to the condition of the materialist because this kind of disappointment occurs frequently.

Prabuddha Muni continues in *Śrīmad Bhāgavatam* 11.3.21 (quoted in HBV 1.32), advising Nimi on the importance of taking shelter of a spiritual master in order to find ultimate spiritual benefit:

tasmād guruṁ prapadyeta
jijñāsuḥ śreya uttamam
śābde pare ca niṣṇātaṁ
brahmaṇy upaśamāśrayam

Therefore, one who is inquisitive about the ultimate good in life should surrender to a spiritual master who has thoroughly understood the purport of the scriptures, who is fixed in divine realization, and has attained peace from the sense impulses.

In this verse, the adjectives *śābde* ("sound") and *pare* ("beyond") are both read with *brahmaṇi* (Brahman). So *śābde brahmaṇi* means the form of God in sound vibration, or the revealed scriptures. The words *pare brahmaṇi* refer to God's transcendental being. The spiritual master must be fully conversant (*niṣṇātam*) with both these aspects of Brahman.

Vishwanatha Chakravarti Thakur comments here that one must take shelter of a guru who has understood the purport of the scriptures (*śābde brahmaṇi niṣṇātam*), that is, the Vedas and the subsequent literature that expands on their meaning, such as the Gita and *Bhāgavatam*. If the spiritual master is not fully knowledgeable and expert in the scriptures, he will not be able to rid the disciple of doubt. As a result, when the disciple becomes inattentive, his faith might weaken. The spiritual master should also have direct experience of the Supreme Brahman, or Krishna (*pare brahmaṇi niṣṇātam*). Without such direct realization of transcendence, the spiritual master's blessings will not be effectual.

The conclusion is that a highly qualified Vaishnava is worthy to be taken as a spiritual master. This is further emphasized elsewhere in the *Bhāgavatam* (11.10.5):

mad-abhijñaṁ guruṁ śāntam
upāsīta mad-ātmakam

> One should worship the guru, who is familiar with My attributes, such as My loving affection for My devotees, through direct experience (*mad-abhijña*), whose mind has been immersed in Me (*mad-ātmaka*), and who has the quality of peacefulness (*śānta*).

The next verse cited in the *Hari-bhakti-vilāsa* (1.34) comes from the *Krama-dīpikā*[7] (4.2). This verse states quite elaborately the characteristics of the guru:

vipraṁ pradhvasta-kāma-prabhṛti-ripu-ghaṭaṁ nirmalāṅgaṁ gariṣṭhāṁ
bhaktiṁ kṛṣṇāṅghri-paṅkeruha-yugala-rajorāgiṇīm udvahantam
vettāraṁ veda-śāstrāgama-vimala-pathāṁ sammataṁ satsu dāntaṁ
vidyāṁ yaḥ saṁvivitsuḥ pravaṇa-tanu-manā deśikaṁ saṁśrayeta

> One who desires to receive the mantra by which the miseries of material life can be overcome should humbly approach an instructor who:

1. Is a *brāhmaṇa*
2. Has defeated all the internal enemies, such as lust, anger, and greed
3. Has a pure body (a body free of disease)
4. Is filled with the deepest devotion, characterized by a passionate love for Lord Krishna's lotus feet
5. Knows the pure path delineated in both the Vedas and the *Pañcarātra Āgamas*
6. Is approved by the society of the pious
7. Is sense-controlled (*dānta*)

The Bhagavad Gita is the essence of all the Vedas. The Bhagavad Gita states that Krishna is the Supreme Person, the object of knowledge of all the Vedic literature. He is the ultimate author of the Vedas and alone

[7] This important work by Keshava Kasmiri is one of the principal sources of the *Hari-bhakti-vilāsa*. Gopala Bhatta Goswami cites it particularly in the chapters on *dīkṣā* and *puraścaraṇa*.

fully knows their purpose. Near the end of the Twelfth Canto of *Śrīmad Bhāgavatam* Vyasadeva states that the *Bhāgavatam* is the essence of the Vedanta (*sarva-vedānta-sāraṁ hi*), the "end of the Vedas," or the *Upaniṣads*. Both the Gita and the *Bhāgavatam* state that one can attain Krishna only through single-pointed devotion. Therefore, the true *brāhmaṇa* is one who has understood the Vedas and realized Krishna (both of which are designated by the word *Brahman*). Only such a person is eligible to accept the designation of guru.

In this connection, it is necessary once again to review this injunction to only take a spiritual master who is a *vipra*, or *brāhmaṇa*. Someone who has taken birth in a *brāhmaṇa* family and has all the qualifications of a spiritual master is certainly eligible to play that role. However, his birth alone is an insufficient qualification. Sri Chaitanya Mahaprabhu clearly indicated this in His conversations with Ramananda Ray:

> *kibā vipra kibā nyāsī śūdra kene naya*
> *jei kṛṣṇa-tattva-vettā, se-i guru haya*

> It does not matter whether one is a *brāhmaṇa,* a sannyasi, or even a *śūdra*. As long as one is knowledgeable about Krishna, he is a guru.

Srila Bhaktisiddhanta Saraswati comments on this text in his Anubhāṣya:

> No matter what caste or class of society one belongs to, if one knows the science of Krishna, he is eligible to act in any category of guru—whether it be the guru who indicates the path of spiritual life (*vartma-pradarśaka-guru*), the initiating (*dīkṣā*) guru, or the instructing (*śikṣā*) guru. The only real consideration in assessing the spiritual master's qualification is his knowledge of the science of Krishna. It has nothing to do with his social station or status.

> One should not think that Mahaprabhu here contradicts the usual scriptural directives. . . . Rather, there are many statements in the *Mahābhārata* and *Bhāgavatam* that confirm this idea, such as the following important text from the *Śrīmad Bhāgavatam* (7.11.35):
>
> *yasya yal lakṣaṇaṁ proktaṁ*
> *puṁso varṇābhivyañjakam*
> *yad anyatrāpi dṛśyeta*
> *tat tenaiva vinirdiśet*
>
> In the foregoing discussion of the four divisions of society, descriptions were given of each of them. If the characteristics so described appear in a member of another caste, they should be taken to indicate the real caste of the person.

Sridhar Swami here says:

> The principal designators of the *brāhmaṇa* are his behavior, namely sense control, etc., and not birth alone. Although normally one is recognized as a *brāhmaṇa* as a consequence of being born into a particular family, this is not the only criterion of someone's *brāhmaṇa*-hood. It is to this end that this statement has been made. In cases where someone has not been born as a *brāhmaṇa* but still has the requisite qualities, these qualities should take precedence in assessing his status. To not do so is an aberration.[8]

[8] *śamādibhir eva brāhmaṇādi-vyavahāro mukhyaḥ, na jāti-mātrāt. yad yadi anyatra dṛśyate taj-jāty-antaraṁ tenaiva lakṣaṇa-nimittenaiva varṇane vinirdiśet, na tu jāti-nimittenety arthaḥ.*

Srila Vishwanatha Chakravarti Thakur comments:

> There are certain general characteristics that indicate the different castes, such as the sense control and self-discipline of the *brāhmaṇa*. These are what are being talked about in this verse, and not the specific activities or duties, such as the *brāhmaṇa's* observance of the *sandhya* three times a day. If the abovementioned general characteristics are seen in someone who has taken birth in another caste, then that person should still be identified as being a *brāhmaṇa*, which here means that he should be given the same degree of respect and honor that would be given to a *brāhmaṇa*. In this case, one should not think that the Gita verse (3.35) applies: "It is better to perform one's own duty imperfectly than another's duty, no matter how perfectly executed. It is better to die in the performance of one's own duty, for the duty of another is fraught with danger." Cultivating the qualities of self-control and self-discipline, etc., are never the duties of "another" but of everyone.

In other words, birth alone cannot be said to determine caste. This is made clear by the use of the optative mood, or *vidhi-liṅ*, which indicates a general instruction (*vidhi*). By the same token, if the qualifications of a guru are seen in someone who is not of the *brāhmaṇa* caste, his qualifications should still be taken to indicate his real status as guru. As such, even someone who by birth is a *śūdra* or some other caste but who knows the teachings of *kṛṣṇa-bhakti* should be considered a guru. This is Sri Chaitanya Mahaprabhu's instruction.

The *Muṇḍaka Upaniṣad* (1.2.11) also clearly shows that what we look for in a spiritual guide are real spiritual qualifications:

tad-vijñānārthaṁ sa gurum evābhigacchet
samit-pāṇiḥ śrotriyaṁ brahma-niṣṭham

> In order to learn the truth, one should take gifts in hand and approach a spiritual master who is learned and fixed in Brahman.

In this verse, the word *tad-vijñāna* means knowing fully the Supreme substance, the Supreme Lord, through the process of devotional service. The words *śrotriyaṁ brahma-niṣṭham* have the same import as *śābde pare ca niṣṇātaṁ brahmaṇy upaśamāśrayam*, found in the *Bhāgavatam* verse quoted above. In other words, the guru is a knower of Krishna (*kṛṣṇa-tattva-vit*). If one finds such a qualified spiritual master, one should go to him and surrender to him fully.

The *Chāndogya Upaniṣad* (6.14.2) also confirms: *ācāryavān puruṣo veda*, "One who has taken a spiritual master knows." In other words, one who has taken shelter and been initiated by a true spiritual master can know the *Param-brahma*."

The *Kaṭha Upaniṣad* (1.3.14) states:

uttiṣṭhata jāgrata prāpya varān nibodhata
kṣurasya dhārā niśitā duratyayā durgaṁ pathas tat kavayo vadanti

> The *Veda Puruṣa* gives the following beneficial instruction to the sages in the following words: "Rise up! Awake! Seize the benefits of this human form of life and become conscious. This path is as difficult to tread as the sharp edge of a razor."

And the *Śvetāśvatara Upaniṣad* (6.23) states:

yasya deve parā bhaktir
yathā deve tathā gurau

tasyaite kathitā hy arthāḥ
prakāśante mahātmanaḥ

Only unto those great souls who have implicit faith in both the Lord and the spiritual master, who is His manifestation and not different from Him, are all the imports of Vedic knowledge automatically revealed.

In the *Caitanya-caritāmṛta* (2.19.151), Mahaprabhu tells Sri Rupa Goswami:

ei rūpa saṁsāra bhramite kono bhāgyavān jīva
guru kṛṣṇa prasāde pāya bhakti-latā-bīja

Wandering in this way through the worlds, some fortunate *jīva* receives the seed of the devotional creeper through the mercy of the guru and Krishna.

In *Caitanya-caritāmṛta* (2.22.25) the Lord says:

tāte kṛṣṇa bhaje kare gurura sevana
māyā jāla chuṭe pāya śrī-kṛṣṇa-caraṇa

Thereupon, he takes up the worship of Krishna and the service of his spiritual master. He thus escapes the nets of Maya and attains Krishna's lotus feet.

In *Caitanya-caritāmṛta* (2.25.270) Krishna Das Kaviraj Goswami says:

caitanya-līlāmṛta pūra kṛṣṇa-līlā-sukarpūra
duṅhe mile haya sumādhurya
sādhu guru prasāde tāhā jei āsvāde
sei jāne mādhurya prācurya

Chaitanya Mahaprabhu's pastimes are full of ambrosia; Krishna's pastimes are the camphor that

> increases their delicious taste. One who relishes that nectar through the mercy of the guru and the saintly Vaishnavas experiences an abundance of sweetness.

In *Caitanya-caritāmṛta* (1.1.45) it is stated:

> *guru kṛṣṇa-rūpa hana śāstrera pramāṇe*
> *guru-rūpe kṛṣṇa kṛpā kare bhakta-gaṇe*

> According to the evidence of the scriptures, the spiritual master is a form of Lord Krishna. In the form of the spiritual master, Krishna gives His blessings to the devotees.

And according to *Śrīmad Bhāgavatam* (11.17.27):

> *ācāryaṁ māṁ vijānīyān*
> *nāvamanyeta karhicit*
> *na martya buddhyāsūyeta*
> *sarva deva mayo guruḥ*

> A disciple should consider his teacher to be My very self and never disrespect him in any way. One should not envy him, thinking him to be an ordinary man, for he is the sum total of all the demigods.

Krishna is the root, the *viṣaya-vigraha*, but in order to show mercy to the devotees, He appears in the form of the spiritual master, the *āśraya-vigraha*. We should never think of the spiritual master as an ordinary human being, for even though he appears to us in human form, he is of the transcendental realm. Our worshipable Srila Prabhupada discussed this verse in his *Vivṛti*:

> When the Supreme Lord takes the role of instructor in His desire to benefit the conditioned souls, he

> is called the *ācārya*. If one shows disrespect to the instructor *ācārya,* or if a disciple or student foolishly thinks himself equal to the spiritual master, envies him, or competes with him, then, because his faith in the teacher is damaged, it will be impossible for him to complete his course of study. One who wishes to fully understand the designated subject matter should worship the spiritual master according to the appropriate regulations, aware that the spiritual master is the Supreme Lord appearing as a devotee but nevertheless of the same substance (*tad-vastu*) as the Supreme Lord. Rather than considering the spiritual master to be the supreme object of devotion, one should consider him to be the reservoir of that devotion. Nevertheless, he is substantially the same.

The last sentence of the above statement should be given special attention. In the seventh verse of *Sri Gurvaṣṭakam,* Vishwanatha Chakravarti Thakur summarizes *guru-tattva* when he writes, "All the scriptures declare the spiritual master to be the Supreme Lord Himself." This is furthermore confirmed by the saintly. Nevertheless, the spiritual master is identified in this way because he is the dearly beloved of the Lord. This means that he is Krishna's *prakāśa-vigraha*—a form through which He makes Himself visible in the world.

So the Supreme Lord Himself has two manifestations: as *viṣaya* and as *āśraya*. Although normally the Supreme Lord is seen as the ultimate object of devotion, when He manifests as the *āśraya-vigraha,* this is called *guru-tattva*. Unless one has grasped the idea of *acintya-bhedābheda,* it is inevitable that one will be confused by this understanding of *guru-tattva*. A pure devotee spiritual master who knows the science of Krishna will deliver his disciple from the clutches of *Mayavada* philosophy by explaining the particularities of Vaishnava theology, or *sambandha-jñāna.*

Śrīmad Bhāgavatam 10.87.33 stresses the necessity of taking shelter of a spiritual master:

vijita-hṛṣīka-vāyubhir adānta-manas tura-gaṁ
ya iha yatanti yantum ati-lolam upāya-khidaḥ
vyasana-śatānvitāḥ samavahāya guroś caraṇaṁ
vaṇija ivāja santy akṛta-karṇa-dharā jaladhau

> Those who try to reign in the wild horse of the uncontrolled mind by conquering the senses and life air become frustrated and confused about how to do so; they are filled with all kinds of anxieties if they refuse to take shelter of a spiritual master, like merchants sailing the ocean on a captainless boat.

This verse is also quoted in the *Hari-bhakti-vilāsa,* where Srila Sanatana Prabhu comments on it: "Even those who have been able to conquer the senses and the life airs through the yoga path are still unable to control the mind, which is like a wild horse. If one tries to do so without taking shelter of a spiritual master, he will only become frustrated. In other words, he remains in the ocean of material life and suffering without a way to escape. Constantly tormented by the sense objects, he suffers endlessly on this ocean like a merchant sailing a boat without a helmsman."

In his *Sārārtha-darśinī,* Vishwanatha Chakravarti Thakur also comments on this verse:

> The question may arise, "Should those seeking to conquer the mind take to the practices of the eightfold yoga system?" The answer is a clear no, for they can more easily quieten the mind through intense devotion to the spiritual master. For it is said in the *Bhāgavatam* (7.15.25), "One can overcome all difficulties through devotion to the spiritual master."[9] In

[9] *sarvaṁ caitad gurau bhaktyā puruṣo hy añjasā jayet.*

> fact, without devotion to the spiritual master, any yoga system is worthless in the matter of conquering the mind. This is what is being said in this verse.

There are several statements in the *Upaniṣads* that support this view. The following verse from the *Kaṭha Upaniṣad* (1.2.9) was spoken by Yamaraja to Nachiketa, who asked for instruction about Brahman:

naiṣā tarkeṇa matir āpaneyā
proktānyenaiva sujñānāya preṣṭha
yāṁ tvam āpaḥ satya-dhṛtir batāsi
tvādṛṅ no bhūyān naciketaḥ praṣṭā

> My most dear one! The determination you have to learn about the Self cannot be achieved through arguments, but only by hearing from another. May I find another pupil like you, Nachiketa, who has the patience to seek the truth.

In this verse, "only from another" (*anyenaiva*) refers to someone who has been able to recognize the difference between the individual and the supreme souls. The intelligence gained by hearing from such a person will lead to "proper knowledge" (*sujñāna*), meaning full knowledge of the supreme soul. The word *bata* in the third line shows Yama's great amazement that Nachiketa was *satya-dhṛti,* or so determined to find the truth that he was able to resist all the temptations Yamaraja offered him in an attempt to distract him. Therefore, Yamaraja asked that he could have other students like Nachiketa with the same determination to achieve supreme knowledge.

The purport of this statement is that knowledge of *sambandha-, abhidheya-,* and *prayojana-tattva* cannot be had by the ascending process of knowledge. One must receive it from a spiritual master by taking shelter of him and being blessed by his mercy.

In his own edition of the *Kaṭha Upaniṣad,* Siddhanti Maharaj gives a number of references that support the need for a guru in his commentary on the verse quoted above. For instance, Lord Krishna says in the Bhagavad Gita (4.34):

> *tad viddhi praṇipātena*
> *paripraśnena sevayā*
> *upadekṣyanti te jñānaṁ*
> *jñāninas tattva-darśinaḥ*

> Try to learn the truth by approaching a spiritual master. Inquire submissively and render service unto him. Self-realized souls can impart knowledge because they are seers of the truth.

And Siddhanti Maharaj quotes other supportive verses:

> *ācāryavān puruṣo veda*

> Only one who has taken a spiritual preceptor can know the Supreme Truth. (*Chāndogya Upaniṣad* 6.14.2)

> *tad-vijñānārthaṁ sa gurum evābhigacchet*
> *samit-pāṇiḥ śrotriyaṁ brahma-niṣṭham*

> In order to realize the truth, one should take gifts in hand and approach a spiritual master who is learned and fixed in Brahman. (*Muṇḍaka Upaniṣad* 1.2.11)

> *yasya deve parā bhaktir*
> *yathā deve tathā gurau*
> *tasyaite kathitā hy arthāḥ*
> *prakāśante mahātmanaḥ*

Only unto those great souls who have implicit faith in both the Lord and the spiritual master, who is His manifestation and not different from Him, are all the imports of Vedic knowledge automatically revealed. (*Śvetāśvatara Upaniṣad* 6.23)

tasmād guruṁ prapadyeta
jijñāsuḥ śreya uttamam
śābde pare ca niṣṇātaṁ
brahmaṇy upaśamāśrayam

Therefore one who is inquisitive about the ultimate good in life should surrender to a spiritual master who has thoroughly understood the purport of the scriptures, who is fixed in divine realization, and who has attained peace from the sense impulses. (*Śrīmad-Bhāgavatam* 11.3.21)

tarko'pratiṣṭhaḥ śrutayo vibhinnā
nāsau ṛṣir yasya mataṁ na bhinnam
dharmasya tattvaṁ nihitaṁ guhāyāṁ
mahājano yena gataḥ sa panthāḥ

Maharaja Yudhisthira said: "Argument alone has no solid foundation. The scriptures contradict each other. No one is considered a sage without having expressed an individual opinion. The truths about religious duty are concealed in the heart. Thus the only true path is the one that has been followed by great authorities." (*Mahābhārata, Vanaparva* 313.117)

Mahaprabhu confirms (CC 2.25.54–55):

parama kāraṇa īśvare keha nāhi māne
sva-sva-mata sthāpe para-matera khaṇḍane

tāte chaya darśana haite tattva nāhi jāni
mahājana jei kahe sei satya māni

> No one wants to accept that the supreme cause of all causes is the Lord. Instead they spend their time trying to establish their own position while tearing down others. As a result, I cannot know the truth from the six philosophical systems. I accept as truth that which the realized souls teach.

In Siddhanti Maharaj's reading of the *naiṣā tarkeṇa* verse, the word *preṣṭha* ("most dear") in the second line is taken as a vocative. In other words, Yamaraja is addressing Nachiketa as "most dear." In the *Hari-bhakti-vilāsa*, however, the word is written with a long *ā* at the end, making it an adjective describing *matiḥ*. Sanatana Goswami comments:

śobhana-jñānāya preṣṭhā parama-yogyatvena
priyatamā eṣā matis tarkeṇa
nija-nyāyena hetunā proktād anyena vidhinā
kṛtvā nāpaneyā apamārge
na praveśanīyety arthaḥ

> The determination (*mati*) that is most dear (*preṣṭhā*) due to being supremely appropriate (*parama-yogya*) is needed in order to attain this salutary knowledge. You should not tread on the path of iniquity by engaging in debate with others whose knowledge is limited.[10]

Narottam Das Thakur writes at the very beginning of the *Prema-bhakti-candrikā*:

[10] *śobhana-jñānāya preṣṭhā parama-yogyatvena priyatamā eṣā matis tarkeṇa nija-nyāyena hetunā proktād anyena vidhinā kṛtvā nāpaneyā apamārge na praveśanīyety arthaḥ.*

guru-mukha-padma-vākya cittete kariyā aikya
āra nā kariba mane āśā
śrī guru caraṇe rati, ei se uttama
gati je prasāde pūre sarva āśā

Fix your mind on the words emanating from the lotus mouth of the spiritual master. Place your hopes in nothing else. Affection for the guru's lotus feet is the ultimate goal, for by his mercy all of one's aspirations are realized.

tad-vijñānārthaṁ sa gurum evābhigacchet
samit-pāṇiḥ śrotriyaṁ brahma-niṣṭham

In order to realize the truth, one should take gifts in hand and approach a spiritual master who is learned and fixed in Brahman. (*Muṇḍaka Upaniṣad* 1.2.11)

Here the word *vijñāna* should be taken to mean knowledge combined with pure loving devotion. The spiritual master, or *sad-guru* is described here as *śrotriyaṁ* and *brahma-niṣṭham*, meaning that he knows the meaning of the Vedic scriptures and is fixed in devotion to Krishna. Finally, the prefix *abhi* means that one should go to the spiritual master in body, mind, and words. In other words, one should approach him physically, but in an appropriately humble frame of mind and with an inquiring spirit.

The *Kaṭha Upaniṣad* (1.2.23) states:

nāyam ātmā pravacanena labhyo
na medhayā na bahunā śrutena
yam evaiṣa vṛṇute tena labhyas
tasyaiṣa ātmā vivṛṇute tanūṁ svām

> This Soul cannot be reached through debate, nor through the intellect, nor through much study. He whom the Soul itself chooses reaches it. To him, the Soul reveals its own form.

This means that one cannot know the Paramatma through debate, reason, or scholarship. When the individual soul turns to God and His service through the shelter of the *sad-guru* and begs for His mercy, only then does the Paramatma reveal to the individual soul His own transcendental form.

All these verses from the *śrutis* clearly indicate the necessity of approaching a spiritual master and taking instruction from him. Similarly, the other great branch of Vedic knowledge, the *Smriti,* makes the same assertion. In the Bhagavad Gita (4.34) Krishna teaches us all through the words He directs at Arjuna:

tad viddhi praṇipātena
paripraśnena sevayā
upadekṣyanti te jñānaṁ
jñāninas tattva-darśinaḥ

> Try to learn the truth by approaching a spiritual master. Inquire submissively and render service unto him. Self-realized souls can impart knowledge because they are seers of the truth.

Krishna is saying, throw yourself at the feet of a spiritual master who has seen the truth. Prostrate yourself before him, please him with sincere service, and beg him to reveal the truths of spiritual life, saying, "O Gurudeva! How have I fallen into this material existence, where I must suffer the three kinds of miseries? How can I be delivered from it?" In response to these heartfelt inquiries, the spiritual master who has direct experience of the Supreme Brahman will divulge his understanding to the disciple.

Verses such as these from the *smṛti* have the same purpose as those like *tad-vijñānārtham*, which are from the *śruti*.

Sri Chaitanya Mahaprabhu instructed the world through His dear associates Sri Rupa and Sri Sanatana in the three kinds of spiritual knowledge, *sambandha*, *abhidheya*, and *prayojana*. The essence of these instructions can be summarized: The Veda is called *āmnāya*, or self-revealed knowledge. Based on this body of knowledge, one should learn about Krishna, Krishna's energies, and the nature of Krishna's relationships with His eternal associates. One should also understand the nature of the individual soul in both its bound and liberated states. Finally, one should conclude his understanding of *sambandha*, or metaphysics, by learning about the fundamental relationship of inconceivable oneness and difference between God and the individual soul. *Abhidheya* is the means by which the soul attains God—through the practice of bhakti. *Prayojana*, or the ultimate state of perfection, is love of God. These points form the ten pillars of Chaitanya Mahaprabhu's teachings.

The *sad-guru* is the great personality who knows these ten principles, and the student should attempt to master these ten divisions of knowledge by studying under his guru. The conclusion of all the scriptures—*śrutis*, *Smritis*, *Purāṇas*, and the *Pañcarātra*—is to worship the Lord under the guidance of a spiritual master.

Lord Brahma says in the *Vāmana-kalpa* (quoted in HBV 4.353):

yo mantraḥ sa guruḥ sākṣāt
yo guruḥ sa hariḥ smṛtaḥ
gurur yasya bhavet tuṣṭas
tasya tuṣṭo hariḥ svayam

The mantra is the guru himself, and the guru is said to be the Lord Himself. If the spiritual master is pleased with his disciple, then the Lord is pleased with that same person.

CHAPTER 3

Qualifications of Sri Guru

The spiritual master's general qualifications are described in the *Mantra-muktāvali,* which is quoted in the *Hari-bhakti-vilāsa* (1.38–40):

> He should be born in a spotless (*avadāta*) family (*anvaya*). In other words, there should be no scandal associated with the family. He himself should be without blemish in his character. He should be faithful to his own religious duties, as ordained by his own spiritual master. Though situated in any one of the four classes of *varṇāśrama* society, he should be fully devoted to Krishna's service. He should be free from anger and know the Vedas and all other scriptures. He should have strong faith and be free from envy. He should speak in a way that is endearing and have a pleasing appearance.
>
> The guru should be pure within and without. He should wear the appropriate dress for someone worshiping the Lord. He should be young and engaged in the welfare of all living beings. The spiritual master should be intelligent and possess a steadiness of will. He should be full in himself [have no desire other than to bring satisfaction to the Lord's senses]. The guru should be nonviolent and have good judgment. He should be virtuous, that is, he should possess virtues like kindness for those who come to take shelter of him. He should be expert and faithful in his worship, grateful, and as affectionate to his disciples as

he would be to a son or daughter. He should be capable of correcting his disciples. He should be devoted to the worship of the Deity. He should be expert in the art of debate. His heart should be pure, for he is always thinking of Krishna. He should be a reservoir of compassion and as deep as an ocean.

The *Hari-bhakti-vilāsa* (1.45–46) quotes the *Viṣṇu-smṛti*:

paricaryā-yaśo-lābha-lipsuḥ śiṣyād gurur nahi

> The person who seeks service, fame, or gain from a disciple is not a guru.

Other Purāṇic sources confirm this:

guravo bahavaḥ santi
śiṣya-vittāpahārakāḥ
durlabhaḥ sad-gurur devi
śiṣya-santāpa-hārakaḥ

> Many are the gurus whose only interest is to steal their disciples' wealth. Rare is the genuine guru who removes his disciple's material miseries.

The *Viṣṇu-smṛti* then goes on to mention the positive qualities one should look for in the guru:

> The true guru is an ocean of mercy, complete in himself, engaged in helping every living creature, without personal aspiration, successful in every way, conversant in all fields of knowledge, able to cut through all doubts, and is not lazy.

CASTE IS NOT A CONSIDERATION

In the eighth chapter of the *Caitanya-caritāmṛta's Madhya-līlā,* Srila Krishna Das Kaviraj recounts the conversation between Ramananda Ray and Sri Chaitanya Mahaprabhu. At the time of their talks, Mahaprabhu was still a young sannyasi, which meant that socially, He was at the pinnacle of the *varṇāśrama* system. Ramananda, although politically influential, was considered a member of the *śūdra* caste and so was socially inferior to Mahaprabhu. Nevertheless, the Lord knew him to be a lover of Krishna, and as soon as He saw him, He embraced him. The two ecstatics remained locked in embrace, shedding tears of joy, for many minutes, causing the politician's retinue to whisper about the impropriety of their behavior. Ramananda, ever the diplomat, suggested that he and the Lord meet at his house, where they could speak about devotional topics in private. When they repaired to Ramananda's quarters, Mahaprabhu surprised Ramananda by asking questions on the nature and goals of devotion. He asked pointed questions, refusing to accept anything but the answers that revealed Ramananda's most intimate understanding of Radha and Krishna's loving exchanges and the process by which one could enter these pastimes, the ultimate goal cherished by all Gaudiya Vaishnavas.

At one point in their conversation, after Mahaprabhu had asked Ramananda to describe Radha and Krishna and to explain divine love and *rasa,* the ecstatic taste of the Divine Couple's loving pastimes, Ramananda said, "I really know nothing at all. You are the one speaking through me. You are the Lord, and I am nothing more than an actor reciting lines, like a parrot repeating what it has been taught. Through my heart, You give me inspiration, and that manifests on my tongue. I don't even know whether what I am saying is good or bad. How can I tell You what You already know?"

The Lord answered with humility: "I am just a *Māyāvādī* sannyasi. I know nothing of devotion, as I have been inundated by this impersonal doctrine. By the grace of Sarvabhauma I came to see the light and My heart has been purified of this misconception. I asked him to tell Me more about the doctrine of devotion, but he sent Me to you, saying that you have a vast understanding of this topic. Now that I have heard you speak, I can understand your greatness. You have shown Me respect as a sannyasi, and have shown humility due to your own birth in a lower caste. But let Me tell you something that is more important to Me than anything to do with one's birth or social station:

kibā vipra kibā nyāsī śūdra kene naya
jei kṛṣṇa tattva vettā sei guru haya

> A person who knows the truths about Krishna is qualified to be guru, whether he is a *brāhmaṇa,* a sannyasi, or a *śūdra*. (CC 2.8.128)

"So don't try to cheat Me by bringing up these matters. You are rich in knowledge of Radha and Krishna and Their love. Please don't deprive Me of this nectar."

Rupa Goswami and Sanatana Goswami were born in an aristocratic *brāhmaṇa* family at the pinnacle of Bengali Hindu society in terms of wealth, education, and influence. Many members of the family were involved with the Muslim—and therefore untouchable for Hindu purists—ruling powers, making them outcastes to the orthodox *brāhmaṇas* of their time. When the shah began his attacks on Hindu temples, however, Rupa and Sanatana Goswami found it impossible to continue aiding and abetting his regime. At the same time, they were attracted by Chaitanya Mahaprabhu's liberal and merciful approach to spiritual understanding. Even so, they never claimed to be qualified by birth or social background, but always spoke of themselves as sinners who had lost whatever piety had led to these advantages. Nevertheless, Mahaprabhu considered them exalted persons who were to play a role of inestimable importance in spreading the flood of divine love throughout the world.

Once, Sanatana came to see Mahaprabhu in Jagannath Puri. In his eagerness to be with the Lord, he took the less populated route through the Jharikhanda jungle in Bihar and Orissa. The climate and conditions were such that he contracted a severe case of scabies. From scratching, his skin became infected, and this made his journey difficult. More painful than the disease, however, was the thought that his condition would make it impossible for him to associate with the Lord and His devotees in Puri. His humility increased as he thought over his actions as minister to the iconoclastic shah. He decided he would commit suicide by throwing himself under the wheel of Lord Jagannatha's cart during the upcoming Ratha-yatra.

Mahaprabhu, being the indwelling Supersoul, understood Sanatana's intention, and one day spoke to him about it. The Lord told Sanatana that he had no right to commit suicide, and doing so would not help him attain *prema*. Nor were the disadvantages arising from his body obstacles to his attaining pure devotion. Mahaprabhu ordered Sanatana to engage in devotional service by hearing and chanting, and to abandon his foolish idea to commit suicide.

Then, in *Sri Caitanya-caritāmṛta* (3.4.66–68) he addressed Sanatana's sense of unworthiness:

nīca-jāti nahe kṛṣṇa-bhajanera ayogya
sat-kula-vipra nahe bhajanera yogya
je bhaje se baṛa abhakta hīna chāra
kṛṣṇa-bhajane nāhi jāti-kulādi vicāra

> Someone born in a low caste is not disqualified from worshiping Krishna. Someone born as a pious *brāhmaṇa* is not especially qualified to worship Him. It is the one who worships the Lord in devotion who is superior, and the one who does not who is lowly. There is no consideration of one's birth or background in Krishna's devotional service.

dīnere adhika dayā kare bhagavān
kulīna paṇḍita dhanīra boro abhimāna

> The Lord has the most compassion for the humble. The noble-born, the scholarly, and the rich are too proud to receive His mercy.

The Lord then told Sanatana that He wished him to serve as a teacher to the Vaishnava community by writing books and by taking important leadership roles. Even today Gaudiya Vaishnavas look on Rupa and Sanatana as founding fathers of the *sampradāya*, recognizing that they played an indispensable part in spreading Mahaprabhu's message and establishing His glories.

In verse 6 of the *Vilāpa-kusumāñjali*, Raghunatha Dasa Goswami offered his respects to Sanatana Goswami as the teacher of *sambandha-jñāna*:

vairāgya-yug-bhakti-rasa-prayatnair
apāyayan mām anabhīpsum andham
kṛpāmbudhir yaḥ para-duḥkha-duḥkhī
sanātanaṁ taṁ prabhum āśrayāmi

> I take shelter of my master, Sanatana Goswami, an ocean of compassion who feels the pain of the suffering. Although I was unwilling and blind, he carefully made me drink the ambrosia of devotion mixed with disinterest in the world.

Sanatana Goswami gave Raghunatha Dasa knowledge of *sambandha*, revealing to him the nature of God and the individual soul.

THE UNQUALIFIED GURU

There is a famous section in the *Bhāgavatam* in which King Rshabhadeva speaks to His sons just prior to His leaving home to live as a forest hermit. In one of His instructions (ŚB 5.5.18) He says:

gurur na sa syāt sva-jano na sa syāt
pitā na sa syāj jananī na sā syāt
daivaṁ na tat syān na patiś ca sa syān
na mocayed yaḥ samupeta-mṛtyum

> No one is truly a guru, nor should one be considered a relative, father, mother, worshipable Deity, or husband if he cannot deliver his dependent from impending death.

In other words, one may already have a guru, but if that guru cannot show his disciples the path to immortality by instructing them properly in devotional service to Krishna, then he cannot be considered qualified. Similarly, if those we consider our relatives, parents, worshipable gods, or other well-wishers or protectors are not capable of delivering us from impending death, they are not fulfilling their true responsibility to us.

Our obligation to such persons is of a different nature than the obligation we owe to Krishna, or to a qualified guru who can help meet our spiritual aspirations. Our duty to the guru is related to our eternal relationship with God, whereas these other relationships merely help us function in the material world.

The fact is that all these mundane relationships tend to entangle us further in the bodily concept of life and, rather than bringing us closer to Krishna, distract us from our eternal duty to Him. We should bear this in mind and keep our priorities straight. If they are spiritual guides, we may take this instruction to mean that if they are unable to bring us to Krishna, then they are unqualified and we should seek out someone who can.

There are many instances of disciples rejecting their materialistic teachers in the *Bhāgavatam*. For example, Shukracharya advised his royal disciple Bali to pursue his selfish interests rather than acquiesce to the incarnation Vamana's request for charity. Shukra warned Bali that if he gave to Vamana he would lose all his possessions. Bali realized his teacher was misleading him and rejected him.

Prahlada was the son of a great demon Hiranyakashipu. Even though it is a son's primary duty to serve and obey his father, when Hiranyakashipu ordered him to reject devotional service to the Lord, Prahlada rejected him. Prahlada continued to reject Hiranyakashipu's order even when his father tried to coerce Prahlada's obedience.

In the *Rāmāyaṇa,* Rama's younger brother Bharata refused to obey his mother Kaikeyi when she told him to take the throne in Rama's place. King Khatvanga refused to obey the gods when they insisted he continue fighting with the demons on their behalf. He rejected this order because he knew his death was imminent and he wanted to engage in direct devotional service to Krishna. The *Bhāgavatam* says that when Khatvanga made this courageous decision, he attained instant spiritual perfection.

The *brāhmaṇas'* wives, whose story is told in the *Tenth Canto* of *Śrīmad Bhāgavatam,* provide another example of persons choosing to practice bhakti instead of bowing to material duty. Once, Krishna and His friends were out pasturing the cows when they started feeling hungry. Krishna sent some of the boys to a nearby village, where Vedic *brāhmaṇas* were performing a sacrifice. Feeding guests is a part of any religious function, and Krishna knew He was sending His friends at a time when feeding them would not contravene any religious strictures. Of course, the privileged guests at any sacrificial feast would be other *brāhmaṇas* and not mere cowherds, so the *brāhmaṇas* refused the boys, thinking they had no obligation to give them charity. They refused the boys even though they knew Krishna had sent them. Puffed up with their own importance and unconcerned about Krishna, they sent the boys back to their Lord.

When Krishna saw the disappointed look on His friends' faces, he knew that they had failed to get sympathy from the priests. He laughed and said, "A mendicant should never expect to get something every time he asks for a handout. You'll just have to try and try again, and eventually you will be lucky."

Krishna knew that the *brāhmaṇas'* wives had long been hearing about Krishna's prowess, beauty, and heroic deeds. He told the boys that they would have more success if they approached these pious women and asked for something to eat on His behalf. "Tell them," he said, "that I have come with Balarama. They are affectionate toward Me, so I am sure they will give you ample food."

The boys returned to the *brāhmaṇas'* compound and this time walked directly to the women's quarters. There they repeated Krishna's words. As soon as the wives heard that Krishna was hungry, they immediately gathered the food they had prepared for the sacrifice and took it to Him, flowing toward Krishna as naturally as a river flows to the sea. Their husbands, brothers, friends, and children tried to block their way, but the wives had so long cherished the desire to see Krishna in person that they could not be stopped.

And, of course, the same dedicated devotion can be said of the *gopīs*, who not only could not be stopped by their family members but could not be turned back even when Krishna told them to go home.

In each of the above cases, these exemplary devotees were able to reject the commands of their authorities because those commands applied only to the relative world. When faced with the opportunity to serve the Absolute, they rejected these conventional authorities. The words used in Sanskrit are *vyavahārika* ("conventional, functional, or relative") and *pāramārthika* ("real, essential, true, related to the highest spiritual truth"). This is the intent of Krishna's final instruction in the Bhagavad Gita: "Give up all other obligations and simply surrender to Me."

King Rshabhadeva's verse quoted above can also be read in another way: not only should you not consider unqualified persons your true authorities, but you should not yourself think of becoming a guru, friend, parent, or husband if you cannot show your dependents to the path to freedom through bhakti yoga.

Another consideration is that one cannot become a guru simply by accumulating a vast fund of knowledge or material scholarship. In His final instructions to His great devotee Uddhava, recorded in *Śrīmad-Bhāgavatam* 11.11.18, Sri Krishna says:

śābde brahmaṇi niṣṇāto
na niṣṇāyāt pare yadi
śramas tasya śrama-phalo
hy adhenum iva rakṣataḥ

> If you have read through all the Vedic scriptures but have not become fixed in the Supreme Truth, then all your efforts to accumulate learning have been fruitless, like those of a farmer who feeds a barren cow.

Vishwanatha Chakravarti points out that *śabde brahmaṇi* can either mean "the revealed knowledge of the Vedic scriptures" (known as *śabda brahma*) or both the revealed scriptures (*śabda*) and the impersonal aspect of God (Brahman). This second interpretation means that one may not only be learned, but he may also be fixed in the impersonal aspect of the Lord. If he does not become fixed in the supreme truth of Krishna's personal aspect, however, then his practice is all a waste.

The word *niṣṇāta* ("immersed") means, according to Vishwanatha, "possessing expertise through direct knowledge." In its second usage in this verse (*niṣṇāyāt*), it means expertise characterized by devotion to Krishna.

Krishna expands on His example in the next verse (ŚB 11.11.19):

gāṁ dugdha-dohām asatīṁ ca bhāryāṁ
dehaṁ parādhīnam asat-prajāṁ ca
vittaṁ tv atīrthī-kṛtam aṅga vācaṁ
hīnaṁ mayā rakṣati duḥkha-duḥkhī

> Truly miserable is that person who has a cow that does not give milk, a wife who is unfaithful, who lives a life of debt and enslavement, has dishonest offspring, wealth not purified by charity, or who speaks words that are not connected to Me.

The advice inherent in this verse is that if we want to become immersed in Krishna, we should reject the pursuit of any knowledge not related to the Lord. The farmer who works hard cutting grass and spending money to feed his cow does so because he expects the cow to calve and thus allow him to milk her, making it possible to earn back his investment by selling the milk. If the cow dries up, then he is *duḥkha-duḥkhī*—made unhappy not only by his labor and expenses but the failure of his plans. If, however, he neglects the barren cow, he becomes subject to even further misery in his next life. Of course, in the time the *Bhāgavatam* was written, it would have been inconceivable for anyone to simply slaughter a barren cow, as has unfortunately become the custom for today's dairy farmers. But in the view of the *Bhāgavatam*, this sinful act will also have long-term consequences for today's farmers, who are ignorant of the suffering they bring to these innocent creatures and thus upon themselves.

Learning, along with other material qualifications such as good family and wealth—and even the ability to perform austerities or self-sacrifice—are only fulfilling when one attains knowledge of the Lord's nature and of devotional service, and then attains love for Him. Without these, material qualifications are as worthless as a pile of broken seashells.

In the *Caitanya-caritāmṛta* (2.19.74 and 75) Krishna Das Kaviraj quotes two verses from the *Hari-bhakti-sudhodaya* (3.11 and 12) to support this understanding:

śuciḥ sad-bhakti-dīptāgni-
dagdha-durjāti-kalmaṣaḥ
śvapāko'pi budhaiḥ ślāghyo
na vedajño'pi nāstikaḥ

A pure devotee, even though an outcaste, is adored by the intelligent because all the sins which resulted in his low birth have been burnt by the blazing fire of his devotion. The same is not true for an atheist though he be a *brāhmaṇa* who has studied the Vedas.

bhagavad-bhakti-hīnasya
jātiḥ śāstraṁ japas tapaḥ
aprāṇasyaiva dehasya
maṇḍanaṁ loka-rañjanam

One may possess a high birth and learning and may meditate on his mantra and perform austerities. Nevertheless, if he is devoid of devotion to the Lord, these things are as useless as beautiful decorations on a dead body.

The conclusion to be drawn is this: if one has taken initiation from a guru purely out of social consideration or some motivation other than attaining pure devotion to Krishna, then he should leave that guru and take initiation again. The *Hari-bhakti-vilāsa* (1.55 and 4.366) states:

gṛhīta-viṣṇu-dīkṣāko
viṣṇu-pūjā-paro naraḥ
vaiṣṇavābhihito'bhijñair
itaro'smād avaiṣṇavaḥ

One can be called a Vaishnava who has taken initiation in the *viṣṇu-mantra* and is engaged in regularly performing puja to the Lord. Anyone who does not fit this definition is not a Vaishnava.

avaiṣṇavopadiṣṭena
mantreṇa nirayaṁ vrajet
punaś ca vidhinā samyag
grāhayed vaiṣṇavād guroḥ

The mantra that was been given by a non-Vaishnava will not lead to auspiciousness. Therefore, one who wishes to attain pure devotional service to Krishna should approach a qualified Vaishnava guru and take initiation again from him.

Abandoning the qualified spiritual master is vehemently condemned in the *Hari-bhakti-vilāsa* (4.363–65):

upadeṣṭāram āmnāyā-
gataṁ pariharanti ye
tān mṛtān api kravyādāḥ
kṛta-ghnān nopabhuñjate

Those who abandon the *mantra-guru* who has come in disciplic succession—whether through family line or as ordained by the Vedic literature—are ungrateful, and when they die, even the crows and jackals will not eat their corpses.

bodhaḥ kaluṣitas tena
daurātmyaṁ prakaṭīkṛtam
gurur yena parityaktas
tena tyaktaḥ purā hariḥ

A person's understanding has become polluted and he shows great bad faith if he abandons his spiritual

> master. One who does so has already renounced Lord Hari Himself.

> *pratipadya guruṁ yas tu*
> *mohād vipratipadyate*
> *sa kalpa-koṭiṁ narake*
> *pacyate puruṣādhamaḥ*

> One who has taken shelter of a true guru and then becomes bewildered and abandons him is such a lowly human being that he is destined to rot in hell for millions of years.

The word *āmnāyāgatam* in the first of the above verses is of some interest. Here, Sanatana Goswami glosses *kula-kramāgataṁ veda-vihitaṁ vā,* "coming in a family line" or "authorized by Vedic injunction." The *kula* guru system has been operative in India for thousands of years. In particular, it is the system that was most current in the Gaudiya Vaishnava *sampradāya* until fairly recently. According to this system, the members of a family, usually non-*brāhmaṇa,* would have a relationship with another family, usually *brāhmaṇa,* who would act as their gurus from one generation to the next. In a time when traditions were maintained faithfully, this system helped to preserve the teachings of the disciplic succession, as fathers passed their teachings on to their sons, who then imparted them to families where worldly considerations made it more difficult to attain a high degree of Vaishnava knowledge. This was especially true in agrarian societies, where few people were even literate and most occupations were passed down in the same lineal way—a carpenter's son would most likely become a carpenter like his father after having been taught his skills by his father.

With the spread of modern education, however, the lineal system started to break down; traditional methods of education began to feel stagnant and sincere disciples found it inadequate to their needs. They thus began to search for teachers who were able to respond to the changing face of society. Our own spiritual master, Srila Prabhupada Om Vishnupada Bhaktisiddhanta Saraswati Goswami Thakur, was such a person who was outspoken in condemning those who think that acting as a spiritual master is based on birthright.

In the Gaudiya Vaishnava *sampradāya,* dynastic guru lines generally establish their legitimacy by claiming to be descended from associates of Sri Chaitanya Mahaprabhu such as Nityananda Prabhu or Advaita Prabhu. Because Nityananda and Advaita are accepted by all Gaudiya Vaishnavas as *viṣṇu-tattva,* and because the guru is to be treated as equal to God Himself, the members of these families consider themselves possessed of some divine prerogative. This is dangerous and can lead to abuses.

Srila Prabhupada pointed all these things out fearlessly. In his *Vivṛti* on *Śrīmad Bhāgavatam* 11.6.26, he wrote about the destruction of the Yadu dynasty at the end of Krishna's *līlā*:

> This story of the *brāhmaṇas'* curse that led to the destruction of the Yadu dynasty marks the end of Krishna's *līlā,* which is dominated by the principle of union. No such destructive curse appears in *gaura-līlā,* which is centered on the principle of separation. Even so, just as Krishna left no direct descendants, so there is no indication that any kind of bloodline of descendants came through Chaitanya Mahaprabhu or any of His associates.
>
> Nityananda Prabhu, the incarnation of Balarama, had only one son, Virabhadra Prabhu, who had no children but spread his teachings through initiated disciples in accordance with the *varṇāśama* system. Similarly, with the one exception of Achyutananda, Advaita Acharya Prabhu did not make any of His own children particularly qualified in the matter of

devotional service. Moreover, although there was no external apocalypse in the bloodlines of Lord Chaitanya and His companions as there was in the case of *kṛṣṇa-līlā,* many of the descendants of these associates of the Lord were cursed to become so involved with mundane society that they were deprived of the supreme goal of *prema,* which Mahaprabhu came to give.

Once, when Sri Gaurasundar went to see Advaita Prabhu in Shantipur, He passed through the village of Lalitpur, where a bearded sannyasi lived. The Lord asked him for a blessing.[1] His purpose was to show the people of this world that there is no need to ask for blessings in order to have any kind of material benefit, all of which simply reveals one's worldly intent. But many of those who claim to have taken shelter of Sri Chaitanya Mahaprabhu in fact interact with a society that has no interest in the Lord's devotional service. In other words, like the Lalitapur sannyasi, they are engaged in offering materialistic people material benefits instead of the supreme gift of *kṛṣṇa-prema*. By acting in this manner, they become subject to a "*brāhmaṇa's* curse" like the Yadus and fall into inauspiciousness, just like any other conditioned soul.

Furthermore, these people insist that they should be treated as though they are on the same level as the Supreme Lord Himself, by which they show themselves to be different from true devotees, who think of themselves as Krishna's servants, or *tadīya,* "His."

[1] See the section below, "The Lalitpur Sannyasi."

> We could thus learn from other *sampradāyas*, such as that of Vishnuswami, where all disciples in the disciplic succession are considered family descendants or eternal children of the founder-*ācārya*. It is this very idea that led Vrindavan Dasa Thakur to use the words *sa-putrāya* ("with His sons") when paying his obeisances to Mahaprabhu, who did not have any children.[2]

The main feature of Srila Prabhupada's instruction in this regard was true to Mahaprabhu's own teaching: one's qualification is measured in terms of one's knowledge of Vaishnava teachings and the depth of one's realization of Krishna. It thus stands to reason that if one is born in an aristocratic Vaishnava family and has all the qualities that one should look for in a spiritual master, then he should not be rejected. Therefore Sanatana Goswami's words *veda-vihitaṁ vā* should also be borne in mind. Family traditions are not the only source of a guru's legitimacy.

So all the strong words in scripture about abandoning the guru refer to the *vyavahārika-guru*. They do not apply to the *pāramārthika-guru*. These two terms are important. They can be translated as "spiritual" and "conventional." In society, one has many senior figures who can be classed as one's gurus—parents and other senior family members, employers, husbands or wives, and respected friends, for example. But if any of these people are unable to give direction to the *paramārtha*, or ultimate spiritual goal of life, then no fault can be incurred by rejecting one's obligations to them and giving priority to the true spiritual master, or *sad-guru*.

---

[2] That verse is: *namas trikāla-satyāya jagannātha-sutāya ca, sa-bhṛtyāya sa-putrāya sa-kalatrāya te namaḥ*: "I bow down to the son of Jagannatha Mishra, the Truth past, present, and future. I bow down to Him along with His servants, wives, and sons" (*Chaitanya-bhagavata* 1.1.2).

Śrīmad Bhāgavatam (11.5.41) says:

devarṣi-bhūtāpta-nṛṇāṁ pitṛṇāṁ
na kiṅkaro nāyam ṛṇī ca rājan
sarvātmanā yaḥ śaraṇaṁ śaraṇyaṁ
gato mukundaṁ parihṛtya kartam

> O King! One who has given up all worldly obligations to take shelter with all his heart of Mukunda, the one worthy refuge, is no longer a servant or debtor to any god, Vedic seer, living creature, relative, human being or forefather.

Generally speaking, the Hindu social system was highly regulated by various religious duties. One is considered to be born a debtor to the gods, the forefathers, the Vedic seers or gurus who gave prescriptions leading to worldly happiness, and so on. By acquitting the five kinds of debts through Vedic ritual, one could expect to find happiness in this world and the next. But seen from the highest perspective—that of our eternal obligation to the Supreme Lord Himself—these obligations become relative, *vyavahārika*.

Thus Krishna tells Arjuna in the Gita (2.46):

yāvān artha udapāne
sarvataḥ samplutodake
tāvān sarveṣu vedeṣu
brāhmaṇasya vijānataḥ

> Whatever purposes are served by a small pond are quickly achieved by great reservoirs of water. Similarly, all the purposes of the Vedas are accomplished by one who has attained love of God.

In the Western world, where the Vedic or *varṇāśrama* system is unknown, people still have a large number of social obligations. However, we must give priority to our supreme obligation toward the Supreme Lord, who is the Soul of our soul—hence the importance of the guru, through whom this relationship is awakened.

Srila Jiva Goswami discusses the matter of rejecting one's guru in the *Bhakti-sandarbha* (210):

> One takes shelter of the *paramarthika-guru* by rejecting one's customary, *vyavaharika-gurus*.[3]

In other words, by taking initiation from a true spiritual master, one changes one's priorities and commits to attaining the ultimate goal of life. This is what is meant by initiation.

Later in the *Bhakti-sandarbha* (238), Sri Jiva writes:

> If one's guru shows himself to be inimical to Vaishnavas, then he is to be rejected, for the scriptures say that a spiritual master who has been contaminated should be abandoned. If he hates Vaishnavas, then he shows himself to be devoid of a Vaishnava nature. Thus he is not a Vaishnava, and is thus subject to the injunction, "The mantra that has been given by a non-Vaishnava will not lead to auspiciousness. Therefore one who wishes to attain pure devotional service to Krishna should approach a qualified Vaishnava guru and take initiation again from him." If there is no properly qualified Vaishnava guru available, then one will be most benefited by regularly rendering service to some great devotee.[4]

---

[3] *tad etat paramārtha-gurv-āśrayo vyavahārika-gurv-ādi-tyāgenāpi kartavyak.*

[4] *vaiṣṇava-vidveṣī cet, parityajya eva–'guror api avaliptasya' iti smaraṇāt. tasya vaiṣṇavabhāva-rāhityenāvaiṣṇavatayā 'avaiṣṇavopadiṣṭena' ity-ādi-vacana-viṣayatvāc ca. yathokta-lakṣaṇasya śrīguror avidyamānatāyāṁ tu tasyaiva* (*Bhakti-sandarbha* 238).

Jiva refers to the following verse in the *Mahābhārata* (5.178.24):

guror apy avaliptasya
kāryākāryam ajānataḥ
utpatha-pratipannasya
parityāgo vidhīyate

A spiritual master who has been affected by the desire for material sense enjoyment and has thus become confused about what to do or not to do, and who has taken to a path other than pure devotion, should be abandoned.

Bhaktivinoda Thakur explains in the *Harināma-cintāmaṇi* (6.39–42) when it may become necessary to abandon one's initiating guru:

tabe jadi e rūpa ghaṭanā kabhu haya
asat saṅge gurura yogyatā haya kṣaya
prathame chilena tini sad guru pradhāna
pare nāma aparādhe hañā hata jñāna

It may happen that for some reason the spiritual master at some time falls into bad company and becomes bereft of a guru's qualifications. When the disciple accepted him as guru, he was highly exalted, but due to committing offenses he has come to lose his spiritual understanding.

vaiṣṇave vidveṣa kari chāḍe nāma rasa
krame krame hana artha kāminīra vaśa
sei guru chāḍi śiṣya śrī-kṛṣṇa-kṛpāya
sad-guru labhiyā punaḥ śuddha nāma gāya

He becomes inimical to the Vaishnavas and loses all taste for chanting the Holy Names, gradually

> he succumbs to desires for wealth and women. The disciple should leave such a guru and, if Krishna is merciful, he will find a *sad-guru* and again sing the pure name.

In the twentieth chapter of the *Jaiva Dharma*, Bhaktivinoda Thakur writes:

> The *dīkṣā-guru* should never be abandoned. This is true. However, there are two circumstances in which he can be rejected. If at the time of initiation, the disciple had not tested the guru for his degree of knowledge of spiritual matters or for his qualifications as a Vaishnava and then subsequently finds out that the guru is of no use whatsoever, then he should leave him. There are many scriptural texts that permit this. For instance, in the *Nārada-pañcarātra* (quoted in HBV 1.101) it is said:[5]
>
> *yo vakti nyāya-rahitam*
> *anyāyena śṛṇoti yaḥ*
> *tāv ubhau narakaṁ ghoraṁ*
> *vrajataḥ kālam akṣayam*
>
> Both the teacher who speaks contrary to the principles of the Vaishnava scriptures and the disciple who hears him with some immoral objectives will spend countless ages in hell.
>
> Bhaktivinoda Thakura then cites the two verses quoted from *Bhakti-sandarbha* above (*guror apy avaliptasya* and *avaiṣṇavopadiṣṭena*).

[5] Sanatana Goswami: *parīkṣām vinā gurusevādiṁ vinā ca mantrasya kathane grahaṇe ca mahān anartha iti likhati–yo vaktīti; nyāyaḥ–dvayor anyo'nya-parikṣaṇa-pūrvaka-gurusevādi-prakāras, tad-rahitaḥ.*

The second reason for which one can leave his spiritual master is if, at the time of being initiated, the spiritual master was indeed qualified both in terms of knowledge and character, but after coming into bad association has been misled into *Mayavada* and other kinds of offensive conceptions. Such a guru is then to be abandoned. If one's guru is not an impersonalist, inimical to the Vaishnavas, or attached to sinful behavior, then even if he is inadequate in terms of his ability to answer all of the disciple's questions on more advanced aspects of the spiritual life, he should not be renounced. One should offer him the respect due his status as one's guru and take permission from him to associate with an advanced Vaishnava from whom he can take instruction about such matters.

SHOULD ONE FOLLOW A FALLEN GURU?

The *Aditya Purāṇa* (as quoted in HBV 4.359) states:

avidyo vā sa-vidyo vā
gurur eva janārdanaḥ
mārga-stho vāpy amārga-stho
gurur eva sadā gatiḥ

> Whether ignorant or learned, the spiritual master is God Himself. Whether he follows the path or not, the spiritual master alone is always our refuge.

Once again, when it is said that the spiritual master is God Himself (*gurur eva janārdanaḥ*), it means that he is worshipable because he is the Lord's dearmost associate and thus the form by which God makes Himself visible in the world (the guru is the Lord's *prakāśa-vigraha*). This *Aditya Purāṇa* verse, however, is somewhat problematic. The line, "Whether he follows the path or not, the spiritual master alone is always our refuge," rings false to our ears. Could it be an interpolation? Perhaps. Or perhaps it has some deeply inscrutable meaning that we have not yet been able to comprehend. How can one treat someone who has fallen away from the devotional path with the honor due a qualified *sad-guru*?

The *Mahābhārata's Udyoga-parva* (5.178.24) states the exact opposite of the *Aditya Purāṇa* verse:

> *guror apy avaliptasya*
> *kāryākāryam ajānataḥ*
> *utpatha-pratipannasya*
> *parityāgo vidhīyate*

> If the spiritual master has been contaminated by the sense objects and can no longer discriminate between what is to be done and what is not to be done, or if he has taken up another path besides that of pure devotion, then he must be abandoned.

How can anyone who seeks the ultimate good expect to attain it if his guide has fallen away from the infallible Lord's lotus feet? This point is stated in the *Hari-bhakti-vilāsa* (2.7), in a verse from the *Viṣṇu-yāmala*:

> If out of affection or greed one accepts a disciple without following the initiation rituals, then both he and his disciple are subjected to the Deity's curse.[6]

Sanatana Goswami clarifies the word *adīkṣayā* in his commentary: *dīkṣā-vidhi-vyatirekeṇa*, "without following the initiation rituals set out in scripture." The words *devatā-śāpa* ("Deity's curse") can refer to the curse of all the gods, or specifically of the god worshiped by the particular mantra being given.

---

[6] *snehād vā lobhato vāpi yo gatoīyād adīk adā*
tasmin gurau sa-śiṣye tu devatā-śāpa āpatet

Again, the *Hari-bhakti-vilāsa* (1.101) quotes the *Nārada-pañcarātra*, which states:

yo vakti nyāya-rahitam
anyāyena śṛṇoti yaḥ
tāv ubhau narakaṁ ghoraṁ
vrajataḥ kālam akṣayam

> Both the guru who instructs with a dishonest purpose and the disciple who receives such instruction with a dishonest purpose commit a grave error and will have to suffer for it.

This verse is specifically about the *dīkṣā-guru*. Thus the word "instruction" here means "initiation into the mantra." Although it is possible to translate *anyāya* in a number of ways—"unreasonable," "illogical," "unethical," "dishonest," or "improper"—Sanatana Goswami explains in his commentary that the word serves as a reference to the spiritual master not examining his disciple properly before initiating him, and the disciple approaching the spiritual master without an appropriate service attitude (*nyāyaḥ dvayor anyonya-parīkṣaṇa-pūrvaka-guru-sevādi-prakāras tad-rāhityam).*

Of course, if the spiritual master becomes inimical to pure devotees, then he most certainly should be abandoned, and one should take reinitiation from a pure devotee *sad-guru*. This is clearly stated by Jiva Goswami in the *Bhakti-sandarbha* (238): *vaiṣṇava-vidveṣī cet parityājya eva.* He goes on to quote the above verse from the *Mahābhārata* (*guror apy avaliptasya*) in support of this statement. He then argues that such a guru's enmity to Vaishnavas proves that he cannot be considered a Vaishnava, and scripture specifically forbids taking initiation from someone who is not a Vaishnava. His evidence is taken from the *Nārada Pañcarātra*:

avaiṣṇavopadiṣṭena
mantreṇa nirayaṁ vrajet

punaś ca vidhinā samyag
grāhayed vaiṣṇavād guroḥ

> Taking the mantra from a non-Vaishnava brings dangerous consequences. So, one in such a position should take initiation again from a Vaishnava guru. (HBV 4.366, Cf. *Padma Purāṇa* 6.226.1–2)

Jiva goes on to say, "If no guru with the qualifications described earlier is available, then one should find some highly advanced devotee and serve him. This will have the most beneficial results. Such a devotee should have the same spiritual goals and also be kindly disposed to the aspirant, for it is clear that without a merciful attitude on the part of the advanced devotee, one will not be attracted to him.

The *Bhakti-rasāmṛta-sindhu* (1.2.229) states:

yasya yat-saṅgatiḥ puṁso
maṇivat syāt sa tad-guṇaḥ
sva-kula-rddhyai tato dhīmān
sva-yūthān eva saṁśrayet

> Like a mirror, a person takes on the qualities of those with whom he comes into contact. One who is intelligent should therefore seek the company of those who have the same ideals in order to develop their good qualities in himself.

In view of all these statements, it is clear that the verse cited above ("Whether ignorant or learned, the spiritual master is God Himself. Whether he follows the path or not, the spiritual master alone is always our refuge") has to be understood in the context of the pure devotee. How can a sincere and honest disciple who is seeking the truth of spiritual life ever keep faith in a guru who has abandoned the path of devotion and taken up destructive practices?

This is why it is so important that the seeker be very careful from the beginning of his spiritual endeavor, for if he chooses his spiritual guide poorly, he may have to regret his choice later. Even so, the disciple must be careful that he does not fall into an attitude of mundane faultfinding with the genuine guru. Appearances can be deceiving, and one should be careful about passing hasty judgments on the guru, which may have a very destructive effect on one's spiritual practice.

The *Hari-bhakti-vilāsa* goes on to discuss the necessity of taking a spiritual master, quoting *Śrīmad Bhāgavatam* 10.87.33:

vijita-hṛṣīka-vāyubhir adānta-manas tura-gaṁ
ya iha yatanti yantum atilolam upāya-khidaḥ
vyasana-śatānvitāḥ samavahāya guroś caraṇaṁ
vaṇija ivāja santy akṛta-karṇa-dharā jaladhau

> O Unborn Lord! Those who try to reign in the wild horse of the uncontrolled mind by conquering the senses and life airs become frustrated and confused about how to do so and filled with all kinds of anxieties if they refuse to take shelter of a spiritual master. They are like merchants sailing the ocean on a captainless boat.

Many of the conditioned souls wandering the universe birth after birth ignorantly think there is no need to accept a spiritual master. There are others who follow the karma, *jñāna*, or yoga path who take just anyone as a spiritual master without understanding the scriptures and what they say about the spiritual master's qualifications. These people simply follow the crowd in their acceptance of someone as guru, sometimes just to satisfy the scriptural requirement that they have a guru.

Once, an old *brāhmaṇa* came from his village to the Ganges to bathe. He saw that, like him, there were many other *brāhmaṇas* there, each with a copper puja plate and cup (*kośākuśi*) in order to perform a ritual after his bath. Afraid that he would not be able to recognize his own plate once he stepped out of the water, he took a handful of clay from the shore and set it on his plate. The other *brāhmaṇas*, who thought this older scholar must be following some tradition they had not learned, followed his example. When the old man came out of the water and saw that every plate was covered with Ganges clay, he laughed and said, "Look at how everyone simply follows the crowd. Rather than finding out why something is done, they simply do what they see someone else do."

When it comes to taking a spiritual master, it seems that most of the world adopts a herd mentality. As a result, playing the role of guru has become a profitable venture. Those unqualified individuals who become guru adjust their philosophy according to time and place, tailoring it to fit an individual disciple's presuppositions and playing the required part. How glorious is the age of Kali! One doesn't know whether to laugh or cry. Although a sham like this is common among the ignorant, guru fads are not absent from among the educated, either.

Dressing up in a sadhu's garb and learning a few lines from scripture is no different from an actor playing Narada Muni in a play. Pure and honest devotees feel real pain at seeing the suffering of the souls in this world and throw their hands up in frustration at seeing this state of affairs. If those who have received the Supreme Lord's mercy and become His servants fail to show the way, then all those who following a false path in search of a guru are destined to be deceived again and again.

The *Bhāgavatam* verse under discussion here—*vijita-hṛṣīka*—has been commented on by Srila Vishwanatha Chakravarti Thakur in his *Sārārtha-darśinī*:

> If anyone thinks that, in order to settle the wandering mind and concentrate it on worshiping the Lord, he should adopt the practices of the eightfold yoga system—mastering various sitting postures, training the breath, and so on—this verse

> tells him that it will not be possible without taking shelter of a pure devotee Vaishnava guru, who is the Lord's manifestation, or *prakāśa-vigraha,* in this world. On the other hand, through devotion to the spiritual master, this kind of sense and mind control are easily achieved, as stated elsewhere in the *Bhāgavatam* (7.15.25):
>
> *rajas tamaś ca sattvena*
> *sattvaṁ copaśamena ca*
> *etat sarvaṁ gurau bhaktyā*
> *puruṣo hy añjasā jayet*
>
> One is said to conquer the modes of passion and ignorance by adopting the practices of the mode of goodness. One should then conquer the mode of goodness by full renunciation. All this is easily achieved by one who is devoted to the spiritual master.
>
> Service to the spiritual master is like the single medicine that cures all ills. In other words, other than devotion to the guru, all methods of mental control are negligible. One who neglects service to the guru and turns to other means is like a merchant with a boat full of goods who tries to sail without a capable helmsman to steer it. The voyage will be full of troubles.

In the Gita, Sri Krishna instructs Arjuna to overcome the powerful mind through *abhyāsa* and *vairāgya,* determination and detachment, which can be thought of as perseverence and patience. In his *Sārārtha-varṣiṇī* (1.12) commentary on this verse, Vishwanatha says:

> A persistent disease needs to be treated by a competent physician, who prescribes medication that must be taken over a long period of time

> according to his direction. Similarly the mind, which is so powerful, can be harnessed through *abhyāsa*, that is, constant cultivation of the yoga of meditation on the Supreme Lord, in accordance with the methods given by the spiritual master as well as by *vairāgya*,[7] or detachment from the sense objects (*viṣayeṣv anāsaṅgena*). This is stated in the *Yoga Sutras: abhyāsa-vairāgyābhyāṁ tan-nirodhaḥ*.

One who surrenders fully to the spiritual master, believing intensely that the spiritual master is his best friend and well-wisher, and takes up the practices of devotional service according to his direction, makes quick advancement in spiritual life. The enemies of this advancement, such as lust and greed, which are hard to overcome, and the mind, which is difficult to control, will both be easily overcome. If I do not believe that "my guru is my best friend and well-wisher," I have not in fact taken shelter of him. How then can I say that I am engaged in *bhajana* according to his direction? Hundreds of thousands of dangers will buffet us like the winds of a hurricane, troubling our every step. This is why it is important to take shelter of a genuine spiritual master.

SIGNS OF A QUALIFIED GURU

In order to facilitate finding a qualified guru, the *Hari-bhakti-vilāsa*, the Vaishnava rulebook, gives a list of attributes one can use to assess a prospective guru's qualifications. The following verses are taken from a book named *Mantra-muktāvalī*:

avadātānvayaḥ śuddhaḥ svocitācāra-tat-paraḥ
āśramī krodha-rahito vedavit sarva-śāstravit
śraddhāvān anasūyaś ca priya-vāk priya-darśanaḥ
śuciḥ suveśas taruṇaḥ sarva-bhūta-hite rataḥ
dhīmān anuddhata-matiḥ pūrṇo'hantā vimarśakaḥ
sa-guṇo'rcāsu kṛtadhīḥ kṛtajñaḥ śiṣya-vatsalaḥ

---

[7] *sad-gurūpadiṣṭa-prakāreṇa parameśvara-dhyāna-yogasya muhur anuśīlanena.*

- *Avadātānvayaḥ*—the guru should be born in a spotless (*avadāta*) family (*anvaya*). In other words, there should be no scandal associated with the family.
- *Śuddha*—the guru should be without character blemishes.
- *Svocitācāra-tat-paraḥ*—the guru should be faithful to the religious duties his own spiritual master has ordained for him.
- *Āśramī*—although adhering to one of the four stages of life in accordance with the *varṇāśrama* system, the guru should be a devotee of Krishna and fully devoted to serving Him exclusively.
- *Krodha-rahita*—the guru should be free from anger. Narottama Das Thakur writes in the *Prema-bhakti-candrikā*: "What havoc can anger not wreak? Therefore always give up anger" (*krodhe vā nā kare kibā, krodha tyāga sadā dibā*). The only place Narottama allows for anger is when it is directed toward those who show the devotees enmity (*krodha bhakta-dveṣī jane . . . niyukta kariba jathā tathā*). In the Gita (3.37) the Lord Himself says:

kāma eṣa krodha eṣa
rajo-guṇa-samudbhavaḥ
mahāśano mahā-pāpmā
viddhy enam iha vairiṇam

> It is lust, which is transformed to anger, that is the mighty, all-devouring source of sin, arising from nature's mode of passion. Know this to be your principal enemy here on earth.

Lust is the overpowering desire to enjoy the sense objects. In certain situations, this desire is transformed to anger. Lust is a product of the mode of passion, but when there are obstacles to gratifying these lusts, the mode of darkness takes over and one becomes possessed by anger. Lust is a ferocious enemy of spiritual life, for it devours all one's self-awareness.

Therefore, in the knowledge that lust and anger are most dangerous, all-consuming enemies, one must guard against them and reject them completely. Then one becomes a *madhyama-adhikārī* with the characteristics described in the *Śrīmad Bhāgavatam*. That is, he shows love for God, friendship to other devotees, and to those who are innocent or lacking knowledge of spiritual truths, he shows mercy by instructing them in spiritual matters and initiating them in the spiritual life. He also ignores those who are inimical to devotees by not cooperating with them. So, being free from anger is a particularly important characteristic of the guru, who follows in the footsteps of Lord Nityananda, known as akrodha paramānanda, "free of anger and full of supreme joy."

- *Veda-vit*—the guru should know the Vedas. Krishna tells Arjuna in Bhagavad Gita 15.15:

sarvasya cāhaṁ hṛdi saṁniviṣṭo
mattaḥ smṛtir jñānam apohanaṁ ca
vedaiś ca sarvair aham eva vedyo
vedānta-kṛd veda-vid eva cāham

> I reside in everyone's heart; from Me alone come remembrance, knowledge, and their loss. I am to be known by all the Vedas, for I am the author of the Vedanta and I alone know the Veda.

Bhaktivinoda Thakur paraphrases this verse as follows:

> "I am seated in the heart of every living creature as the Lord. According to the *jīva's* past piety or impiety, I bestow on him remembrance, knowledge, or forgetfulness. Therefore I am not simply the all-pervading Brahman but the Supersoul in the heart who awards every *jīva* the fruits of his work. Then again, I am not simply the worshipable object of the *jīvas* in the form of the underlying Brahman or Paramatma, but I am their instructor also. I am the Supreme Person, Bhagavan, who is the aim of all the Vedic

> knowledge. I am the compiler and knower of Vedanta, and I am the knower of the Vedas. Therefore I, the Supreme Lord, in order to bring about the greatest auspiciousness for all living beings, manifest as the all-pervading Brahman in the material nature, as the Paramatma in the *jīva*'s heart, and finally as the Supreme Person, the giver of life's ultimate meaning. In these three forms I deliver the conditioned soul from his bondage."

The Lord, who is the ultimate object of the Vedic knowledge, composed the Vedanta through Vyasadeva. Vyasadeva is the Lord's empowered incarnation; therefore the Lord composed the Vedic literature through him. He is also the knower of the Vedas and their purport. As Vishwanatha Chakravarti says in his commentary on this verse, "No one but Krishna knows their true meaning" (*matto'nyo vedārthaṁ na jānāti*).

Therefore only he to whom Krishna reveals its meaning can truly understand the Vedic scriptures. As such, the blessings and grace of the Lord are the only source of true spiritual knowledge.

At the very end of the Gita's eighteenth and last chapter, Krishna speaks of the most confidential knowledge (*sarva-guhyatamaṁ jñānam*). There He states the ultimate teaching: "Give up all other duties and simply surrender unto Me" (*mām ekaṁ śaraṇaṁ vraja*). This means that devotion to God, characterized by the surrendering process (*śaraṇāgati*), is the true religion or duty of the spirit soul. This is the principal sign of spiritual knowledge, or being a *veda-vit*, and this is why it has been given as one of the most important characteristics to look for in a spiritual master.

The Vaishnava poet, Nayanananda Thakur, wrote several verses expressing these principles:

cāri veda ṣaḍ-daraśana paṛiyāche
se jadi gaurāṅga nāhi bhaje
kibā tāra adhyayana locana-vihīna jena
darapaṇe andhe kibā kāje

Someone who studies the four Vedas and the six philosophical systems, but does not worship Lord Gauranga, has wasted his time in study. Of what use is a mirror to a blind man?

veda vidyā dui kichui nā jānata se jadi gaurāṅga jāne sār
nayanānanda bhaṇe sei se sakali jāne sarva siddhi karatale tār

Whereas one who has no knowledge of the Veda or any other matter, if he knows just this, that Gauranga is the essence of all things, then, says Nayanananda, he knows everything that needs to be known and all perfections are within his grasp.

The *Caitanya-caritāmṛta* (2.20.124–25) also describes the essence of Vedic knowledge:

veda-śāstra kahe sambandha abhidheya prayojana
kṛṣṇa prāpya sambandha bhakti prāptyera sādhana
abhidheya-nāma bhakti prema prayojana puruṣārtha-
śiromaṇi prema mahā-dhana

The Vedic knowledge is subdivided into three parts known as *sambandha* ("relations"), *abhidheya* ("signification"), and *prayojana* ("the aim or end"). The knowledge of Krishna as the goal of spiritual life is called *sambandha*. The knowledge that devotion is the means of attaining Him is called *abhidheya*. The ultimate goal of life, or *prayojana*, is love of Krishna, or *prema*. This *prema* is the greatest treasure of spiritual life and is foremost among all the objectives of human life.

To know this essence, then, is to know the Vedas. Simply memorizing many verses from the Vedas does not make one a knower of the Vedas.

- *Sarva-śāstravit*—the guru should know all the scriptures.

> *bhārate sarva-vedārtho bhāratārthaś ca kṛtsnaśaḥ*
> *gītāyām asti teneyaṁ sarva-śāstra-mayī matā*

> All the meaning of the Vedas is contained in the *Mahābhārata*. The essence of the *Mahābhārata* is contained in the Bhagavad Gita. Therefore the Bhagavad Gita is the equal of all the scriptures. (From Nilakantha's commentary on Bhagavad Gita 1.1)

Because this nectar of the Gita emanated from the mouth of the lotus-naveled Lord Himself, one should drink it with great care. It is said that the *Upaniṣads* are like a cow, Arjuna (to whom Krishna spoke the Gita) like its calf, and Krishna its milkman. The milk is the nectar of spiritual knowledge, and the drinker of the divine ambrosia the intelligent seeker of truth.[8]

The Supreme Lord is the one who bestows on us the intelligence that gives us a sense of certainty—what in the Gita is called *vyavasāyātmikā buddhi*. The Lord says, "To those who are constantly devoted and worship Me with love I give the intelligence by which they can attain Me. In order to bless them, I, dwelling in their hearts, destroy the darkness of their ignorance with the lamp of knowledge." (Gita 10.10–11)

But we know that the *Śrīmad Bhāgavatam* is the explanation of the Gita. It synthesizes all the Vedas and the Vedanta. *Śrīmad Bhāgavatam* is the final offering of Vedavyasa, who was inspired to compose it while in the deepest trance of divine vision. The *Garuḍa Purāṇa* states that the *Bhāgavatam* contains the explanation of the *Vedānta-sūtras*, points to the essential contents of the *Mahābhārata*, is the commentary on the *Gāyatrī* mantra (said to be the mother of the Vedas), and contains the meaning of all the Vedas. Therefore, if one wishes to understand the true meaning of the Vedas, one should look to the *Bhāgavatam*.

---

[8] *sarvopaniṣado gāvo, dogdhā gopāla-nandanaḥ, pārtho vatsaḥ sudhīr bhoktā, dugdham gītāmṛtaṁ mahat* (*Gītā-māhātmya* 5).

The *Bhāgavatam* (1.3.42) itself says that in its words one can find the essence of all the Vedas as well as epics like the *Mahābhārata.*[9] The conclusion is that one who knows the *Bhāgavatam* knows all the scriptures.

- *Śraddhāvān*—the guru should possess strong faith.

pūrva ājñā veda dharma, karma, yoga jñāna
saba sādhi avaśeṣa ājñā balavān
ei ājñā bale bhaktera śraddhā jadi haya
sarva karma tyāga kari se kṛṣṇere bhajaya

Faith (*śraddhā*), according to Krishna Das Kaviraj, means belief in the word of God. In the twenty-second chapter of the *Caitanya-caritāmṛta's Madhya-līlā* (2.22.59–60), Krishna Das says that in the Gita, Krishna first instructs Arjuna to follow the paths of karma, yoga, or *jñāna*. The final conclusion, however, is that bhakti is the true process for attaining God. If a devotee has faith in this last order of the Lord, then he abandons all other duties and simply worships Him.

tāvat karmāṇi kurvīta na nirvidyeta yāvatā
mat-kathā-śravaṇādau vā śraddhā yāvan na jāyate

As long as one has not renounced material desire, one should engage in one's prescribed *varṇāśrama* duties until he develops faith in hearing and chanting about Me. (ŚB 11.20.9)

śraddhā-śabde kahe viśvāsa sudṛḍha niścaya
kṛṣṇa-bhakti kaile sarva-karma kṛta haya

---

9 *sarva-vedetihāsānāṁ sāraṁ sāraṁ samuddhṛtam.*

The word *śraddhā* refers to a firm and confident belief that by engaging in devotion to Krishna alone, all of one's duties will be fulfilled. (CC 2.22.62)

śraddhāvān jana hoy bhakti-adhikārī uttama,
madhyama, kaniṣṭha śraddhā anusārī
śāstra yuktye sunipuṇa dṛḍha śraddhā jāra
uttama adhikārī sei tāraya saṁsāra
śāstra yukti nāhi jāne dṛḍha śraddhāvān madhyama
adhikārī sei mahā-bhāgyavān
jāhāra komala śraddhā se kaniṣṭha jana krame
krame teṅho bhakta haibe uttama

A faithful person is eligible for the practice of devotion according to the degree of his faith—superior, intermediate, or fledgling. One who has mastered the reasoning of the scriptures and has strong faith is called the superior candidate, and he easily crosses over the material ocean. One who does not have clear knowledge of the scriptures but has strong faith is the intermediate candidate, who is nevertheless very fortunate. One's whose faith is weak is called the inferior candidate, but he also gradually becomes superior. (CC 2.22.64–67)

- *Anasūyaḥ*—the guru is free from envy. According to the dictionary, the word *asūyā* means "seeing fault where there is virtue." The word also means "enmity" and "anger." The word is used in the famous *Bhāgavatam* verse where Krishna says, "Know the *ācārya* to be Me, and never envy him by thinking him an ordinary man" (*ācāryaṁ māṁ vijānīyāt na martya-buddhyāsūyeta*).
- *Priya-vāk*—the guru speaks pleasingly. Krishna is dear to everyone. Therefore Krishna's names, forms, virtues, and pastimes are subjects most pleasing to all souls. Those nondevotees who follow the practices of karma, *jñāna*, or yoga have no taste for hear-

> ing about Krishna, but this does not mean that the guru speaks to them on other subjects simply to coddle them. He prefers to remain silent and meditate on Krishna.

There is something more that needs to be said here: Sri Chaitanya Mahaprabhu could not abide statements that went against the conclusions of the scripture or inaccurately presented the flavors of devotion.

rasābhāsa haya jadi siddhānta-virodha
sahite nā pāre prabhu mane haya krodha

> If any statement contained perverted reflections of the transcendental aesthetic or went against the doctrines of the *Bhāgavatam,* Sri Chaitanya Mahaprabhu found it intolerable and would become angry. (CC 3.5.97)

jadbā-tadbā kavira vākye haya rasābhāsa
siddhānta-viruddha śunite nā haya ullāsa
rasa rasābhāsa jāra nāhika vicāra
bhakti-siddhānta-sindhu nāhi pāya pāra

> Some poets think that they can write anything that comes into their mind. In their writings there is usually an incorrect presentation of the divine loving relationships. There is no pleasure in hearing words that are contrary to the scriptural conclusions. Anyone who cannot distinguish between the genuine sacred aesthetic and its reflection will be unable to ever cross the ocean of scriptural conclusions which lead to devotional service. (CC 3.5.102–103)

kṛṣṇa-līlā gaura-līlā se kare varṇana
gaura-pāda-padma jāṅra haya prāṇa-dhana

> Only persons who have enshrined Mahaprabhu's lotus feet within their hearts as their life and soul are qualified to narrate Krishna's and Gauranga's pastimes. (CC 3.5.106)

The conclusion is that only the speech of one who has surrendered his soul to Gauranga Mahaprabhu sounds like ambrosia to the ears of another devotee. Such speech, which is connected to Gaura and Govinda, is alone pleasing and is a defining characteristic of a pure devotee spiritual master.

- *Priya-darśanaḥ*—the guru should have a pleasing appearance. The spiritual master's appearance should inspire one to feel devotion. Krishna resides in the heart of His devotee. As Narottama Das says, "Govinda rests in your heart" (*tomāra hṛdaye sadā govinda viśrāma*). Krishna's presence in the heart has an inexplicable effect on the guru's external appearance and renders him attractive to all who are seeking the Lord.
- *Śuciḥ*—the guru is pure within and without. The *Garuḍa Purāṇa* (2.47.52) states:

apavitraḥ pavitro vā
sarvāvasthāṁ gato'pi vā
yaḥ smaret puṇḍarīkākṣaṁ
sa bāhyābhyantara-śuciḥ

> Whether one is pure and saintly or not, if one remembers the lotus-eyed Lord in all circumstances, then he is factually pure both within and without.

Lord Chaitanya also quotes the *Hari-bhakti-sudhodaya* (3.12, 19), which states:

śuciḥ sad-bhakti-dīptāgni-
dagdha-durjāti-kalmaṣaḥ

śvapāko›pi budhaiḥ ślāghyo
na vedajño'pi nāstikaḥ

A pure devotee, even though an outcaste, is adored by the intelligent, for all the sins that resulted in his low birth have been burned to ashes by the blazing fire of his devotion. The same is not true for an atheist, even though he be a *brāhmaṇa* who has studied the Vedas.

bhagavad-bhakti-hīnasya
jātiḥ śāstraṁ japas tapaḥ
aprāṇasyaiva dehasya
maṇḍanaṁ loka rañjanam

One may possess high birth and learning and may meditate on his mantra and perform austerities. Nevertheless, if he is devoid of devotion to the Lord, these good works are as useless as beautiful decorations on a dead body.

The conclusion is that devotion to Krishna is true purity.

- *Suveśaḥ*—the guru wears the appropriate dress for someone who is worshiping the Lord. This means, at least minimally, that he wears clean clothes. Being appropriately dressed has nothing to do with one's clothes being expensive; expensive clothes have no intrinsic value for those who are absorbed in the Lord's service. There is a Bengali saying, "The fancier the costume, the bigger the cheat" (*bāhirer sāja joto, bhitarer phāṅki toto*). If one's essential being is devoid of love of God, then no amount of dressing up will camouflage it. When Sanatana Goswami came to Benares, he exchanged his expensive mohair blanket for a torn quilt, an act of renunciation that brought Mahaprabhu great joy. However, this does not mean that someone comes to possess the quality of being nicely dressed (*suveśa*) simply by taking on the dress of a monk or sadhu. Rather, one has to have achieved true inner renunciation. Mahaprabhu would never approve of false renunciation (*phālgu-vairāgya*).

- *Taruṇaḥ*—the guru is young. In other words, in his enthusiasm to serve the Lord he is as vigorous as a youth.
- *Sarva-bhūta-hite rataḥ*—the guru is engaged in serving the welfare of all living beings by extensively glorifying Krishna's names, forms, qualities, and pastimes, for their benefit.
- *Dhīmān*—the spiritual master is intelligent. As Srila Bhaktivinoda Thakur sings in *Kalyāṇa-kalpa-taru*:

> *ata eva māyā moha chāṛi buddhimān nitya tattva*
> *kṛṣṇa-bhakti karun sandhāna*

> The intelligent person should therefore cast aside the enchantments of this illusory world and seek out the eternal truth of devotion to Krishna.

- *Anuddhata-matiḥ*—the guru possesses a steadiness of will without being aggressive.
- *Pūrṇaḥ*—the guru is "full." His heart is so full of the wealth of devotion and divine love that he feels no need for whatever is valued in this world, such as profit, adoration, and prestige. The guru has no desire for anything other than to give Krishna's senses pleasure.
- *Ahantā*—the guru is nonviolent.
- *Yimarśakaḥ*—the guru has good judgment.
- *Sa-guṇaḥ*—the guru is virtuous. That is, he possesses virtues like kindness toward those who come to take shelter of him.
- *Arcāsu kṛta-dhīḥ*—the guru is expert and faithful in his worship.
- *Kṛtajñaḥ*—the guru shows gratitude toward others, especially to his own guru and the Vaishnavas.
- *Śiṣya-vatsalaḥ*—the guru is as affectionate to his disciples as he would be to a son or daughter and does everything to further their advancement in devotional life.

- *Nigrahānugrahe śaktaḥ*—the guru knows how to both reprimand and bestow mercy on his disciples.
- *Homa-mantra-parāyaṇaḥ*—the guru is devoted to the performance of sacrifice and the recitation of mantras.
- *Ūhāpoha-prakāra-jñaḥ*—the guru is expert in the art of debate.
- *Śuddhātmā*—the guru's heart is pure, for he is always thinking of Krishna.
- *Kṛpālayaḥ*—the guru is a reservoir of compassion.
- *Garimā-nidhiḥ*—the guru is as deep as an ocean.

DOES THE GURU NEED TO BE A HOUSEHOLDER?

Some people think the word *āśramī* contained in the above verses means that the guru should be a householder, while others take it to mean he should be a renunciant. Even others think the guru must be a *brāhmaṇa*. But in His conversations with Ray Ramananda, Chaitanya Mahaprabhu clarifies this point:

kibā vipra kibā nyāsī śūdra kene naya
jei kṛṣṇa tattva vettā sei guru haya

> A person who knows the truths of spiritual life is qualified to be guru, whether he is a *brāhmaṇa*, sannyasi, or *śūdra*. (CC 2.8.128)

In his *Anubhāṣya*, Srila Prabhupada writes:

> It does not really matter what one's caste or stage of life is, whether one is a *brāhmaṇa, kṣatriya, vaiśya,* or *śūdra, brahmacārī, gṛhastha, vānaprastha,* or sannyasi. Anyone can be a guru if he is knowledgeable about Krishna. By guru is meant any kind of guru—the one who shows the way (*vartma-pradarśaka*), the initiating guru (*dīkṣā-guru*), or the instructor in spiritual matters (*śikṣā-guru*). The spiritual master's qualification is based on whether or not he knows Krishna and not

on any material consideration such as birth or status. This statement by Mahaprabhu does not contradict the scriptures. He Himself, as a *gṛhastha* named Vishwambhara Mishra, was initiated by a sannyasi named Ishwara Puri. Nityananda Prabhu was similarly initiated by Madhavendra Puri, a sannyasi (although according to others, he was initiated by Lakshmipati Tirtha). Advaita Acharya, although a *gṛhastha*, was initiated by Madhavendra Puri, and Sri Rasikananda, although born in a *brāhmaṇa* family, was initiated by Shyamananda Prabhu, who was not born in a caste *brāhmaṇa* family. Ganga Narayana Chakravarti and Ramakrishna Bhattacharya, both caste *brāhmaṇas*, took initiation from Narottama Das, who was not a caste *brāhmaṇa*. Other such examples are Yadunandana Chakravarti of Katwa, who took *pañcarātrika* initiation from a non-*brāhmaṇa* named Gadadhara Das. In the *Mahābhārata*, even outcastes like the wise hunter (*dharma-vyādha*) were not rejected as *śikṣā-gurus* because of their caste or profession.

As Mahaprabhu told Srila Sanatana Goswami (CC 3.4.66–67):

nīca-jāti nahe kṛṣṇa-bhajanera ayogya
sat-kula-vipra nahe bhajanera yogya
je bhaje se baṛa abhakta hīna chāra
kṛṣṇa-bhajane nāhi jāti-kulādi vicāra

Someone born in a low caste is not disqualified from worshiping Krishna. Someone born as a pious *brāhmaṇa* is not especially qualified to worship Him. The person who worships is superior, whereas one who does not is lowly. In the worship of Krishna, one's birth or background is not a question.

By this standard, the superiority or inferiority of an individual is based not on consideration of birth, background, wealth, or mundane education; these are immaterial when it comes to devotion to the Lord. Everyone without exception has the right to worship the Lord, for it is the eternal constitutional position of the *jīva* to be the Lord's servant. The scriptural injunction is to take shelter of a genuine spiritual master and to become established in one's constitutional position.

The *Hari-bhakti-vilāsa* (1.42–44) quotes a few more verses—taken from the *Agastya-saṁhitā*—to add further information about the guru's qualifications:

> A householder can be called a guru if he is engaged in the worship of God, is peaceful, holds no aspiration for sense objects, and possesses spiritual knowledge. He should know the Vedic mantras and be conversant with their meaning. He should be the best of *brāhmaṇas*, capable of saving or destroying someone. He should know the science of mantras and yantras, be able to discern the essence of a matter, and possess esoteric knowledge. He should have performed *puraścaraṇa*, be perfect in the performance of sacrifices and mantra, and know the various applications of both. He should be austere and truthful.[10]

Since it is clearly stated in the *Hari-bhakti-vilāsa* that in the case of chanting Vaishnava mantras there is no need to perform *puraścaraṇa*, and that the best *puraścaraṇa* is service to the guru, the statement that "the guru must have performed *puraścaraṇa*" means he should have faithfully served his guru. As Sanatana Goswami writes, "Only through the mercy

[10] *devatopāsakaḥ śānto viṣayeṣv api niṣpṛhaḥ*
adhyātma-vid brahma-vādī vedaśāstrārtha-kovidaḥ
uddhatuṁ caiva saṁhartuṁ samartho brāhmaṇottamaḥ
tattvajño yantra-mantrāṇāṁ marma-bhettā rahasya-vit
puraścaraṇa-kṛd homa-mantra-siddhaḥ prayoga-vit
tapasvī satya-vādī ca gṛhastho gurur ucyate.

of the guru can one attain complete success in *puraścaraṇa*" (*kevalaṁ śrī-guru-prasādenaiva puraścaraṇa-siddhiḥ syāt*).[11]

The word *gṛhī* means householder. Some people think that using this word in relation to the guru means that the guru should be a householder. In an earlier verse, it was said that the guru should be an *āśramī*, or situated in one of the four *āśramas*, *brahmacārī*, *gṛhastha*, *vānaprastha*, or *sannyāsa*. In other words, he must be following the rules of the stage of life in which he is situated and not indifferent to those regulations.[12]

Another *Purāṇa* states:

guravo bahavaḥ santi
śiṣya-vittāpahārakāḥ
durlabhaḥ sad-gurur devi
śiṣya-santāpa-hārakaḥ

> Many are the gurus whose only interest is to steal their disciples' wealth. Rare is the genuine guru who removes his disciples' material miseries.

The *Hari-bhakti-vilāsa* (1.45–46) cites the following text with more signs of the qualified guru from the *Viṣṇu-smṛti*:

paricaryā-yaśo-lābha-lipsuḥ śiṣyād gurur nahi
kṛpā-sindhuḥ susampūrṇaḥ sarva sattvopakārakaḥ
niḥspṛhaḥ sarvataḥ siddhaḥ sarva vidyā viśāradaḥ
sarva saṁśaya saṁchettā nalaso gurur āhṛtaḥ

---

[11] See articles 2.09, *Caitanya Vāṇī* 22.10 (1984), pp. 187–93 and 2.10. *Caitanya Vāṇī* 27.11 (1989), pp. 204–208.

[12] See article 2.16, *Caitanya Vāṇī* 32.2 (1994), p. 26.

> The person who seeks service, fame, or gain from a disciple is not a guru. The true guru is an ocean of mercy, complete in himself, engaged in helping every living creature, without personal aspiration, successful in every way, conversant in all fields of knowledge, able to cut through all doubts, and is not lazy.

Here, Sanatana Goswami writes in his *Dig-darśanī* commentary: "The person who possesses all the other qualities appropriate to a guru should nevertheless be avoided if his only interest in the disciple is receiving some benefit from him. The verse can be read in two ways: with *śiṣyāt* as a verb, meaning 'would initiate' ('a person who would initiate desiring service, fame, or gain is not a guru'), or as a noun, in which case it means 'from the disciple' ('a person who desires service, fame, or gain from his disciple is not a guru')."

In the *Nārada Pañcarātra* (as quoted in HBV 1.47–50), in the conversation between the Lord and Narada Muni, the Lord says:

brāhmaṇaḥ sarva-kāla-jñaḥ kuryāt sarveṣv anugraham
tad-abhāvād dvija-śreṣṭhaḥ śāntātmā bhagavan-mayaḥ
bhāvitātmā ca sarvajñaḥ śāstrajñaḥ sat-kriyā-paraḥ
siddhi-trayam āyukta ācāryatve'bhiṣecitaḥ
kṣatra-viṭ-śūdra-jātīnāṁ kṣatriyo'nugrahe kṣamaḥ
kṣatriyasyāpi ca guror bhāvād īdṛśo yadi
vaiśyaḥ syāt tena kāryaś ca dvaye nityam anugrahaḥ
sajātīyena śūdreṇa tādṛśena mahā-mate
anugrahābhiṣekau ca kāryau śūdrasya sarvadā

> O best of the twice-born! A caste *brāhmaṇa* who knows all the times (i.e., who knows the five aspects of the *Pañcarātra* doctrine and practice) may show compassion (in the form of giving instruction in the mantra) to people of all other castes.

> In the absence of such a *brāhmaṇa*, a *kṣatriya* may fulfill this function of giving initiation to those in the *vaiśya*, *kṣatriya*, or *śūdra* castes if he shows the qualities of peacefulness, absorption in the Supreme Lord, and mental purity, and he is all-knowing [according to Sanatana, in the sense that he knows all the proper *dīkṣā* rituals], attached to good works, has attained the three kinds of perfection [that is, perfection in the discipline of chanting the mantra, service to guru, and worship of the Deity through *puraścaraṇa* and other practices], and has been consecrated in the functions of the *mantra-guru* by his own spiritual master.
>
> If a qualified *kṣatriya* of the above description cannot be found, then *vaiśyas* and *śūdras* may take initiation from a qualified *vaiśya*. If no such *vaiśya* is found, a *śūdra* may initiate and give *abhiṣeka* to another *śūdra*.

Here, *abhiṣeka* means the authorization a guru gives a disciple to allow that disciple to take his own disciples or to become the guru's successor. Sanatana Goswami says that the guru should ordain his disciple after he has performed the *puraścaraṇa*.

Further precisions are given in verses 1.51–52 of the *Hari-bhakti-vilāsa*:

> *varṇottame'tha ca gurau sati yā viśrute'pi ca*
> *svadeśato'tha vānyatra nedaṁ kāryaṁ śubhārthinā*
> *vidyamāne tu yaḥ kuryāt yatra tatra viparyayam*
> *tasyehāmutra nāśaḥ syāt tasmāc chāstroktam ācaret*
> *kṣatra-viṭ-śūdra-jātīyaḥ prātilomyaṁ na dīkṣayet*

> If someone from a superior caste possesses the qualities listed above, whether in the immediate area or elsewhere, then someone from the lower castes

> should not initiate disciples. If someone does initiate when there are members of superior castes present, then his hopes for both this world and the next will be ruined. Therefore, *kṣatriyas*, *vaiśyas*, and *śūdras* should act in accordance with the scriptures and not initiate anyone in castes higher than their own.

However, Sanatana quotes the *Padma Purāṇa* in the *Hari-bhakti-vilāsa* (1.53–54), which says:

> *mahā-bhāgavataḥ śreṣṭho brāhmaṇo vai gurur nṛṇām*
> *sarveṣām eva lokānām asau pūjyo yathā hariḥ*
> *mahā-kula-prasūto'pi sarva-yajñeṣu dīkṣitaḥ*
> *sahasra-śākhādhyāyī ca na guruḥ syād avaiṣṇavaḥ*

> The topmost *bhagavata* (devotee of *Bhagavan*) is a *brāhmaṇa,* who is therefore the legitimate guru of all humankind. Such a person is to be revered by the entire world, as is the Lord Himself. On the other hand, a *brāhmaṇa* who is not a Vaishnava, even though he was born into an impeccable lineage, has been initiated into all the great sacrificial rites, and has studied the thousand branches of the Vedic lore, cannot be admitted as a guru.

In his *Dig-darśanī* comment on these verses, Sanatana Goswami states that the "topmost bhagavata is one who is engaged in all the aspects of Vaishnava practice and who truly knows the Lord's glories (*aśeṣa-vaiṣṇava-dharma-rataḥ śrī-bhagavan-māhātmyādi-jñānavāṁś ca*).

The *Padma Purāṇa* (quoted in HBV 1.55) gives another, minimum definition of the Vaishnava:

> *gṛhīta-viṣṇu-dīkṣāko*
> *viṣṇu-pūjā-paro naraḥ*

vaiṣṇavo'bhihito'bhijñair
itaro'smād avaiṣṇavaḥ

> Someone who has himself taken initiation into the *viṣṇu-mantra* and is engaged in the worship of the Lord is called a Vaishnava by the wise. All others are non-Vaishnavas.

The *Pañcarātra* states:

avaiṣṇavopadiṣṭena
mantreṇa nirayaṁ vrajet
punaś ca vidhinā samyag
grāhayed vaiṣṇavād guroḥ

> One who receives a mantra from a non-Vaishnava goes to perdition. To avoid this, he should once again ask to be given the mantra by a Vaishnava guru.

In this verse, the use of the prescriptive form of the verb in the words *vrajet* and *grāhayet* shows the absolute necessity of taking shelter and being initiated by a proper guru. Therefore initiation is not a trifling matter. Those who have a genuine desire to engage in the Lord's worship must sincerely pray to the Lord in the heart to find such a guru. The Lord is like a wish-fulfilling tree; He will certainly answer this prayer.

In India, there are many caste rules, and some people refuse to eat or drink anything offered by someone who is not initiated. So some householders feel it necessary to take initiation just so that they will be accepted socially. On the other hand, these same people think, "We are fallen souls in this age of Kali. We are just householders surrounded by our wives and children, whom we have to maintain by whatever means possible. How can we possibly follow all the restrictions laid out in the scriptures? We had better look around for a guru who does not make too many dietary prohibitions so that we don't make too much trouble for ourselves."

However, if we take a guru who acts in ways that are considered reprehensible in the scriptures and is thus outside the disciplic succession, then we must ask whether the purpose of initiation has been achieved. What are the results of not following scriptural injunctions? Krishna tells Arjuna in the Gita (16.23–24):

> *yaḥ śāstra-vidhim utsṛjya vartate kāma-cārataḥ*
> *na sa siddhim avāpnoti na sukhaṁ na parāṁ gatim*
> *tasmāc chāstraṁ pramāṇaṁ te kāryākārya-vyavasthitau*
> *jñātvā śāstra-vidhānoktaṁ karma kartum ihārhasi*

> He who rejects the scriptural injunctions and lives only as his desires prompt him, attains neither spiritual perfection, worldly happiness, nor the supreme destination. Therefore the scriptures are the reliable source of information in deciding what is to be done or not to be done. You should therefore learn which activites are enjoined by the scriptures and engage in them.

Srila Vishwanatha Chakravarti summarized the essence of the Gita's sixteenth chapter in his *Sārārtha-varṣiṇī* commentary:

> *āstikā eva vindanti sad-gatiṁ santa eva te*
> *nāstikā narakaṁ yāntītyadhyāyārtho nirūpitaḥ*

> Believers in the scriptural teachings meet an auspicious end, for they are saintly. Nonbelievers go to hell. That is the purport of this chapter.

CHARACTERISTICS THAT DISQUALIFY A GURU

Although we have been discussing a guru's qualifications, we must constantly bear in mind Mahaprabhu's dictum that the most important qualification a guru needs is that he know Krishna (*jei kṛṣṇa tattva-vettā se guru hoy*). So when seeking a guru, this is the primary quality to look for. If we pay excessive attention to considerations of caste or social position, then we may be deceived when it comes to real spiritual understanding. This is something that we must be particularly vigilant about.

The *Hari-bhakti-vilāsa* (1.56–58) next turns to the question of what characteristics disqualify one from acting as guru. The first citation is taken from the *Tattva-sāgara*:

bahv-āśī dīrgha-sūtrī ca viṣayādiṣu lolupaḥ
hetu-vāda-rato duṣṭo'vāg-vādī guṇa-nindakaḥ
aromā bahu-romā ca ninditāśrama-sevakaḥ
kāla-danto'sitauṣṭhaś ca durgandhi-śvāsa-vāhakaḥ
duṣṭa-lakṣaṇa-sampanno yadyapi svayam īśvaraḥ
bahu-pratigrahāsakta ācāryaḥ śrī-kṣayāvaḥaḥ

> All the good fortune of a disciple will be destroyed if he takes a guru who eats too much, who is a procrastinator, who is greedy for sense gratification, who is given to useless arguments, who is immoral, who enjoys gossiping about other people's sinful activities and then turns others' virtues into vices, who is either devoid of bodily hair or has too much hair, who takes up a condemned way of life, who has black teeth or lips, who has bad breath, and who, although quite capable of giving in charity, is attached to taking money from his disciples or other rich people.

Some of these flaws are worth discussing.

- *Bahv-āśī*—one who eats too much. One who is addicted to good-tasting foods and filling his belly will inevitably become subject to the pushings of the genitals. Sri Chaitanya Mahaprabhu said:

jihvāra lālase jebā iti uti dhāya
śiśnodara-parāyaṇa kṛṣṇa nāhi pāya

One who runs here and there looking for good things to eat becomes attached to his sex organs and belly and will never attain Krishna. (CC 3.6.222–27)

- *Dīrgha-sūtrī*—one who puts off to tomorrow what can be done today.
- *Viṣayādiṣu lolupaḥ*—one who is excessively attached to his wife and children or to the sense objects related to taste, touch, sight, smell, and sound.
- *Hetu-vāda-rataḥ*—one who engages in useless speculation or argumentation. The *Hayaśīrṣa-pañcarātra* (quoted in HBV 1.71–72) says:

jaiminiḥ sugataś caiva nāstiko nagna eva ca
kapilaś cākṣapādaś ca ṣaḍ ete hetu-vādinaḥ
etan-matānusāreṇa vartante ye narādhamāḥ
te hetu-vādinaḥ proktās tebhyas tantraṁ na dāpayet

There are six philosophers who are called *hetu-vādins*, or dry speculators. They are Jaimini (father of the *Pūrva-mīmāṁsā*), Sugata (the Buddha), Charvaka (the atheist), Mahavira (father of *Jainism*), Kapila (founder of the *Sāṅkhya* philosophy), and Akshapada, or Gautama (founder of the *Nyāya* school). Those lowly humans who follow these teachers are also called dry speculators (*hetu-vādīs*). One should not give initiation to, nor take initiation from, such persons.

- *Duṣṭa*—this is glossed in the commentary as "envious, violent, and vengeful."
- *Avāg-vādī*—according to Sanatana Goswami's commentary, this means someone who likes to talk about others' sinful activities.
- *Guṇa-nindakaḥ*—someone who out of envy finds fault even in another's virtues. In the *Caitanya-caritāmṛta* (3.8.79), Ramachandra Puri was described as having this quality:

jāhāṅ guṇa śata āche tāhā nā kare grahaṇa
guṇa-madhye chale kare doṣa āropaṇa

> If someone had a hundred virtues, he would show no interest in any of them. Rather, he would find some reason to criticize one virtue or another, and make it look like a vice.

- *Ninditāśrama-sevaka*—one does not compromise with people who are engaged in sinful activities to make a living in order to gain personal benefit.

THE LALIPUR SANNYASI

When Sri Chaitanya Mahaprabhu was still known as Vishwambhara and was living in Nabadwip, he proposed to Nityananda Prabhu that They visit Advaita Acharya in Shantipur, about twenty-five kilometers south along the Ganges. Halfway there, They came to the village of Lalitpur where, on the banks of the river lived a householder dressed in saffron, like a sannyasi. Such so-called sannyasi are sometimes called *ghara-pāgalā*, or "householder madmen"; they practice a kind of left-handed tantric spirituality, which includes drinking liquor and consorting with women. These unorthodox practices are not considered Vedic.

Saraswati Thakur comments in his *Gauḍīya-bhāṣya* on *Chaitanya-bhagavata* 2.19.43:

> Such householder sannyasis are practitioners of a kind of tantra in the mode of ignorance, practicing illicit sex and the keeping of women, and yet they call themselves renunciants, or *tyāgīs*. According to some *Śakta* texts, these sannyasis claim that their practices are legitimate and according to the scriptures. Nowadays, the Pandita Sri Annada Charan Mitra wears saffron, although he is a householder, and in Vrindavan, Sri Madhusudan Goswami also wears saffron, claiming that he does so for the sake of preaching.

In fact, the wearing of saffron is prescribed for renunciants following the *vidhi-marga* (*maryādā patha*), or path of scriptural injunctions. All the great *ācāryas* of the Middle Ages thus wore saffron. Rupa and Sanatana Goswami initiated the path of *rāgānuga-bhakti* (*anurāga-patha*), and naturally gravitated toward the transcendental practices of the *paramahaṁsa*. They thus rejected even the kind of *sannyāsa* that Chaitanya Mahaprabhu Himself took (the *eka-daṇḍa sannyāsa* of the *Advaita sampradāya*), and wore the white cloth symbolic of those completely transcendental to the four orders of the *varṇāśrama* system.

Gopala Bhatta Goswami's spiritual master was Prabodhananda Saraswati, who also wore saffron, but he belonged to the triple-staff (*tridaṇḍa*) order of sannyasis. This is appropriate for those who are functioning as *ācāryas* or gurus. Nevertheless, he too showed that he considered the *rāgānugā* path and the transcendental attitude and white dress of Rupa and Sanatana to be superior.

In other words, wearing saffron cloth is appropriate only for those in the renounced order of life, who appropriately function as spiritual masters to society. Nevertheless, those such as Prabodhananda Saraswati indicated that the transcendental position, or *paramahaṁsa* state, symbolized by the white *bahirvāsa* of the Six Goswamis, is superior. In both these renounced conditions, however, there is no room for sannyasis to cohabit with women.

Acting as though They did not know this, Sri Chaitanya and Nityananda entered the sannyasi's compound, as it is a pious act to see a man who has dedicated his life to the service of God. On seeing him They offered Their obeisance. The sannyasi was enchanted by Vishwambhara's charming appearance, perfectly shaped limbs, and radiant smile and so joyfully blessed Him, saying, "May You enjoy wealth, a good marriage, many descendants, and vast learning."

Mahaprabhu immediately replied, "*Gosāi*, this is not a real blessing. Bless Me instead that I receive Krishna's grace. A blessing that brings one loving devotion to Lord Krishna is inexhaustible and indestructible. You are a sannyasi, so it is not becoming for you to bless Me with such mundane benefits."

Srila Bhaktisiddhanta Saraswati comments:

> In the opinion of these householder sannyasis, a blessing means getting married, overcoming poverty, wealth, higher social status, mundane education, and other such things. Gaurasundara showed no favor to this particular group of "householder madmen," and His intent here was to show the flaws in their way of offering blessings. Worldly people seeking material advantages are unable to understand the mentality of the Vaishnava *paramahaṁsas*, who are free of all such desires, and so think they are just like them.

Sannyasis of this sort gravitate toward the doctrine of *jāti gosvāmī,* the claim of hereditary guru privilege. Mahaprabhu had absolutely no affection for such ideas, but nevertheless, He sought to teach the sannyasi a lesson: that Krishna's pleasure is the greatest blessing of all. Mundane people think that the insignificant ashes of material desire are glorious—anything but devotion to Krishna. As they are unable to understand the glories of *bhāgavata-dharma,* which is beyond material desires, they confuse the superficial Vishnu worship rituals of the caste *brāhmaṇas* (*smārtas*) with pure *Vaishnavism.*

These sannyasis, like those who claim hereditary guru privilege, are eager to receive the title *Gosvāmī* or *gosāi.* Mahaprabhu addressed the householder sannyasi as *gosāi* in mock respect, but the truth is that such people do not deserve this title, which is reserved for those who have mastered the senses. The *Bhāgavatam* (7.5.30) says that those with uncontrolled desires descend into darkness (*adānta-gobhir viśatāṁ tamisram*).

Rupa Goswami's definition of the term *gosvāmin* is given in the first verse of the *Upadeśāmṛta*:

vāco vegaṁ manasaḥ krodha vegaṁ
jihvā vegam udaropastha vegam
etān vegān yo viṣaheta dhīraḥ
sarvām apīmāṁ pṛthivīṁ sa śiṣyāt

One who has the ability to tolerate the urges of speech, mind, anger, taste, the belly, and the genitals is able to instruct the entire world.

On hearing Mahaprabhu's reply, the sannyasi changed his attitude and answered with a snort. "I have heard of people like You. You try to say something nice to them and they give you a kick in return. This is exactly how this young *brāhmaṇa* is behaving. I happily wished for Him to become rich, but He simply criticizes me.

"Tell me, young *brāhmaṇa*, why did You find fault with my blessings? What is the point of living if You haven't enjoyed sex with a beautiful woman or You have insufficient money? I wished these things for You, but You find that embarrassing? And even if Your body is filled with devotion to Krishna, what will You live on if You have no money? Tell me that!"

The Lord simply smiled and placed His hand on His forehead in amazement at the sannyasi's foolishness. He then took the occasion to teach the world that one should not ask for anything other than devotion to Krishna. He said, "Listen, *Gosāi*, we will get whatever food we get automatically as the result of our past deeds. In this world, people desire to have money and a wife and children, but they still have to leave everything at death. On the other hand, no one wants fevers, so why do we suffer from them? The reason for all this is karma, although not many people know it.

"Most people think that they can become wealthy or have family happiness by chanting God's name and bathing in the Ganga. It's true that the Vedas promise such material results, but the ultimate purpose of all the Vedic injunctions is to bring us to Krishna."

The householder sannyasi smiled and thought that perhaps Vishwambhara had been brainwashed. He suspected that Nityananda Prabhu, who was also dressed as a sannyasi, had mesmerized him. Aloud he said, "I have traveled around the world. I have been to Ayodhya, Mathura, Badarikashram, Benares, and even Sri Lanka. But this young pup is going to teach me right and wrong?"

Nityananda Prabhu managed to cool the householder sannyasi's temper with sweet words, and then the two Prabhus bathed in the Ganges and offered some fruit for Their noon meal. But when the sannyasi showed his true colors as a left-handed tantrik by offering Them liquor, They made Their escape.

Srila Prabhupada writes in his *Gauḍīya-bhāṣya* on *Chaitanya-bhagavata* (2.19.86):

> Those who follow the *vāmācāra*, or left-handed tantra, have several practices that are not approved by orthodox Hindus of any tradition. Specifically, they use what are called the "five M's" (*pañca-ma-kāra*), namely meat (*māṁsa*), fish (*matsya*), alcoholic beverages (*madya*), sexual relationships (*maithuna*), and fried grain (*mudrā*). They also use a woman's menstrual blood in their ritual worship of the woman. The *Ācāra-bheda-tantra* says that one is to place the red sign of the goddess on one's forehead and hold the wine cup in one's right hand and then drink while meditating on the *śākta* guru and the goddess. There is a mantra that one is to recite to the cup five times before drinking. One is advised not to drink beyond the point that one's senses can remain steady. Then there are mantras that are to be recited afterwards in order to pacify the senses. More instructions on this matter can be found in the *Prāṇa-toṣaṇī-tantra* and the *Kulārṇava-tantra*.

Concluding this story, Vrindavan Das states that the Lord is merciful even to drunkards and materialists, but He is not so merciful to the *Mayavadis*. Bhaktisiddhanta Saraswati comments in his *Gauḍīya-bhāṣya* on *Chaitanya-bhagavata* (2.19.95): "Ordinarily, those in the mundane concept of life who have strong ideas about morality have greater respect for monistic philosophers than for womanizers and the like. The most merciful Lord, however, does not support this superficial point of view. Mahaprabhu opposed the views of the Vedantists, who detest the personal Lord and are inimical to devotion. Even though someone may be weak and fall prey to a life of sensuality or drink, the Lord still considers such a person better than one whose heart has been hardened by the impersonalist or atheist doctrine."

Bhaktivinoda Thakur writes in his *Śaraṇāgati* (*Varjanātmikā* 27):

viṣaya-vimūḍha āra māyāvādī jana
bhakti-śūnya duṅhe prāṇa dhare akāraṇa
ei dui saṅga nātha nā haya āmāra
prārthanā kariye āmi caraṇe tomāra

Both those who are bewildered by the promise of sense enjoyments and *Māyāvādī* impersonalists are devoid of devotion. Their lives have no purpose. I pray at Your feet, O Lord, that I never be subjected to the association of either one or the other.

se du'yera madhye viṣayī tabe bhāla
māyāvādī-saṅga nāhi māgi kona kāla

Of the two, however, I would rather be with a sensualist than with a *Māyāvādī*. I hope never to be subjected to the company of a *Māyāvādī*.

viṣayī-hṛdaya jabe sādhu-saṅga pāya
anāyāse labhe bhakti bhaktera kṛpāya

A sensualist may be transformed by the association of a devotee, whose mercy can easily turn him to a life of devotion.

māyāvāda doṣa jāra hṛdaya paśila
kutarke hṛdaya tāra vajra-sama bhela

But once the impersonalist contamination has touched the heart, the heart becomes as hard as stone, fortified by all manner of false argument.

bhaktira svarūpa āra viṣaya āśraya
māyāvādī anitya boliyā saba kaya

The *Māyāvādī* considers devotion, the devotee, and the object of devotion to be temporary manifestations of the material world.

dhik tāra kṛṣṇa-sevā śravaṇa-kīrtana
kṛṣṇa aṅge vajra hāne tāhāra stavana

I curse his so-called service to Krishna, his hearing of the *Bhāgavatam,* and his chanting of the Holy Names. His prayers to Krishna rain like thunderbolts on Krishna's body.

māyāvāda sama bhakti pratikūla nāi
ataeva māyāvāda saṅga nāhi cāi

There is nothing more harmful to devotion than *Māyāvāda* philosophy. Therefore I do not wish to ever be with people who subscribe to that philosophy.

bhakativinoda māyāvāda dūra kari
vaiṣṇava-saṅgete baise nāmāśraya dhari

Bhaktivinoda hereby rejects *Māyāvāda* philosophy and takes shelter of the Holy Names in the association of devotees.

CHAPTER 4

Qualifications of the Disciple

The *Hari-bhakti-vilāsa,* after describing the difference between the true guru and the pretender, turns to the disciple's qualifications. Following these descriptions, Bhaktivinoda Thakur summarizes the principal qualities of both guru and disciple in *Jaiva Dharma* (chapter 20):

> The principal thing to retain here is that an aspiring disciple should be of good moral character and have faith. The guru should be a practitioner of pure devotional service; he should be knowledgeable in the theology of Krishna, of unblemished character, honest, free of greed, unaffected by the impersonalist conception of the Deity, and expert in attaining results in the practice of devotion (*kārya-dakṣa*). A *brāhmaṇa* who possesses such qualities and is in good standing in society can act as guru for all the other castes. If a prospective disciple cannot find a guru to his liking among the *brāhmaṇas,* then he may take a spiritual master from one of the other castes. The conclusion here is that one can leave all caste considerations aside and concentrate on the principal qualification of the guru: his worthiness to guide one on the path of devotional service. A person who is involved with conventional Hindu society might find it more practical to have a spiritual master who is a *brāhmaṇa,* but he should still look for the central characteristic of a devotee, for this is the real qualifications of a guru. The scriptures have prescribed the testing of both the disciple and the spiritual master and have

> also allowed for periods of time for such testing. The goal here is that the guru and disciple should formalize their relation by initiation only when the spiritual master has determined that the aspiring disciple is qualified (has the *adhikāra*) and the disciple has come to the point of believing the spiritual master is a pure devotee and has faith in him.

In the *Hari-bhakti-vilāsa* (1.74) the following verses from the *Tattva-sāgara* summarize the virtues possessed by an ideal disciple:

> *amāny amatsaro dakṣo nirmamo dṛdha-sauhṛdaḥ*
> *asatvaro'rtha-jijñāsur anasūyur amogha-vāk*
>
> The disciple should have the following characteristics: he should be humble, nonenvious, expert, detached, determined, friendly, patient, inquisitive, nonenvious, and does not waste words.
>
> *tayor vatsara-vāsena jñātānyonya-svabhāvayoḥ*
> *gurutā śiṣyatā ceti nānyathaiveti niścayaḥ*
>
> By living together for a year, the spiritual master and the disciple will be able to understand each other's character and know whether they are capable of acting as spiritual master and disciple respectively. Without such close association, it will be impossible to be certain about such things.

The *Upaniṣads* also say that the spiritual master should not initiate anyone who has not lived with him for at least a year (*nāsaṁvatsara-vāsine deyāt,* quoted in HBV 1.75). The *Hari-bhakti-vilāsa* (1.77) quotes an ancient text, the *Sāra-saṅgraha,* that gives a reason for such care being taken before initiating disciples:

rājñi cāmātyajā doṣāḥ
patnī-pāpaṁ sva-bhartari
tathā śiṣyārjitaṁ pāpaṁ
guruḥ prāpnoti niścitam

The flaws of a minister are taken by the king and the sins of a wife are taken by her husband. In the same way, the sins committed by a disciple are most certainly taken by the spiritual master.

Some people ask how this is possible if the spiritual master is beyond the modes of material nature and fixed at Krishna's lotus feet. It is true that a powerful spiritual master is able to eradicate a disciple's sins along with the disciple's sinful nature. Out of mercy, he may take unqualified disciples and transform them without even going through the customary testing period. However, not everyone who is called to act as guru can afford to be so generous. This scriptural warning is to remind those who take on the role of guru to remain careful, for if one takes many disciples only for the profit, adoration, and prestige he can gather from them, he will make unworthy disciples who will not only ruin his reputation over time but also reflect badly on the entire Vaishnava community.

Some scriptures are even stricter in their demands for testing. Sanatana Goswami quotes the *Sāradā-tilaka,* which states that *brāhmaṇas* should be tested for a year, *kṣatriyas* for two years, *vaiśyas* for three, and *śūdras* for four. Yet another text triples these numbers! In our age of Kali, life is short and few people have the patience to undergo such long periods of testing. Nevertheless, the instruction needs to be taken seriously, because the dangers a guru faces when taking unqualified disciples, or a disciple faces when taking an unqualified guru, have repercussions that negatively affect the spiritual lives of everyone in the community.

THE DISCIPLE'S BEHAVIOR

The *Hari-bhakti-vilāsa* (1.90) then lists the kinds of service a disciple may perform for the spiritual master. He can fetch water, grass, flowers for Deity service, wood for the sacrificial fire or cooking. He can wash or repair the guru's living quarters or clothing. He can prepare the guru's toothbrush (generally, the twig of a neem tree) or other toiletry items.

The *Hari-bhakti-vilāsa* also summarizes a number of points of etiquette that should not be neglected when it comes to knowing how to behave in the spiritual master's presence.

> Do not sit on or step over the spiritual master's bed, seat, remnants, eating plate and utensils, or bath-water. It goes without saying that one does not use the spiritual master's cups or plates for oneself. One should never sit on the same seat as the spiritual master; nor should one sit on a seat more elevated than the guru's. One should not stretch out one's legs, stretch one's body, yawn, laugh or joke, or crane one's neck in the guru's presence. One should not worship another person in the guru's presence or treat another person as the guru's equal.
>
> As soon as one sees the spiritual master, one should fold one's hands and offer obeisance, falling to the ground like a tree that has been chopped down at the roots.

śreyas tu guruvad vṛttir
nityam eva samācaret
guru-putreṣu dāreṣu
guroś caiva sva-bandhuṣu

> The disciple should treat his guru's wife and children, friends and relatives, with the same respect he affords the guru, seeking their well-being. (HBV 1.84)

Most Gaudiya Maths follow the standards set by their founder-*ācārya*, Srila Bhaktisiddhanta Saraswati, which are principally set up as residences for *brahmacārīs* and sannyāsīs. Since most Gaudiya Math *ācāryas* are in the renounced (*sannyāsa*) *āśrama*, the question of respecting and serving the guru's wife, children, and relatives is not one that their disciples usually have to face. However, the disciples who have been initiated earlier by one's guru become a new disciple's family—they are part of the *acyuta-gotra,* or divine family of Vaishnavas. These devotees are one's older brothers and sisters and should be respected as one would have respected the guru's children in the times of the *Upaniṣads*. Serving godbrothers and godsisters who are engaged in the spiritual master's service should not be seen as separate from serving the spiritual master himself. Serving all Vaishnavas is an essential element on the path of devotion (*chāṛiyā vaiṣṇava-sevā, nistāra pāiyāche kebā*). Those who have taken shelter of the same guru are likely to be Vaishnavas with the same inclination, or *ruci* (*sajātiyāśaye*), and due to their common connection they are also likely to be affectionate (*snigdha*). Therefore these devotees will be natural objects of service, association, and veneration.

The *Hari-bhakti-vilāsa* (1.89) follows this discussion with another important instruction:

dīkṣāṁ vyākhyāṁ prabhutvaṁ ca
guror agre vivarjayet

> When the guru is present, one should not give initiation, explain the scriptures, or exercise one's powers as a master.

Of course, in some extraordinary cases, the spiritual master may ask his students to explain something in order to test their knowledge; he may even ask trusted disciples to initiate on his behalf or to make their own disciples while he is still present. But no disciple should arrogantly think that he can initiate anyone without the direct permission of his spiritual master.

One should not imitate the spiritual master's movements or speech. When in the presence of one's spiritual master's seniors, one should treat these devotees with the same respect one would accord one's guru, but when in the presence of one's own seniors, such as one's parents or teachers, one should not show these persons honor in the guru's presence without first receiving the guru's permission.

The *Hari-bhakti-vilāsa* (1.94–95) also discusses some other points of etiquette. In the presence of the guru or even away from him, one should not speak his name without using appropriate honorifics. One should also not speak his name without a devotional attitude. Gaudiya Vaishnavas generally use the words "*Oṁ Viṣṇupāda Śrī*" before saying their guru's name, as well as adding other titles. If one is asked for his guru's name, he should use his guru's full title. Generally, any titles that reveal the honor and respect in which one holds one guru are a sufficient show of that honor and respect. The *Hari-bhakti-vilāsa* adds that one should bow one's head and fold one's hands when saying the guru's name.

Here are some of the titles for the guru used in the Gaudiya Math:[1]

- *Oṁ viṣṇupāda*: the Vedic mantra *oṁ* is recited first to remind the disciple of the spiritual master's divine nature and his identification with Krishna or Viṣṇu. *Viṣṇupāda* means "one who sits at the feet of Lord Viṣṇu. In other words, when the disciple says *oṁ viṣṇupāda*, he reminds himself of the extreme respect in which he holds his divine preceptor.
- *Paramahaṁsa*: "supreme swan." This title may be given to anyone who is in the highest stage of the renounced order. Using this term, the disciple shows his appreciation for the guru's spiritual achievements. It should not be used if one's guru is a householder.
- *Parivrājakācārya*: like *paramahaṁsa*, this word is used to designate a stage of the *sannyāsa-āśrama*, referring to one who travels in order to teach the conditioned souls about devotional service to Krishna.

[1] As part of this list of titles, spelling includes diacritics.

- *Aṣṭottara-śata-śrī*: this title is used when speaking of one's spiritual master or other gurus in one's disciplic succession. It means "one who possesses 108 opulences"—in other words, one who possesses unlimited glory and good fortune.
- *Śrī/Śrīla (Sri/Srila):* in India, these two honorifics are commonly given to people due respect. Of the two, the latter is particularly reserved for saints and those respected for spiritual accomplishments. It should be noted that in Bengal, *Śrīmān* is generally used by older persons when they introduce those younger to them. It should not be confused with *Śrīmat* or *Śrīmad*, which are appropriate when speaking of a senior personality.
- *Gosvāmī* (*Goswami*): in the Gaudiya Math, this title is exclusively reserved for those in the renounced order. It means "one who has mastered the senses." It is a reminder of the connection in disciplic succession to Sri Chaitanya's intimate disciples, the Six Goswamis of Vrindavan. *Gosvāmī* and *Swami* are found in the *Muktika Upaniṣad*'s list of 108 names given to *tridaṇḍi sannyāsīs*. Two well-known disciples of Srila Prabhupada were given these titles: Sri Bhakti Saranga Goswami Maharaja and Sri Bhaktivedanta Swami Maharaja. However, both names are often added to the list of titles offered to all sannyāsīs.
- *Mahārāja* (*Maharaja*): "great king." The spiritual master is the greatest of kings, in the sense that he is the lord of the transcendental realm. The disciple is dependent on his mercy as much as the humble citizen is dependent on the king's mercy. This title is also used throughout northern India as an honorific for people in the renounced order of life.
- *Ṭhākura* (*Thakur*): although this title (which means "Deity" or "divinity") is used widely in Bengal as an honorific offered to senior religious figures, in the Gaudiya Math it has been used for only a few persons—devotees such as Srila Vrindavana Dasa Thakur, Srila Vishwanatha Chakravarti Thakur, Srila Bhaktivinoda Thakur, and Srila Prabhupada Bhaktisiddhanta Saraswati Thakur.
- *Prabhupada*: once again, although this title is used in wider Bengali Vaishnava society to designate one's own guru (generally, one's

caste guru), in the Gaudiya Math it is used almost exclusively for the founder of all the Gaudiya Mathas, Srila Bhaktisiddhanta Saraswati Goswami Prabhupada. Out of supreme respect for him, there are very few in the Gaudiya Matha who would allow their disciples to address them by this title.

The *Hari-bhakti-vilāsa* (1.93, 100) summarizes:

na guror apriyaṁ kuryāt
tāḍitaḥ pīḍito'pi vā
nāvamanyeta tad-vākyaṁ
nāpriyaṁ hi samācaret

> Never act in a way that is displeasing to your guru, even if he chastises or punishes you. Do not disregard his words, nor avoid acting for his pleasure.

ācāryasya priyaṁ kuryāt
prāṇair api dhanair api
karmaṇā manasā vācā
sa yāti paramāṁ gatim

> One who acts to please his guru, using his life energies, his wealth, in his acts, thoughts, and words attains the supreme destination.

The *Mantra-muktāvalī* (quoted in HBV 1.59–62) gives the following characteristics of an ideal disciple:

śiṣyaḥ śuddhānvayaḥ śrīmān vinītaḥ priya-darśanaḥ
satya-vāk puṇya-carito'dabhra-dhīr dambha-varjitaḥ
kāma-krodha-parityāgī bhaktaś ca guru-pādayoḥ
devatā-pravaṇaḥ kāya-mano-vāgbhir divā-niśam
nīrujo nirjitāśeṣa-pātakaḥ śraddhyānvitaḥ
dvija-deva-pitṛṇāṁ ca nityam arcā-parāyaṇaḥ

yuvā viniyatāśeṣa-karaṇaḥ karuṇālayaḥ
ity ādi-lakṣaṇair yuktaḥ śiṣyo dīkṣādhikāravān

> The ideal disciple should come from a good family, should be handsome, well-mannered, pleasing in appearance, truthful, pious in character, clear in his intelligence, without arrogance, free from lust and anger, devoted to the guru's service, inclined to the Deity in body, mind, and words, day and night. He should be healthy, free from all sinful tendencies, faithful, a constant worshiper of the *brāhmaṇas,* the gods and the forefathers, young, self-controlled, and compassionate. Such a disciple is worthy of being initiated.

In the earlier mentioned *Śrīmad-Bhāgavatam* verse (11.10.6, quoted in HBV 1.63) it states:

amāny amatsaro dakṣo
nirmamo dṛḍha-sauhṛdaḥ
asatvaro'rtha-jijñāsur
anasūyur amogha-vāk

> The disciple should be humble, nonenvious, expert, detached from wife and family, deeply affectionate toward the guru, not rushed in the performance of tasks, eager to learn, nonenvious, and does not waste words.

The last of these, *amogha-vāk*, means that an ideal disciple is disciplined in speech and does not waste his words by gossiping or speaking about trivial matters; he speaks only about Krishna.

There is a reason why the virtue of humility (*amānī*) is listed first. When Krishna was about to leave Hastinapur to return to Dwaraka, Arjuna's mother, Kunti Devi, offered beautiful prayers. In one of those verses, she stressed the important characteristics of an ideal disciple—of one who wishes to attain spiritual perfection and the mercy of the Lord:

janmaiśvarya-śruta-śrībhir
edhamāna-madaḥ pumān
naivārhaty abhidhātuṁ vai
tvām akiñcana-gocaram

> The person whose intoxication with high birth, power, learning, and wealth is constantly increasing is incapable of calling out to You, O Lord, for You are only perceived by those who are dispossessed. (ŚB 1.8.26)

Srila Vishwanatha Chakravarti Thakur comments that calling out the names of Krishna and Govinda is not something a person who is attached to worldly prestige and reputation can do. The dispossessed (*akiñcana*) are those who have nothing but Krishna. These devotees have no material pride. In the following verse, Kunti Devi uses the word *akiñcana* a second time: "I bow down to You, the wealth of the dispossessed." In this first verse the word *aiśvarya* is used to mean either power or riches. *Śruta* means "what has been heard," and in this case refers to education, scriptural knowledge, and scholarship. The word *Sri* can mean either wealth or beauty. So, people seek birth in an aristocratic or reputable family, with learning and power, scholarship, physical beauty, and so many other such things, but possessing these attributes inflates them with pride and they become intoxicated. Material pride prevents such persons from attaining Krishna.

Nonenvy is also important for a disciple. Envy is defined as the distress one feels on seeing others succeed and prosper. Envy brings with it hatred, enmity, and anger. The *Bhāgavatam* states at its very beginning that only saintly persons who are free of envy can comprehend the Supreme Truth, in whom all illusion has been overcome.

Śrīmad Bhāgavatam (1.1.2) states:

> *dharmaḥ projjhita-kaitavo'tra paramo nirmatsarāṇāṁ satāṁ*
> *vedyaṁ vāstavam atra vastu śivadaṁ tāpa-trayonmūlanam*
> *śrīmad-bhāgavate mahā-muni-kṛte kiṁ vā parair īśvaraḥ*
> *sadyo hṛdy avarudhyate'tra kṛtibhiḥ śuśrūṣubhis tat-kṣaṇāt*

> The spiritual path described in this *Bhāgavatam* is entirely devoid of any dishonest purpose; it is held in adoration by the saints who are free of the flaw of enviousness. The only subject dealt with here is the Supreme Substance, the one Supreme Truth that brings all auspiciousness and uproots the miseries of material life. What need then is there for any scripture other than this *Śrīmad Bhāgavatam*, composed by the great sage Vyasadeva? The pious trap the Lord in their hearts from the very moment they even desire to hear this greatest of all scriptures.

Envy is one of the six great enemies of the *jīva*, and a fearsome one at that. One who has not become free from envy cannot even begin to understand a single word of the supreme religion of pure devotional service described and explained in *Śrīmad Bhāgavatam*, which was composed by the Lord Himself. When the other five enemies—lust, anger, greed, intoxication, and illusion—have become extremely powerful, they attain their fullness in envy. Therefore, one who has been overcome by envy is completely deprived of the mercy of the Lord's internal potency. Therefore only someone who is free from envy is genuinely qualified to become a disciple.

Sanatana Goswami says that a guru may initiate a person who has taken shelter of him with intense devotion, even if he does not possess all the virtues described above. However, there are some character flaws serious enough to stop a guru from taking a person as a disciple. These are listed in the *Hari-bhakti-vilāsa* (1.64–67), quoted from the *Agastya-saṁhitā*:

- *Alasa*: laziness. Being indifferent to the effort needed to make progress in spiritual life.
- *Malina*: unclean. There are numerous rules governing the cleanliness of body and dress. Someone who ignores such regulations is unacceptable as a disciple. The saying "Cleanliness is next to godliness" is applicable here. However, this does not mean that excessive absorption in one's bodily appearance is condoned.

- *Kliṣṭa*: the need to burden oneself with unnecessary tasks.

gardabhera mata āmi kari pariśrama
kāra lāgi eta kari nā ghucila bhrama

I labor like a mule. I don't know why my illusion has still not come to an end. (Bhaktivinoda Thakur, *Kalyana-Kalpataru* 2.4.5)

- *Dāmbhika*: in his commentary on Bhagavad Gita 16.4, Vishwanatha Chakravarti defines *dāmbhika* as hypocrisy, or advertising oneself as religious when in fact one is not.[2]
- *Kṛpaṇa*: miserliness. This refers to someone who is reluctant to spend money. The *Upaniṣads* say that the person who leaves this world without having attained self-knowledge and knowledge of the Supreme Truth, the goal of life, and how to achieve it, is called a miser. But this is also applicable to those who are unaware of how to spend money in ordinary and spiritual matters. Such people are said to be possessed by *Yakṣas*.
- *Daridra*: poverty. Real poverty is expressed when one does not make the effort to earn the wealth of love for God. Mahaprabhu told Raghunatha Das:

sadā nāma labe yathā lābhete santoṣa
ei mātra ācāra kare bhakti-dharma-poṣa

---

[2] *svasyādharmikatve'pi dhārmikatva-prakhyāpanam.*

> Always chant the name of the Lord and be satisfied with whatever comes to you. Only this attitude will nourish your devotional life. (CC 1.17.30)

- *Rogī*: sickliness.
- *Ruṣṭa*: anger.
- *Rāgī*: attachment to material sense objects.
- *Bhoga-lālasa*: greed for material sense gratification.
- *Asūya-grasta*: vengefulness.
- *Matsara-grasta*: envy.
- *Śaṭha*: treachery. This refers to someone who is two-faced, a cheater, or someone who acts sweetly but who has a nefarious purpose.
- *Paruṣa-vādī*: the speaking of harsh words.
- *Anyāyopārjita-dhana*: earning money by illegal or immoral means.
- *Para-dāra-rata*: attachment to the wives of other men. Mahaprabhu says:

asat-saṅga-tyāga ei vaiṣṇava ācāra
strī-saṅgī eka asādhu kṛṣṇābhakta āra

> The rejection of unholy company is the essence of Vaishnava behavior. The unholy are divided into those who are attached to sex life and those who are against the principle of devotion to Krishna. (CC 2.22.87)

- *Viduṣāṁ vairī*: envy. Refers to one who is inimical to those who know more than him.
- *Ajño paṇḍita-mānī*: the pride of thinking oneself learned, despite the fact that one is drowning in an ocean of ignorance.
- *Bhraṣṭa-vrata*: being incapable of keeping one's word or maintaining the principles that are favorable to devotional life.
- *Kaṣṭa-vṛtti*: having great difficulty making a living. Those who make little or no effort to advance in material life sometimes take

shelter of a spiritual master in order to extract some benefit for themselves and their family. Their apparent efforts at spiritual life are simply a show; their real concern is their material survival.

- *Piśuna*: backbiting; slanderous, calumnious, treacherous behavior.
- *Khala*: giving pain to others, like a poisonous snake that is by nature dangerous to everyone. Someone with this kind of viciousness does not seek to help or do others good but spontaneously tries to hurt or cause others trouble.
- *Bahv-āśī*: gluttony. Here again:

> *jihvāra lālase jebā iti uti dhāya*
> *śiśnodara-parāyaṇa kṛṣṇa nāhi pāya*

> One who runs here and there looking for good things to eat becomes attached to his sex organs and his belly and will never attain Krishna. (CC 3.6.27)

> One who is attached to his tongue and its tastes will eventually become attached to filling the belly. Addiction to the belly leads to increased sex desire. There are six urges we all feel: the urge to speak, the urge to dwell on things in the mind, the urge to become angry, the urge of the tongue to taste a variety of flavors, the urge of the belly to be filled, and the urge of the sex organs. One who can resist these urges is said to have controlled the senses and become a goswami. Those who are dominated by the urges of the tongue and belly have a difficult time making spiritual advancement. Only the most powerful spiritual master should dare take on such a disciple; for others, such a disciple could prove extremely dangerous.

- *Krūra-ceṣṭa*: engaging in cruel activities, like murder.
- *Durātmā*: wickedness.

- *Nindita*: engaging in activities that make one universally despised or criticized.
- *Puruṣādhama*: attachment to illicit sex and other despised activities.

akṛtyebhyo'nivāryāś ca
guru-śikṣāsahiṣṇavaḥ
evaṁ-bhūtāḥ parityājyāḥ
śiṣyatve nopakalpitāḥ

The *Hari-bhakti-vilāsa* (1.68–70) states:

> Finally, those who cannot be turned away from sinful actions and who cannot tolerate the directions of the spiritual master are to be rejected, as they are not worthy of being disciples.
>
> Those gurus who take such persons as disciples out of greed or some other unsavory motivation are affected by their disciples' flaws. It is said that the gods become angry and curse them, they become poor and lose their children and wives, and when they die they go to hell and are subsequently born into animal species.[3]

---

[3] *yady ete hy upakalperan devatākrośa-bhājanāḥ*
bhavantīha daridrās te putra-dāra-vivarjitāt
nārakāś caiva dehānte tiryañcaḥ prabhavabti te.

CHAPTER 5

Examining Sri Guru and the Disciple

The *Hari-bhakti-vilāsa* (1.73) then turns to the subject of the guru and disciple examining each other.

tayoḥ parīkṣā cānyo'nyam
ekābdaṁ saha-vāsataḥ
vyavahāra-svabhāvānu-
bhavenaivābhijāyate

Spiritual master and disciple should test each other over a period of a year, during which time they should live together. During this time, the testing takes the form of experiencing each other's behavior and character.

The *Mantra-muktāvalī* (quoted in HBV 1.74) states:

tayor vatsara-vāsena
jñātānyonya-svabhāvayoḥ
gurutā śiṣyatā ceti
nānyathaiveti niścayaḥ

By living together for a year, it is possible for them to know each other's nature and personality and thus whether they are worthy of acting as guru and

> disciple respectively. There is no other way to do this.

The *śrutis* also say that the guru should not give the mantra to anyone who has not lived with him for a year (*nāsaṁvatsara-vāsine deyāt*). Another text, the *Sāra-saṅgraha* (quoted in HBV 1.76), similarly states that a genuine guru tests a disciple who has taken shelter of him for one year (*sad-guruḥ svāśritaṁ śiṣyaṁ varṣam ekaṁ parīkṣayet*).

The *Krama-dīpikā* (4.3, quoted in HBV 1.78) states:

santoṣayed akuṭilārdretarāntarātmā
taṁ svair dhanaiś ca vapuṣāpy anukūla-vāṇyā
abda-trayaṁ kamala-nābha-dhiyā'tidhīras
tuṣṭe vivakṣatu gurāv atha mantra-dīkṣām

> The disciple should patiently please the spiritual master for a period of three years, acting in complete sincerity and honesty, offering him his wealth, his body, and favorable words, thinking of him as a direct manifestation of the lotus-naveled Lord. Then, when the spiritual master is pleased with him, the disciple can ask him for initiation into the mantra.

Those who ignore all these directions ordering spiritual master and disciple to examine each other for an extended period of time, will, for the most part, come to regret their actions. This has happened in the past, is happening in the present, and will go on happening in the future with the same result. Of this there is no doubt. However, there are some extraordinarily powerful devotees who are especially close to the Lord and thus beyond the restrictions and limitations placed on them by scriptural regulations. They engage in whatever they do by the desire of the Lord Himself. No sin can taint their transcendental lives. We, on the other hand, are tiny *jīvas* with limited powers. If we imitate such great souls, then we will surely come to regret it.

There is a popular saying in Bengal, "You can easily find thousands of teachers, but it is hard to find even one student" (*guru mile lākh lākh, śiṣya mile eka*). This means there are many people who think they know everything, especially when it comes to the meaning of life, but it is hard to find anyone who is actually serious about learning a subject properly. Still, in reality, it is just as hard to find a qualified spiritual master as it is to find a qualified student. The *Kaṭha Upaniṣad* (1.2.7) states:

śravaṇāyāpi bahubhir yo na labhyaḥ
śṛṇvanto'pi bahavo yaṁ na vidyuḥ
āścaryo vaktā kuśalo'sya labdhā-
ścaryo jñātā kuśalānuśiṣṭaḥ

> The subject matter of the Self is one that not many get to even hear about. And most of those who do hear do not get to understand it. If one finds a speaker who can teach him about God, that is a most wonderful thing. And if one submits to such a teacher and becomes a knower of God, that is an even greater wonder.

So, both a genuine teacher and a genuine student are rarities in this world. Elsewhere, it is said:

guravo bahavaḥ santi
śiṣya-vittāpahārakāḥ
durlabhaḥ sad-gurur devi
śiṣya-santāpa-hārakaḥ

> Many are the gurus whose only interest is to steal their disciples' wealth. Rare is the guru who removes his disciple's material miseries.

The point here is that those who make a living by giving a mantra, explaining scriptures such as *Śrīmad Bhāgavatam* or Bhagavad Gita, singing the kirtan of the *mahā-mantra* or hymns composed by the great Vaishnavas, are acting as enemies of transcendental spirituality. Of this there is no doubt. Whoever takes the mantra from a false guru or listens to him speak on the scripture or sing will never get any real spiritual benefit. These persons are to be thought of as undesirable association in the way we think of *karmīs, jñānīs,* and yogis who are only interested in sense enjoyment, liberation, and mystic powers as undesirable association. In the *Prema-vivarta* (7.1–9), Jagadananda Pandita writes:

> O brother! You cannot chant the Holy Name in the association of nondevotees. The sounds of the Holy Name may come out of your mouth, but it will not really be the name. It will sometimes be the name's reflection (*nāmābhāsa*) and sometimes the offensive chanting (*nāmāparādha*) of the name. But brother, you should know that in either case, this kind of chanting interferes with the attainment of pure devotion to Krishna. If you want to chant the Holy Names, then associate with pure devotees and keep your desires for sense enjoyment, liberation, and yogic powers at a distance.
>
> Give up the ten offenses to the Holy Name as well as worrying about receiving respect or criticism. Consume what you need without attachment and always chant the Holy Name. Accept everything that favors devotion to Krishna and reject everything that interferes with its practice. Abandon any efforts for liberation or mystic power as well as devotion that has been diluted by fruitive desire or by superficial ritual. Above all, give up the false renunciation of the monkeys in which bodily consciousness and attachment to sense gratification remain strong. Remain strong in the knowledge that Krishna is always taking care of you. Offer yourself to Krishna completely in humility and become free from all entanglements.

It is very difficult for an ordinary person to find the association of genuine saintly persons. Krishna knows this and so He kindly came to Nadia in the form of a saintly devotee. An intelligent person takes shelter of Gauranga's lotus feet, for he knows that other than Gauranga, there is no true saint or spiritual master.[1]

The *Hari-bhakti-vilāsa* (8.265) confirms that kirtan should not be used to make one's livelihood:

gīta-nṛtyāni kurvīta deva-dvijādi-tuṣṭaye
na jīvanāya yuñjīta vipro pāpa-bhiyā kvacit

> One should engage in singing and dancing for the pleasure of the Lord and the *brāhmaṇas*, their servants. But a *brāhmaṇa* should never do so for making a living, for fear of incurring sin.

Sanatana Goswami comments in his *Dig-darśinī*, "One should never at any time engage in such activities for the sake of making a living. The reason for this is given here: for fear of committing a sin. In other words, by doing so, one is committing a sin."

Similarly, in the essence of all the Vedas, Vedānta, epics, and *Purāṇas*, the *Śrīmad Bhāgavatam* (7.13.8, quoted in BRS 1.2.112), it is said:

na śiṣyān anubadhnīta
granthān naivābhyased bahūn
na vyākhyām upayuñjīta
nārambhān ārabhet kvacit

---

[1] *asādhu-saṅge bhāi kṛṣṇa-nāma nāhi haya | nāmākṣara bāhirāya baṭe tabu nāma kabhu naya ||*
kabhu nāmābhāsa haya sadā nāma-aparādha | e saba jānibe bhāi kṛṣṇa-bhaktira bādha ||
jadi karibe kṛṣṇa-nāma sādhu-saṅga kara | bhukti-mukti-siddhi-vāñchā dūre parihara ||
daśa-aparādha tyaja māna-apamāna | anāsaktye viṣaya bhuñja āra laha kṛṣṇa-nāma ||
kṛṣṇa-bhaktira anukūla saba karaha svīkāra | kṛṣṇa-bhaktira pratikūla saba kara parihāra ||
jñāna-yoga-ceṣṭa chāḍa āra karma-saṅga | markaṭa-vairāgya tyaja yāte deha-raṅga ||
kṛṣṇa āmāya pāle rākhe jāna sarva-kāla | ātma-nivedana dainye ghucāo jañjāla ||
sādhu pāyoā kaṣṭa baḍa jīvera jāniyā | sādhu-bhakta-rūpe kṛṣṇa āilā nadīyā ||
gorā-pada āśraya karaha buddhimān | gorā bai sādhu-guru āche kebā āna ||

> The sannyāsī should not make disciples; nor should he study many different books. The sannyāsī should not make one's living by explaining the scriptures; nor should he start many great undertakings.

The commentators say that even though this verse appears in the context of the dharma of sannyāsīs or other renunciants, since bhakti in general promotes detachment, these statements are applicable to Vaishnavas in all stations of life. Sridhar Swami says that "not making disciples" means that sannyāsīs should not offer bribes or other types of unsavory forms of coercion to attract unworthy persons as disciples.

The following verse from the *Brahma-vaivarta Purāṇa,* in the eleventh chapter of the *Prakṛti-khaṇḍa,* confirms this:

śūdrāṇāṁ sūpakārī ca yo harer nāma-vikrayī
yo vidyā-vikrayī vipro viṣa-hīno yathorasaḥ

> Both *śūdras* who are not devotees of Vishnu but who are engaged as cooks, and *brāhmaṇas* who sell the Holy Name of Krishna or their knowledge, are like snakes without poison.

This verse requires some explanation. A snake that has no poison still resembles a snake, so ignorant people will fear it even though it can do no harm. Similarly, a *brāhmaṇa* who makes his living from giving initiation or teaching scripture may resemble a guru, but he will not actually be able to empower his disciples to attain the highest spiritual goal. The wise are not deceived by their pretense.

"Selling the Holy Name" means either giving initiation into a *kṛṣṇa-mantra* or the *mahā-mantra,* or earning money by singing kirtan of the Holy Name in concerts or door to door. Professional lecturers on the *Bhāgavatam* and other scriptures make contracts to speak for a specific length of time. This type of speaking has an extremely negative effect on one's devotion. Devotion is about pleasing Krishna's senses. If one's purpose in speaking the *Bhāgavatam* is to satisfy one's own senses, then that takes one in the opposite direction from bhakti and gives no pleasure to *Bhakti Devi* or her Lord.

The *Bhāgavatam* verse quoted above also says that one should not start "many great undertakings." The commentaries explain: "Do not start building temples and *maṭhas* (or *āśramas*)." This means that one should not get caught up in building fancy temples at great cost in order to increase one's own prestige and reputation. Whatever one's endeavors, they should not interfere with efforts to preach the message of Chaitanya Mahaprabhu, which is beneficial for the entire world.

In *Śrīmad Bhāgavatam* (11.11.38–41), Lord Sri Krishna tells His dear friend Uddhava:

> These are devotional activities that bring eternal benefit: having faith in the establishment of My Deity form in a temple and spontaneously working, either alone or with others, towards establishing gardens, orchards, or parks around the temple; sweeping the temple and washing it, sprinkling scented water in the temple, drawing auspicious designs with rice paste, and engaging in other kinds of service in the temple without false pride, thinking of oneself as a servant; freedom from pride and hypocrisy, not boasting of the service one has done for Me; never using the lamp that has been lit in the temple for any other purpose; and finally, offering to Me whatever is dearest to oneself. When one offers Me what one loves oneself, then it leads one to immortality.

Therefore, this instruction to not build temples and *maṭhas* is for those who contravene the principle of serving the Lord, the spiritual master, and the Vaishnavas, and who instead seek profit, adoration, and prestige.

What is meant by the word scripture? Madhvacharya answers this question in his commentary on the Bhagavad Gita:

ṛg yajuḥ sāmārthavāś ca bhārataṁ pañcarātrakam
mūla-rāmāyaṇaṁ caiva śāstram ity abhidhīyate
yac cānukūlam etasya tac ca śāstraṁ prakīrtitam
ato'nya-grantha-vistāro naiva śāstraṁ kuvartma tat

> Scripture (śāstra) includes the four Vedas—*Ṛg, Sāma, Yajur,* and *Atharva,* the *Mahābhārata,* the *Pañcarātra,* and the original *Rāmāyaṇa* by Valmiki. Other texts that follow the conclusions of these works are also considered scripture. All other books are not considered scripture, for they lead in the wrong direction.

Elsewhere, Madhva cites the following verse from the *Nārada Purāṇa*:

pañcarātraṁ bhārataṁ ca
mūla-rāmāyaṇaṁ tathā
purāṇaṁ ca bhāgavataṁ
viṣṇur veda itīritaḥ

> The *Pañcarātra,* the *Mahābhārata,* the original *Rāmāyaṇa* by Valmiki, and the *Bhāgavata* and *Viṣṇu Purāṇas* are all accepted as Veda.

The *Padma Purāṇa*, as quoted in the *Bhakti-sandarbha* (314) states:

śruti smṛtī mamaivājñe
yas te ullaṅghya vartate
ājñā-cchedi mama dveṣī
mad-bhakto'pi na vaiṣṇavaḥ

> The *śruti* and *smṛti* are My direct orders. Anyone who does not abide by them goes against My order and is envious of Me. Even if he is My devotee he is not a Vaishnava.

Earlier we gave a verse from the *Nārada Pañcarātra,* as it is quoted in the *Hari-bhakti-vilāsa* (4.366), that states that a Vaishnava is anyone who has received initiation into a *viṣṇu-mantra* and is engaged in regular worship of the Deity. Other than these people, everyone else is a non-Vaishnava. One cannot take initiation from a person who is not situated in a holy disciplic succession, but if one has done so, he should take reinitiation from someone who is rightly situated. If he does not do so, he will not derive benefit from his mantra.

avaiṣṇavopadiṣṭena
mantreṇa nirayaṁ vrajet
punaś ca vidhinā samyag
grāhayed vaiṣṇavād guroḥ

> The mantra that has been given by a non-Vaishnava will not lead to auspiciousness. Therefore one who wishes to attain pure devotional service to Krishna should approach a qualified Vaishnava guru and take initiation again from him.

This verse has been commented on in the *Gauḍīya-kaṇṭha-hāra*:

> Milk is a very pure food. By taking it, one feels satisfaction, nourishment, and the end of hunger. But if such a fine food is touched by a serpent, then it has poisonous effects. In the same way, the holy words of the scripture and the saints normally awaken devotional tendencies in a living entity, but if heard from the lips of an offender to the Holy Name, it may seem to give rise to *hari-kathā,* but that *kathā* will simply be an offense to the Holy Name. One should never listen to offensive chanting of the Holy Name. Should one do so, it will not only not bring the *jīva* auspiciousness, but as with milk touched by a snake, it will bring him misfortune.

THE SAGE AYODA DHAUMYA TESTS HIS DISCIPLES

Aruni Udalaka

yasya deve parā bhaktir
yathā deve tathā gurau
tasyaite kathitā hy arthāḥ
prakāśante mahātmanaḥ

> Only to those great souls who have implicit faith in both the Lord and the spiritual master, who is His manifestation and not different from Him, are all the imports of Vedic knowledge automatically revealed. (*Śvetāśvatara Upaniṣad* 6.23)

In ancient times, there was a great sage named Ayoda Dhaumya. He had three students, Upamanyu, Aruni, and Veda. The story of this guru and his disciples is told near the beginning of the *Mahābhārata* (*Ādi-parva*, chapter 3, *Pauśya-parva*). It tells how the guru tested each of them and how, by his mercy, they were able to understand the scriptural teachings. On hearing this story, one cannot help but be amazed.

One day, Dhaumya bade Aruni, who came from Panchala, to stop the water from flowing out of a rice field by repairing a breach in the dyke. In India, paddy fields are normally surrounded by low clay dykes. This keeps the seedlings under at least a few centimeters of water, something the rice needs in order to grow.

Aruni took his guru's order seriously and immediately went to the spot. He did everything he could think of to stop the water from flowing out of the paddy field, but the earth with which he filled the breach was simply washed away by the strong current. When after numerous attempts he was unable to stop the water from draining out of the field, he became worried that he had failed to do his guru's bidding. He decided the best thing to do was lie down in the breach and block the hole with his body. This was successful in holding the water back.

After some time, when Aruni did not return from his errand, Dhaumya started to worry, for he was affectionate toward his disciples. So he set off for the paddy fields with Upamanyu and Veda, calling out, "Aruni, where are you? Come hither, my child."

On hearing his guru's voice, Aruni stood up and came to him, bowing at his feet. On being asked where he had been, he answered, "I was lying down in the dyke to stop the water from going out, as I was unable to find any other means. I remained there until I heard your voice and then came here. The water is now escaping again, so please tell me what I should do."

Dhaumya was pleased with Aruni and blessed him: "O Aruni, since you arose from the ditch and reopened the course of water, you shall henceforth be called Udalaka as a mark of my favor. And because you have been obedient to me, I bless you that you shall obtain all good fortune and that the meaning of all the Vedic scriptures will shine in you."

Upamanyu

Another day, Ayoda Dhaumya ordered his second disciple, Upamanyu, "Go, my child, and look after the cattle." Upamanyu immediately did as he was told. From that day on, he went every morning with the cows and watched them graze until evening, when he returned to his guru's ashram. On his arrival, he would respectfully salute Dhaumya.

One day, when Upamanyu had offered his obeisance, Dhaumya remarked that the boy was looking quite sturdy. "My child, what are you doing for food during the day? You are looking rather plump."

Upamanyu answered, "Master, I support myself by begging." Dhaumya said, "Nothing a disciple obtains in alms should be taken without first offering it to his guru."

From that day on, whatever alms Upamanyu received from begging he offered to Dhaumya, who took it all without leaving anything for

Upamanyu. Even so, the young lad made no complaint and went on attending the cattle from morning to night, returning in the evening to pay homage to his guru.

After a few days, Dhaumya observed that Upamanyu was not losing weight, so he asked him again, "My child, I take everything you obtain by begging without leaving you anything at all. So how are you feeding yourself? I see that you are still looking rather plump."

Upamanyu replied, "Master, after I give everything I obtain in alms to you, I go begging a second time so that I can eat."

Dhaumya replied, "This is most improper. By doing this, you are making it more difficult for other beggars. You have shown yourself to be quite greedy."

Thereafter, Upamanyu stopped going to beg a second time. A few days later, Dhaumya observed that his disciple was still looking fat, so he again asked him, "My child, I take everything you obtain by begging, without leaving you anything at all. You have stopped begging alms a second time. And yet I see that you are still quite plump. What are you eating now?"

Upamanyu answered, "Master, I am now living on the cows' milk." Once again, Dhaumya said, "It is not proper for you to take the milk of the cows without first obtaining my consent."

Upamanyu once again acknowledged his guru's criticism and stopped taking milk from the cows. However, after a few days, when Dhaumya observed that he was still fat, he said, "My child, you no longer eat alms and you do not drink milk, and yet you are still fat. What are you doing for your subsistence now?"

This time Upamanyu said, "Prabhu, when the calves suckle their mother's teats, their faces become covered with froth. I lick this froth to keep body and soul together."

Again his guru said, "This too is improper and unjust. Calves are by nature generous creatures. Seeing your hunger, they do not drink their fill so that more froth will be left for you. As a result, they go hungry. I want you to stop taking this froth."

Upamanyu nodded, and the next day he went as before to tend the cows. Now left with no other option, Upamanyu became so hungry that after a few days he began to eat fruits and leaves. Not knowing which were edible and which were not, he ate some milkweed leaves that caused him to go blind. Then, having lost his ability to see, he fell into an abandoned well and was unable to get out.

That evening, after sunset, Dhaumya saw that Upamanyu had not yet come home, so he set off with his two other disciples to find him. They called and called. Finally they heard Upamanyu's weak voice rising from the bottom of the well. Dhaumya asked him how he had fallen into the hole. When Upamanyu told him, Dhaumya said, "Pray to the Ashvini Kumaras, the twin physicians of the gods, and they will restore your sight."

Thus directed by his preceptor, Upamanyu sang a Vedic hymn to invoke the Ashvinis. Shortly after, they appeared to him and said, "We are satisfied. Take this cake and eat it. It will restore your sight."

Upamanyu answered, however, "O Ashvinis, I believe you are telling me the truth, but I dare not eat this cake without first offering it to my spiritual master."

The Ashvinis told him, "You know, your guru once invoked us just as you did. We gave him a cake like this one and he took it without offering it to his master. Why don't you do as he did?"

Upamanyu refused to be swayed, however. "O Ashvinis!" he said. "Forgive me, but I have vowed to take nothing without first offering it to my preceptor."

The Ashvinis said, "We are pleased by your devotion to your guru. Your sight shall be restored and you shall enjoy all good fortune."

When he had recovered his sight, Upamanyu climbed out of the well and bowed to his spiritual master. Dhaumya was pleased with him for passing all the tests he had set and said, "You shall obtain all the prosperity the Ashvinis have blessed you with. Moreover, all knowledge of the Vedas and the *dharma-śāstras* will illuminate your heart."

Veda

Then it was the turn of the third disciple, Veda, to be tested. Dhaumya told Veda to stay in his house and act as his servant. Veda did as he was told and served in his guru's household faithfully for many years, bearing heat and cold, hunger and thirst, without complaint. This was the trial devised by Ayoda Dhaumya to test his pupil's resolve. Years passed, and Veda did all his chores uncomplainingly. Dhaumya was very much pleased with Veda's dedication, so he instructed him in all the wisdom contained in the scriptures, until Veda equaled his guru in knowledge.

Veda then returned to his hometown, where he himself became a preceptor. One of his disciples was Janamejaya, the descendant of the Pandavas and king of the Kuru dynasty, who later served as the principal audience for the *Mahābhārata*, which he heard from Vaishampayana.

In the past, spiritual masters tested their disciples in this way. When they saw their disciples' sincere service attitudes they blessed them with knowledge so that nothing remained for them to learn. Although times have changed, the principle remains the same. A sincere disciple should show the same commitment to his spiritual master's service as these disciples offered Dhaumya.

It is said that the spiritual master's order is to be obeyed without argument (*ājñā gurūṇām avicāraṇīyā*). From the transcendental point of view, a disciple who takes shelter of a saintly Vaishnava guru should pray for nothing but pure devotional service and divine love.

Vishwanatha Chakravarti sings, "The spiritual master's pleasure leads to the pleasure of Krishna. If the spiritual master is displeased, there is nowhere else to go."

The glories of service to the spiritual master have been sung in all the scriptures, especially in the *Upaniṣads* and *Purāṇas*. The disciple who is indifferent to serving his spiritual master will never get Krishna's mercy. The *Bhāgavatam* recounts that even Krishna set the example of how to serve the spiritual master.

After Krishna had returned to Mathura and killed Kamsa, he was reunited with His parents Vasudeva and Devaki. Since He and Balarama had spent Their childhood in the cowherd community, They had not received an education befitting their new life as princes. Not only that, They had not received the sacred thread, as was befitting young men of Their caste. Vasudeva sent the two boys to Avantipur, where the renowned teacher Sandipani Muni lived. In a very short time, the two brothers mastered all that Sandipani could teach Them.

Later in the *Bhāgavatam*, the story is told of Sudama Vipra, who had been a student with Krishna at the Avantipur school. Sudama was afflicted by poverty, and his wife told him to take advantage of his childhood friendship with Krishna in order to get some material benefit. When Sudama came to Dwaraka and met with the Lord, the two spent some time reminiscing about their days at their guru's *āśrama*.

Krishna remembered one experience that the two of them had shared. Once, Sandipani had asked Krishna and Sudama to fetch wood for fuel to be used in the sacrificial fire, which was kept perpetually lit. The two boys had gathered large bundles of wood and were carrying them on their heads when a heavy thunderstorm broke, leaving them stranded in the forest. The two were forced to spend the entire night in the rain without shelter, setting an unparalleled example of service to the guru. The *Upaniṣads* say that the wind blows out of fear of the Lord, the sun shines out of fear of the Lord, Indra sends the rains out of fear of the

Lord, and fire does its work of burning out of fear of the Lord. Even time fears the Lord. Yet here, the Supreme Master of the fourteen spheres, the most worshipable Deity Himself, demonstrated how to tread the path of religion.

Krishna's own words show the lesson His behavior was meant to demonstrate:

nāham ijyā-prajātibhyāṁ
tapasopaśamena ca
tuṣyeyaṁ sarva-bhūtātmā
guru-śuśrūṣayā yathā

> I, the soul of all beings, am not as pleased by the performance of the prescribed duties of the four *āśramas*, i.e., sacrifices, service to the family, austerities, and renunciation, as I am by service to the guru. (ŚB 10.80.34)

When morning came and the rain stopped, Sandipani Muni and his disciples went into the woods to look for Sudama and Krishna. The two students were in a pitiable state. Sandipani showed his appreciation for their sacrifice, and his words, recorded in *Śrīmad Bhāgavatam* (10.80.41–42) stand as a testimonial to the value of selfless service to the spiritual master:

> My children! Every living creature takes care of its body as its most dear possession. Out of love for me, however, you two have ignored your desire for ease and comfort. Such behavior is verily the duty of a good disciple who seeks to repay his debt of gratitude to his guru. O best of the twice-born! You have pleased me, and so I bless you that all your desires will be fulfilled and that all you have learned will never be forgotten, in either this life or the next.

This, then, is how a disciple who has taken the instruction of *Śrīmad Bhāgavatam* to make the guru his personal worshipable Deity (*gurv-ātma-daivataḥ*) attains all perfections by the mercy of his spiritual master. *Śrīmad Bhāgavatam* (10.80.32–33) states:

sa vai sat-karmaṇāṁ sākṣād
dvijāter iha sambhavaḥ
ādyo'ṅga yatrāśramiṇāṁ
yathāhaṁ jñānado guruḥ

The father who gives us birth is our first guru. The second guru is the one who gives second birth through initiation and instructs us in his specific duties in *varṇāśrama-dharma*. Such a guru is as worshipable as I am. But the giver of knowledge to everyone in the world, in other words, the giver of universal and transcendental spiritual knowledge, is directly a manifestation of Me.

nanv artha-kovidā brahman
varṇāśramavatām iha
ye mayā guruṇā vācā
taranty añjo bhavārṇavam

O *brāhmaṇa*! Assuredly, those persons are the most clever who even within the *varṇāśrama* system cross over the ocean of material suffering by hearing the guru's words, for I am the guru.

MADHAVENDRA PURI AND HIS DISCIPLES

In chapter eight of the *Caitanya-caritāmṛta's Antya-līlā*, Krishna Das Kaviraj tells a most instructive story, one that compares the results achieved by two disciples of the same guru—one of whom received his master's grace and the other who incurred his displeasure. This story is most salutary and gives pause to all who have taken shelter of a divine preceptor, teaching how they should behave with him.

Srila Madhavendra Puripada was the greatest spiritual leader of his time. An ocean of love for Krishna, he was able to give guidance to the entire universe. However, his disciple Ramachandra Puri was unable to avail himself of the benefit of his guru's exalted status. Rather, by causing his guru distress, he displeased him, was deprived of his mercy, and thus became known as a great faultfinder and backbiter.

When Madhavendra Puri was approaching the end of his sojourn in the world of mortals, he displayed the ecstatic pastime of feeling divine separation. The separation of the devotee from the Lord, although it appears to ordinary eyes to be suffering, is in fact sublime joy, for the devotee is aware of Krishna's presence. The devotee's meditation on the Lord's form, pastimes, virtues, and qualities is heightened by his sense of unworthiness and deprivation.

Ramachandra Puri was present as Madhavendra Puri was feeling this exalted emotion. He saw his guru chanting the Holy Name and crying out, "I could not attain Mathura!" Saraswati Thakur comments in his *Anubhāṣya* (3.8.20):

> Ramachandra Puri was unable to comprehend the flashes of divine separation that his guru was experiencing. Seeing his tears and cries superficially, he took them for the pain felt by conditioned souls when overpowered by grief, regret, or other sense of material lack. Being naïve about his guru's emotional and theological sophistication, Ramachandra thought he could relieve his suffering by instructing him in knowledge of Brahman. Madhavendra took this as evidence of his disciple's stupidity and furthermore as deliberate insolence. The result was that he stopped feeling benevolent toward him and rejected him.

Krishna Das tells the story in the *Caitanya-caritāmṛta* (3.8.16–23):

> Previously, when Madhavendra Puri was preparing to leave this world, Ramachandra Puri came to his hermitage. Madhavendra was chanting the names of the Lord and crying out, "Alas, I have not attained the land of Mathura." Ramachandra then started to instruct him—although a disciple, he shamelessly gave his guru advice without any fear. "You are one with the universal spirit," he said. "By nature you are complete in yourself, full of joy. You should know this, so why are you crying?"
>
> When he heard this, Madhavendra lashed out at him. "Get away from me, you sinful creature!" he said angrily. "I have been deprived of Krishna's grace and unable to attain His abode. I am about to die and I am suffering from my failure to attain Krishna, and you have come here to add to my suffering? Don't show your face to me again. Go wherever you like, but if I see you at the time of death, my next birth will surely be inauspicious. I am dying from the distress of not having attained Krishna and this cursed fool is giving me lessons about Brahman."

In this way, Madhavendra Puri was induced to withhold his blessings from Ramachandra Puri. In fact, Ramachandra's offense resulted in various material desires awakening in him. The word Kaviraja Goswami uses for "material desire" is *vāsanā*, which refers to latent desires in our subconscious that are the result of deep conditioning. Bhaktivinoda Thakur explains that in Ramachandra's case, this was a desire for liberation and knowledge of Brahman, which led him to despise the devotees. Thinking himself superior to them, he engaged in constant criticism, looking for any sign of sensuality or falldown in them.

In the *Bhakti-sandarbha*, Jiva Goswami quotes from the *Bhagavat-pariśiṣṭa* that support the possibility of a falldown like Ramachandra Puri's:

jīvan-muktā api punar bandhanaṁ yānti karmabhiḥ
yady acintya-mahā-śaktau bhagavaty aparādhinaḥ
jīvan-muktāḥ prapadyante kvacit saṁsāra-vāsanām
yogino vai no lipyante karmabhir bhagavat-parāḥ

> Those who have attained the liberated state while still in this world may still become entangled again as a result of their actions. This can happen if they commit offenses to the inconceivably powerful Supreme Lord. Those who have attained the liberated state while still in this world sometimes have desires. True yogis, however, are never affected by karma if they are fixed in devotion to the Lord.

Such persons may either become dry philosophers and criticize devotees, or materialists addicted to sex life and other enjoyments. In this particular case, Ramachandra Puri became addicted to the dry practice of philosophical speculation and a critic of all and sundry. He became so attached to faultfinding that he cultivated it like an art. Wherever he went, he would find something to criticize in Vishnu and the Vaishnava. Of such persons it is said:

śata śata guṇa ache tāhā nā kare grahaṇa
guṇa-madhye-o chale kare doṣa āropaṇa

> Although someone may have hundreds and hundreds of virtues, they do not accept them, but rather find ways of turning their virtues into faults.

In *Sri Caitanya-caritāmṛta* (3.8.27–31), Kaviraja Goswami then contrasts Ramachandra's behavior with that of Madhavendra's other disciple, Ishwara Puri, who later became the spiritual master of Sri Chaitanya Mahaprabhu.

Ishwara Puri served his spiritual master's lotus feet, cleaning his stool and urine with his own hands. He constantly helped him to remember Krishna's name, and talked about Krishna's pastimes and singing Krishna's names unceasingly. Madhavendra Puri was so pleased that he embraced Ishwara Puri and gave him a benediction, "May you have divine love for Krishna." Thenceforward, Ishwara Puri was an ocean of *prema*, while Ramachandra Puri became a fountain of blasphemy. For the edification of the world, these two served as examples of the guru's blessings and his punishment.

Madhavendra Puri was the root of the tree of *prema*. The verse on his lips at the time he left this world, although simple, is still a perfect sample of his intense mood of divine separation:

ayi dīnadayārdra nātha he
mathurānātha kadāvalokyase
hṛdayaṁ tvad-aloka-kātaraṁ
dayita bhrāmyati kiṁ karomy aham

> O Lord, whose heart softens at seeing the condition of the unfortunate! O Lord of Mathura, when will I ever see you? My heart is filled with pain from not seeing you, my love, and am confused. What can I do? (CC 3.8.32, quoted as *Padyāvalī* 330)

In *Caitanya-caritāmṛta* (2.4.194–195), Chaitanya Mahaprabhu sings this verse. In fact, Krishna Das Kaviraj says that only Srimati Radharani, Chaitanya Mahaprabhu, and Madhavendra Puri have the capacity to relish this verse:

ei śloka kahiyāchena rādhā ṭhākurāṇī
tāṅra kṛpāya sphuriyāche mādhavendra purī
kibā gauracandra ihā kare āsvādana
ihā āsvādite āra nāhi cauṭha jana

> This verse was spoken by Srimati Radharani, by whose mercy it appeared on the tongue of Madhavendra Puri. Gaurachandra then relished these words, but other than these three, no one else can truly understand them.

Srila Bhaktivinoda Thakur explains this verse in his *Amṛta-pravāha-bhāṣya* (2.4.197):

> Those who follow the path of pure devotion and adhere to the Vedānta are divided into four disciplic families. Of these four, Madhavendra Puri accepted the authenticity of the line of Madhva by taking *sannyāsa* in this line. From Madhva to Lakshmipati (Madhavendra Puri's guru) this disciplic line lacked the mood of *śṛṅgāra-rasa,* or erotic love. This is evident from the conversation Mahaprabhu had with the Tattvavadis (followers of Madhva's line) during His tour of South India. Until Mahaprabhu's time the popular conception of the Absolute Truth was *viṣṇu-bhakti,* worshiping the Lord in the mood of awe and reverence.
>
> With this beautiful verse, Madhavendra Puri sowed the seed of bhakti in *śṛṅgāra-rasa.* He became one with the mood of Sri Radhika as She experienced intense separation from Krishna after He had left Vrindavan to become a prince in Mathura. To cultivate Her feelings of separation is the highest expression of devotion. A devotee immersed in this *rasa* considers himself poor, humble, and always begs Krishna to be kind to him. This is why Madhavendra addresses the Lord as *dīna-dayārdra-nātha,* "one who is kind to the poor."
>
> Inasmuch as we are separated from Krishna, this mood is the most natural way to feel while performing acts of devotion. When Krishna departs for Mathura, Sri Radhika's heart is trembling with anxiety from not being able to see Him. Yearning to behold His beautiful face, She laments, "My love, My heart is

> sorrowful and agitated because I can't see You. What do I have to do to see You again? You know that I am helpless, so please be kind to Me!"
>
> It can easily be seen that the mood expressed here by Madhavendra Puri resembles that of Mahaprabhu in the mood of Sri Radha in Vrindavan, especially when She saw Uddhava. Our preceptors have said that the root of the tree of *śṛṅgāra-rasa* is Madhavendra Puri; Ishwara Puri is its sapling, Mahaprabhu is its trunk, and His followers are its branches.

This same mood awakened in Mahaprabhu on His way through Remuna. Those pure-hearted disciples who follow in the line of disciplic succession from Srila Bhaktivinoda Thakur, who was particularly dear to Sri Chaitanya and the foremost follower of Srila Rupa Goswami, can experience the same intensity of feeling. The fact is that by taking sincere shelter of genuine spiritual masters expert in devotional service in this rich, emotional spirit of separation, and by following in the spirit described in the *Bhāgavatam*—*guru-daivatātmā*, making the spiritual master one's personal Deity—one will be able to dive into the ocean of transcendental devotional nectar and have the good fortune of tasting ambrosia.

NAROTTAMA DAS, AN IDEAL DISCIPLE

Devotion to the spiritual master can also be found in our disciplic succession in the person of Narottama Das Thakur. His life is perfectly representative of a *sādhaka*'s life. Although Narottama was the son of a landowner so rich they called him a rāja, he did not hesitate to clean Lokanatha Goswami's toilet area in order to win his compassionate glance. This story is told in the *Prema-vilāsa*.

Narottama was the son of a rich landowner in Rajshahi, now in Bangladesh. He was devoted to Sri Chaitanya Mahaprabhu and Krishna from an early age, but his parents wished to see him take responsibility for the family's holdings. Narottama, however, had a different idea and ran away to Vrindavan when still a teenager. In Vrindavan, he studied under Jiva Goswami, who told him to take initiation from one of the many exalted Vaishnavas living there at the time. Jiva himself, although he was the principal authority on the Vaishnava scriptures and the most respected member of the Gaudiya community in Vrindavan, had vowed not to initiate anyone.

Narottama visited nearly all the great Vaishnavas in the area, but no one impressed him more than Lokanatha Goswami, who was not only the embodiment of renunciation but unequaled in his devotion to his Deity, Radhavinoda. Lokanatha was so renounced that he never stayed in the same place for two nights in a row, remaining under a different tree each night. One day, however, the Lord came personally to give Lokanatha a Deity, telling him that its name was Radhavinoda.

Lokanatha wondered where he would keep his Deity, as he was constantly wandering through the land of Vraja. Finally he decided to make a large bag, which he made into Radhavinoda's temple. Wearing the bag around his neck, he was able to keep his worshipable Deity close to his heart, like a necklace. When the people of Vraja saw the affectionate relationship between Lokanatha and his Lord, they were attracted to him and asked if they could build a house for him and Radhavinoda. Lokanatha refused. His spirit of renunciation was so strong that he declined to accept anything except what he absolutely needed for the Deity's service.

Like Jiva, Lokanatha had also taken a vow not to accept disciples. But Narottama was equally determined to accept initiation from no one other than his chosen guru. Narottama repeatedly asked Lokanatha to initiate him, but the saint remained firm. Finally, Narottama decided that even if Lokanatha would not give him initiation, he would serve him in some special way in order to get Krishna's favor, and if he could win his favor, so much the better.

That night, Narottama began to clean the area Lokanatha used as a toilet. Narottama went to that place and sifted the soil to make a fine, clean earth with which Lokanatha could clean his hands. Each night, he swept the place clean, his heart filled with joy. He considered it most fortunate that he could do this service; indeed, he felt it made his life worthwhile, and he held the broom to his chest, repeating, "This is where I will get the strength to attain my lord's lotus feet." As he said these words, torrents of tears washed over his chest.

Lokanatha was so surprised to see the place being kept clean that he was curious to find out who was doing the service. One evening, he went and hid behind some bushes, chanting *japa* into the night while he waited for the anonymous servant to come.

At midnight, Lokanatha saw someone begin to clean the place. When he saw who it was, Lokanatha was astonished that Narottama, the son of a rāja, was engaged in such a filthy task. He felt embarrassed and asked him his purpose in doing the service. Narottama began to cry. He fell at Lokanatha's feet and said, "My life is useless unless I obtain your mercy." When Lokanatha saw Narottama's humility and pain, his resolve to never initiate anyone softened and he imparted the mantras to him. Thus Narottama Das gave an outstanding example to the world of how one should behave in the service of one's spiritual master.

Lokanatha was a renounced Vaishnava, but he saw in Narottama someone who was not only cultured but enthusiastic with a taste for dealing with people. As a result, he asked him to go back to his homeland to preach Krishna consciousness.

Those who have taken full shelter of the Supreme Lord and are situated on the transcendental platform in full service to the Lord usually have no enthusiasm for helping people on the bodily platform. When a devotee of Narottama Das's caliber goes against this principle, then such welfare activities themselves are honored and increase in prestige. So Narottama returned to northern Bengal on his spiritual master's order and began to preach pure devotional service and thus deliver the people of his homeland.

A humble disciple never thinks that he has finished his service to his spiritual master. In this respect, a song by Narottama Das, addressed to his guru, is particularly worth remembering:

ki rūpe pāiba sevā mui durācār
śrī-guru-vaiṣṇave rati nā haila āmār
aśeṣa māyāte mana magana hailo
vaiṣṇavete leśa-mātra rati nā janmilo
viṣaye bhuliyā andha hainu divā-niśi
gale phāṅsa dite phire māyā se piśācī
māyāre kariyā jaya chāṛāno nā jāy
sādhu-kṛpā vinā āra nāhiko upāy
adoṣa-daraśi prabho patita-uddhār
ei bāra narottame koroho nistār

> How can a wicked soul like me ever attain service to the Lord? I have no affection for the service of the spiritual master and the Vaishnavas. My mind has remained absorbed in this world of unlimited illusion and so been unable to develop even a drop of attachment for the association of devotees. I have totally forgotten myself in sense gratification and have become blind, both day and night. In the mean-time, the witch Maya follows me around, looking for a chance to place a noose around my neck. There seems to be no way to be free of her. Other than the mercy of the saintly, there is nothing that can help me to conquer Maya. O Gurudeva, you see no fault in anyone and you deliver even the most fallen. Please, O Gurudeva, it is now time to save Narottama Das.

Of course, Ishwara Puri, Narottama Das, and other great souls in our disciplic succession are eternally perfect and have no need for spiritual practices meant to bring one to perfection. The examples they set us are only for our instruction and edification.

The ultimate object of service is the Supreme Person, Krishna. He appears in the form of the spiritual master, also known as the guru or *ācārya*, who acts as Krishna's servant. In the form of the guru Krishna teaches through both example and precept how to cultivate devotional service to Him. He has done this in the past, is doing so in the present, and will continue to do so in the future. Although the *viṣaya-vigraha* takes on the appearance of the *āśraya-vigraha*, it is essential to remember that both truths are simultaneously manifest in the spiritual master. If one fails to understand this, he will surely become confused and end up with unwanted results in his spiritual practice. It is Krishna's divine compassion that He takes the form of a devotee in the person of the spiritual master. Krishna Das Kaviraj Goswami explains this point in the *Chaitanya-charitamrita* (1.1.45):

guru kṛṣṇa-rūpa hana śāstrera pramāṇe
guru-rūpe kṛṣṇa kṛpā kare bhakta-gaṇe

According to the scriptures, the spiritual master is a form of Krishna. Krishna takes the form of the guru to bestow His mercy on the devotees.

We offer obeisance to our spiritual master with the words *śri-gaura-karuṇā-śakti-vigrahāya namo'stu te*: "I bow down to you, the embodiment of Gauranga Mahaprabhu's compassionate potency."

However, it is not enough to simply make a show of taking shelter of the spiritual master. Even a slight deviation from the principle of loyalty to the spiritual master will cause suffering. The scriptures say:

tāṅra upadeśa-mantre māyā-piśācī palāya
kṛṣṇa-bhakti pāya kṛṣṇa nikaṭe jāya
tāte kṛṣṇa bhaje kare gurura sevana
māyā jāla chuṭe pāya kṛṣṇera caraṇa

> The witch of material illusion flees at the utterance of the mantra the guru has given. Through his instructions one attains devotion to Krishna and goes to Krishna. So worship Krishna and serve the guru. You will escape Maya's net of illusion and attain Krishna's lotus feet.

The guru knows about Krishna. He instructs us in the *sambandha-, abhidheya-,* and *prayojana-tattvas*. In order to attain this knowledge, we must approach him with humility, with a spirit of sincere inquiry and service. The Bhagavad Gita (4.34) states:

tad viddhi praṇipātena
paripraśnena sevayā
upadekṣyanti te jñānaṁ
jñāninas tattva-darśinaḥ

> "Try to learn the truth by approaching a spiritual master. Inquire submissively and render service to him. Self-realized souls can impart knowledge because they are seers of the truth."

> In this context, one should realize that it is not enough to bow down and ask questions; one must also serve the spiritual master, and one should do so from a basis of trust and affection. Service without trust and affection has no merit. Therefore, Narottama Das prays, "How will I attain service to Krishna? I am so sinful that I have no affection for the guru and Vaishnavas."

JABALA SATYAKAMA GAINS KNOWLEDGE OF BRAHMAN

The *Chāndogya Upaniṣad*[2] tells the story of how a young boy named Satyakama attained knowledge of Brahman. According to Sripada Shankaracharya, who wrote the principal commentary on the *Chāndogya Upaniṣad*, "The purpose of this story is to teach that faith (*śraddhā*) and penance (*tapas*) are the two principal elements in the worship of Brahman."[3] This story is about faith in the guru and a willingness to accept austerities in his service.

In the *Bhakti-rasāmṛta-sindhu* (1.2.74), Srila Rupa Goswami writes:

guru-padāśrayas tasmāt
kṛṣṇa-dīkṣādi-śikṣaṇam
viśrambhena guroḥ sevā

> First take shelter of a spiritual master. Then take initiation from him in the Krishna mantra and instruction from him in the three aspects of knowledge related to the path of devotion: *sambandha, abhidheya*, and *prayojana*. Then serve the spiritual master with faith and devotion.

The word *viśrambha* here means firm faith—and this is what Shankaracharya means when he says "faith and penance." The spiritual master is to be seen as nondifferent from Krishna, as the Lord's *prakāśa-vigraha*, or the form in which He reveals Himself to the world. When one has *viśrambha*, firm faith, one serves the spiritual master knowing that by so doing he can attain all success in his spiritual endeavors.

Krishna Das Kaviraj Goswami defines *śraddhā* in the *Caitanya-caritāmṛta* (2.22.62):

---

2 The chapters in the *Chāndogya Upaniṣad* are called *prapāṭhas*, "readings," and the subsections are called *khaṇḍas*.

3 *śraddhā-tapasor brahmopāsanāṅgatva-pradarśanāyākhyāyikā.*

śraddhā-śabde kahe viśvāsa sudṛḍha niścaya
kṛṣṇa-bhakti kaile sarva-karma kṛta haya

> [T]he firm and confident belief that by alone engaging in devotion to Krishna, all one's duties will be fulfilled.

When describing the sequence by which one attains perfection in spiritual life, Rupa Goswami lists, *ādau śraddhā tataḥ sādhu-saṅgo'tha bhajana-kriyā:* "The progressive development of *prema* begins with faith (*śraddhā*), firm faith in the shastras, and the teachings of sādhus." The association of sādhus indicates taking shelter of a spiritual master, through which one can truly begin the process of spiritual life.

kono bhāgye kono jīve śraddhā yadi hoy
tabe sei jīva sādhu saṅga karaya
sādhu saṅga hoite hoy śravaṇa kīrtana

> If by some good fortune a *jīva* develops faith, then he associates with devotees, in whose company he is able to engage in hearing and chanting about Krishna.

The word *bhāgya*, when used in this context, refers to the accumulated piety that comes from activities that lead to or awaken devotion. *Bhāgya* usually takes the form of fortuitous association with devotees or hearing the Holy Names or something of that nature. If someone is predisposed to practice devotion through such contacts, then faith in bhakti wells up inside him. This leads him to seek out the company of devotees and, through such company, to engage in devotional activities.

Śrīmad-Bhāgavatam (10.80.34) states:

nāham ijyā-prajātibhyāṁ
tapasopaśamena ca

tuṣyeyaṁ sarva-bhūtātmā
guru-śuśrūṣayā yathā

I, the soul of all beings, am not as pleased by the performance of the prescribed duties of the four ashrams, i.e., sacrifices, service to the family, austerities, and renunciation, as I am by service to the guru.

In His conversation with His *brāhmaṇa* friend Sudama, recorded in *Śrīmad Bhāgavatam* (10.80. 35–38), Krishna recalls how they were blessed by their spiritual master as a result of the special service they offered him:

api naḥ smaryate brahman vṛttaṁ nivasatāṁ gurau
guru-dārais coditānām indhanānayane kvacit
praviṣṭānāṁ mahāraṇyam apartau su-mahad dvija
vāta-varṣam abhūt tīvraṁ niṣṭhurāḥ stanayitnavaḥ

O *brāhmaṇa,* do you remember what happened to us while we were living with our spiritual master? One day, his wife sent us to fetch firewood, and when we entered the vast forest, an unseasonal storm arose, with fierce wind and rain and harsh thunder.

sūryaś cāstaṁ gatas tāvat tamasā cāvṛtā diśaḥ
nimnaṁ kūlaṁ jala-mayaṁ na prājñāyata kiñcana

Then, as the sun set, the forest was covered by darkness in every direction, and on account of the flooding we could not distinguish high land from low.

vayaṁ bhṛśaṁ tatra mahānilāmbubhir
nihanyamānā muhur ambu-samplave
diśo'vidanto'tha parasparaṁ vane
gṛhīta-hastāḥ paribabhrimāturāḥ

> Constantly besieged by the powerful wind and rain, we lost our way amid the flooding waters. We simply held each other's hands and, in great distress, wandered aimlessly about the forest.

The word *paribabhrima* ("wandered aimlessly") can be taken in different ways. Sridhar Swami derives it from a different verb root (*bhṛ*), which means "to carry." Krishna and Sudama were carrying a load of cut wood, as they had been requested by their spiritual master's wife (guru mother). So even though it was pouring rain and they were lost in the woods, they never thought for a moment of putting the wood down and abandoning their service.

When the sun came up the next morning, Sandipani Muni had all his students go out and look for the lost boys. When they were found, he poured profuse blessings on them, his heart melting with gratitude for their sacrifice and compassion for the difficulties they had undergone.

Narottama Das Thakur was the son of a rich landlord, and yet he cleaned his guru's toilet in order to obtain his mercy. Ishwara Puri was similarly ready to do menial service for his guru by cleaning his body when he was incontinent in his old age and nursing him through his illness until the end of his life. The *Caitanya-caritāmṛta* (3.8.26) confirms:

īśvara purī kare śrī-pāda-sevana
sva-haste karena mala-mutrādi mārjana

> Ishwara Puri served his spiritual master's lotus feet. He even cleaned his stool and urine with his own hand.

Not only that, but Ishwara Puri comforted his guru by recounting to him Krishna's pastimes, singing songs about Krishna, and reciting Krishna's names, thus making his guru's last days as comfortable as possible. Madhavendra was so satisfied with Ishwara Puri's service that he gave his disciple the greatest blessing:

tuṣṭa haiyā purī tāṅre kailā āliṅgana
vara dilā kṛṣṇe tomāra hauka prema-dhana

Madhavendra Puri became pleased with him and embraced him. Then he blessed him, saying, "May the treasure of love for Krishna be bestowed upon you." (CC 3.8.28)

The scriptures give many, many such examples of sincere service to the spiritual master and the resultant mercy given to the disciple by him. This story about Satyakama shows his commitment to his spiritual master and how he attained knowledge of Brahman through it. There is a saying: *ājñā gurūṇāṁ hy avicāraṇīyā*, "The order of the spiritual master is not to be questioned." The spiritual master is connected to the Lord, and one who is mindful about following his spiritual master's directions places himself in a position to receive God's mercy. Thus it is said, *guru rūpe kṛṣṇa kṛpā karen bhakta-gaṇe*: "Krishna appears in the form of the guru to bless the devotees." Through the guru, the Lord helps the disciple attain perfection.

SATYAKAMA TAKES SHELTER OF HIS SPIRITUAL MASTER

Once there was a boy named Satyakama, who was the son of Jabala. Satyakama had heard people say that those who wish to attain all auspiciousness should dedicate themselves to learning about Brahman. So he made up his mind to follow a spiritual path and to find a guru who would educate him about the soul. Satyakama asked his mother, Jabala, a question:

brahmacaryaṁ bhavati vivatsyāmi
kiṁ-gotro nv aham asmi

Revered mother, I would like to live with my teacher, becoming a student and studying the sacred lore so that I can attain spiritual knowledge. Please tell me about my family lineage, so that I can properly identify myself.[4]

[4] This story can be found in the *Chāndogya Upaniṣad* (4.4.1).

In India, a *brāhmaṇa* has to know his family lineage, or *gotra,* in order to be accepted as a student of the Vedic literature. Satyakama had to know his father's name, at the very least, in order for his guru to teach him.

His mother replied:

> I do not know what *gotra* you belong to. When I was a young girl, I served many men. I was still very young when I had you, so I have no idea what your *gotra* is. My name is Jabala and you are Satyakama. You can identify yourself as Satyakama, the son of Jabala.[5]

In the sentence, *bahv ahaṁ carantī paricāriṇī yauvane tvām alabhe,* Jabala explains why she did not know who her son's father was. This sparse phrase leaves much room for speculation. Shankaracharya's commentary therefore expands on it:

> When her son asked her about his father, Jabala answered, "I don't know in which *gotra* you were born." Her son then asked, "Why don't you know?" She answered, "In my husband's house, I used to be so busily engaged in housework, serving guests and so on, and I was too absorbed in service to remember things like the name of your father's *gotra*. Then I had you and you were still young when your father died. So now I am a widow and I never had the chance to find out your *gotra*. My name is Jabala and you are Satyakama. You can tell your teacher that you are Jabala-Satyakama when he asks you."[6]

---

[5] *nāham etad veda tāta yad-gotras tvam asi. bahv ahaory can be found in the Chnt to leave this.āham etan na veda yad-gotras tvam asi. jabālā tu nāmāham asmi. satyakāmo nāma tvam asi. sa satyakāma eva jābālo bravīthā iti* (*Chāndogya Upaniṣad* 4.4.2).

[6] *evaṁ pṛṣṭā jabālā sā hainaṁ putram uvāca—nāham etat tava gotraṁ veda. he tāta! yad-gotras tvam asi. kasmān na vetsi? ity uktāha—bahu-bhartṛ-gṛhe paricaryā-jātam atithy-abhyāgatādi caranty ahaṁ paricāriṇī paricarantīti paricaraṇa-śīlaivāham. paricaraṇa-cittatayā gotrādi-smaraṇe mama mano nābhūt. yauvane ca tat-kāle tvām alabhe labdhavaty asmi. tadaiva te pitoparataḥ. ato'nāthāhaṁ sāham etan na veda yad-gotras tvam asi. jabālā tu nāmāham asmi, satyakāmo nāma tvam asi. sa tvaṁ satyakāma evāhaṁ jābālo'smīty ācāryāya bruvīthāḥ. yad yācāryeṇa pṛṣṭa ity abhiprāyaḥ.*

The Sri Vaishnava scholar, Ranga Ramanuja Muni, also wrote a commentary on this *Upaniṣad*, the *Prakāśikā*. His comments agree substantially with Shankaracharya's:

> She said, "I was so busily engaged in serving all the guests and visitors in my husband's house, serving the guru and others, that I never learned about my husband's *gotra*. I was very young when you were born, and so I do not know your *gotra*. You should tell your guru that your name is Satyakama, your mother's name is Jabala, and that you don't know your *gotra*."

Although some people present Jabala as a prostitute or unwed mother, neither the great Shankara nor Ranga Ramanuja confirm this. Instead, she was a young widow.

Be that as it may, Satyakama Jabala approached his guru, Haridrumata Gautama, and said, "O *bhagavān*! I wish to live with you as a *brahmacārī*. This is why I have come to you." Sometimes in the *śrutis* highly revered saints and sages are addressed as *bhagavān*. Although it is a title usually reserved for God, in this case, it is being used in its other sense, for a highly honored person.

As expected, Gautama inquired, "O gentle one, what is your *gotra*?"

Satyakama replied truthfully. "I do not know anything about my father's family. I asked my mother, but she told me, 'I begot you when I was very young and was busy serving in my husband's household. Therefore I never found out the details about your father's ancestry. My name is Jabala and your name is Satyakama, so give your name as Satyakama, son of Jabala.'"

Gautama replied, "My dear son, no one but a *brāhmaṇa* could speak truth such as you have just spoken. Therefore, O gentle one, go and bring wood for a sacrifice. Because you have not avoided nor stretched the truth but have spoken straightforwardly, I can understand that you are born of a brāhmaṇa family. So even though you do not know your *gotra*, your truthfulness testifies to your true status as a *brāhmaṇa*. I shall gladly give you the sacred thread." And so Gautama invested Satyakama with the sacred thread in the *upanayana* ritual.[7]

Gautama had a herd of cows, many of which were weak and sickly. He selected four hundred of those in the poorest health and gave them to Satyakama, saying, "My child, please take care of these cows."

Satyakama took the herd Gautama had given him and said, "Master, I shall not return home until these four hundred cows have increased and become a thousand." After saying these words with folded hands, Satyakama offered obeisance to his guru and left with the cows. He then began to feed them with the best grains, grasses, and water that he could. He took them through woods that were safe from wild beasts, absenting himself from his guru's *āśrama* for several years. Gradually, the cattle regained their health and started to reproduce until they numbered a thousand, throughout which time Satyakama accepted the hardships of living in the forest and watching over the herd. All this was done in the spirit of a surrendered disciple.

tomāra sevāya duḥkha haya jata,
seo ta parama sukha
sevā sukha duḥkha parama sampad
nāśaye avidyā duḥkha

> All miseries faced in the course of Your service are actually the source of great happiness. Both feelings of happiness and distress in Your service are riches, for they both destroy the misery of ignorance. (Bhaktivinoda Thakur, *Śaraṇāgati* 18)

The surrendered disciple accepts the order of the spiritual master without question. When the spiritual master sees such a sincere disciple, his

[7] *taṁ hovāca — naitad abrāhmaṇo vivaktum arhati samidhaṁ somyāharopa tvā neṣye na satyād agā iti.*

heart becomes pleased. His pleasure makes Krishna's pleasure possible. When there were a thousand cows, the wind god, Vayu, entered one of the bulls and began to speak to Satyakama: "O Satyakama! Our number has now reached a thousand. You have made good your promise to your guru, so take us back to his ashram. But first I would like to say something to you about one of the feet of Brahman."

Satyakama answered, "Please go on," so Vayu, still speaking through the bull, said, "The eastern region is one quarter, the western region is one quarter, the southern region is one quarter, and the northern region is another quarter. O gentle one, these four quarters are one foot of Brahman, known as *prakāśavat* ('endowed with splendor')."

The bull continued, "One who knows this and meditates on the foot of Brahman, consisting of four quarters, with the name *prakāśavat,* also becomes endowed with splendor in this world. In other words, whomever knows and meditates on this foot of Brahman by the name of *prakāśavat,* consisting of four quarters, conquers the resplendent worlds."

After having completed his instructions, Vayu said, "Tomorrow, the fire will tell you of another of Brahman's feet." And with that, the bull fell silent.

The next day, Satyakama completed his daily rituals and resumed driving the cows toward his teacher's home. When evening fell, he decided to camp for the night. He penned the cows, then went to gather firewood. He then lit a fire and sat facing it, meditating on the bull's words.

At that moment, the god Agni called to him from the fire, "Satyakama, O gentle one, I would like to instruct you on one of the feet of Brahman."

When Satyakama humbly indicated his desire to listen, Agni said, "The earth is one quarter, the sky is a second quarter, heaven the third, and the ocean the fourth. This is the second foot of Brahman, also consisting of four quarters. It is called *anantavat* ('possessing no end'). One who knows this and meditates on this foot of Brahman, consisting of four quarters, by the name *anantavat,* becomes endless in this world—that is, he takes on infinite qualities. And whomever knows this and meditates on this foot of Brahman named *anantavat,* consisting of four quarters, conquers over the unlimited, indestructible worlds after his death."

Agni added, "Tomorrow a swan will instruct you on another foot of Brahman," and fell silent.

The next day, Satyakama completed his daily rituals and then continued to drive the herd toward his teacher's home. Once again evening fell before he arrived, so he sought out a suitable place to camp for the night. He gathered firewood, lit a fire, and sat facing it, meditating on the words Agni had spoken to him.

As he sat there, the sun god appeared to him in the form of a swan. According to Shankara, the sun is also known as *haṁsa,* "swan," partly because of its clarity and partly because it appears to fly in the sky. The swan said, "My child, I shall instruct you on another foot of Brahman."

When Satyakama humbly indicated his desire to listen, the swan said: "Fire is one quarter, the sun a second, the moon the third, and lightning the fourth. This is a foot of Brahman, consisting of four quarters and called *jyotiṣmat* ('full of light'). One who knows this and meditates on this foot of Brahman, consisting of four quarters, by the name *jyotiṣmat,* becomes luminous in this world. After death, whoever knows this and meditates on the foot of Brahman known as *jyotiṣmat,* consisting of four quarters, conquers over the luminous worlds."

Then the sun god in the form of a swan said, "Tomorrow, a diver-bird will instruct you in the last remaining foot of Brahman," and fell silent.

The next day, Satyakama set off again with the cows. When it became evening, he again gathered wood, lit a fire, and sat down to meditate. As he sat, a diver-bird, known in Sanskrit as a *madgu,* flew near and called, "Satyakama!" The *madgu* was in fact the personification of prana, the life airs.

He said, "Dear one, I will instruct you in the last foot of Brahman!" When Satyakama showed his enthusiasm for his next lesson, the diver-bird said, "Breath is one quarter, the eye another, the ear yet another, and the mind the last. This last foot of Brahman, consisting of four quarters, is called *āyatanavat* ('having a refuge or place'). Anyone who knows this and meditates on this foot of Brahman, consisting of four quarters, with the name *āyatanavat*, becomes possessed of a home in this world. (Or, as Shankaracharya interprets it, becomes capable of giving shelter to a great many others.) After dying, he conquers the worlds that offer a home. These benefits come to whomever knows this and meditates on this foot of Brahman, consisting of four quarters and given the name *āyatanavat*."

In this way, Satyakama learned about the four feet of Brahman while walking to his guru's home. Four times four make sixteen. The number sixteen, or two to the power of four, is the sign of fullness. In India, if one says something has its sixteen parts, that means it is missing nothing.

When Satyakama arrived with his thousand cows, his guru saw that his body was illuminated with knowledge. He asked, "Satyakama, you are filled with light, like someone who has come to know Brahman. Who has instructed you in this knowledge? I would like to know."

Someone who has come to know Brahman is satisfied in his senses, has a smiling face, is free of worry, and has a sense of fulfillment. Satyakama's guru recognized these symptoms in his disciple and so wanted to know where he had received his knowledge. Satyakama was devoted to the truth, so he answered without hesitation: "Master, I was not given instruction by any human being but by gods. Even so, please give me the instructions I desire."

Acharya Shankara comments that Satyakama's intended to say, "Knowing that I am your disciple, what other human, no matter how learned, would dare to instruct me? In other words, there is no one in the world capable of instructing me other than you. Therefore, give me the instruction I desire. That is, please instruct me in that for which I came to take shelter of you. What need have I of anyone else's instructions be those teachers gods or men? I care nothing for them."[8]

Knowledge of Brahman is received from the spiritual master. The disciple who is single-mindedly devoted to the spiritual master is eligible to receive it. One can obtain such knowledge from the worshipable *dīkṣā-guru* by showing exclusive reverence, asking questions on the subject to show a deep interest in it, and serving him devotedly. This is the process for receiving the spiritual master's mercy, and if one continues to obediently follow the directives given by the spiritual master, one will quickly be able to attain spiritual perfection. Although Satyakama had received instructions from Vayu, Agni, Aditya, and Prana in the forms of a bull, fire, a swan, and a diver-bird, receiving a full understanding of the four aspects of Brahman, he did not consider his education complete, as he had not heard of this directly from his initiating spiritual master.

Therefore Satyakama said, "O Master! I have heard from other seers, who like you are equal to the Lord, that lessons taken from one's own *ācārya* have the most auspicious results.[9] So I implore you, please instruct me in knowledge of Brahman."

When Haridrumata Gautama heard these words, which were full of sincere and affectionate devotion for him, he was greatly pleased and unhesitatingly reiterated everything his disciple had already heard from the gods, not leaving any aspect of the teaching untouched.

After initiating Satyakama, the son of Jabala, Gautama had chosen the weakest and sickliest cows he had and gave them to Satyakama to take care of. Satyakama had left his spiritual master, promised not to come

[8] *ko'nyo bhagavac-chiṣyaṁ māṁ manuṣyaḥ sann anuśāsitum utsahetety abhiprāyaḥ. ato'nye manuṣyebhya iti ha pratijajñe pratijñātavān. bhagavāṁs tv eva me kāme mamecchāyāṁ brūyāt kim anyair uktena nāhaṁ tad gaṇayāmīty abhiprāyaḥ* (Shankara on *Chāndogya Upaniṣad* 4.9.2).

[9] *śrutaṁ hy eva me bhagavad-dṛśebhya ācāryād dhaiva vidyā viditā sādhiṣṭhaṁ prāpatīti tasmai haitad evovācātra ha na kiṁcana vīyāyeti vīyāyeti* (*Chāndogya Upaniṣad* 4.9.3).

back until the herd had grown to a thousand, and dedicated himself to serving the cows, abandoning all thought of his own happiness and accepting all pain and difficulty without complaint. He never lost faith in or affection for his spiritual master, and by executing his service with diligence, he was able to win his guru's pleasure and blessings.

Someone who serves the spiritual master in this manner also attracts the blessings of the gods. Satyakama received instructions from the gods in a totally unexpected way, yet even though he had received knowledge of Brahman by their blessings, he could not think of himself as fully blessed until he had heard the same knowledge from his guru.

A disciple does not think much of the gods' gifts without also receiving the blessings of his spiritual master. Indeed, the disciple has no interest in the mercy of Krishna without receiving the mercy of his spiritual master. He considers the Lord's mercy to be the Lord's trick. Krishna's mercy rains down on a disciple through his spiritual master. Krishna without the guru, like Krishna without Radha, is as impossible as sun without heat or light. Satyakama could only think of himself as fulfilled when he heard the transcendental knowledge directly from his own preceptor.

The lesson we should take from this if we desire auspiciousness for ourselves is to seek to serve and please Krishna by serving the spiritual master—by making the spiritual master the supreme object of worship. A disciple's qualifications immediately disappear as soon as he starts seeing even the slightest insufficiency in his guru's appearance, virtues, learning, intelligence, eloquence, capabilities, caste, spiritual realization, or popular acceptance, or as soon as he feels any doubt about any of these. Thinking of the spiritual master as an ordinary man is the offense known as "disrespecting the guru." As soon as one deviates even slightly from obedience to the spiritual master, one will have no ability to advance even slightly on the extremely difficult path of spiritual life. All our efforts at *sādhana* and *bhajana* will be as meaningless as clarified butter poured onto ashes. The only means a genuine disciple has to advance in devotional life is his having exclusive affection for a bona fide spiritual master. The following verse by Narottama Das Thakur is particularly important to meditate on:

ki rūpe pāibo sevā mui durācāra
śrī-guru-vaiṣṇava rati nā hoilo āmāra

> How will I ever get service to Krishna? I have no attachment to either the spiritual master or the Vaishnavas.

WHAT IS BRAHMAN?

About this story from the *Upaniṣad* it is worth saying a few things about the word Brahman. The immediate meaning of this word is not the same for everyone. Those who have attained knowledge, however, understand it to mean Krishna, the personal form of God, who is sometimes called "*Param Brahma.*" To be complete, knowledge of Brahman must include *sambandha*, *abhidheya*, and *prayojana*. *Sambandha-jñāna* includes seven categories of knowledge—the proper understanding of Krishna, Krishna's energies, Krishna's relationships, the individual soul, the individual soul's bound and liberated states, and the inconceivable simultaneous oneness of and difference between the individual soul and God. *Abhidheya-jñāna* is knowledge of devotional service to Krishna. *Prayojana-jñāna* is knowledge of divine love for Krishna.

kṛṣṇa āra tāṅra śakti traya jṣāna
jāṅra āche tāṅra nāhi kṛṣṇete ajṣāna

> One who has knowledge of Krishna and His three potencies is complely free from ignorance about Krishna.

Krishna, the Supreme Brahman is self-manifest and self-luminous. This is the meaning of the first foot taught to Satyakama, which Vayu called *prakāśavān*. Although Krishna is unlimited, He appears before a devotee in a medium-sized form; under the pressure of His devotee's love, He becomes finite, although He is infinite. Even so, His name, form, qualities, and pastimes are spiritual, undivided, and without end. This is the true meaning of the second foot of Brahman, *anantavān*. The third foot was *jyotiṣmat* ("full of light"). Krishna is as luminous and effulgent as a thousand suns, yet to His devotees, whose eyes are anointed with the salve of love, He appears in a gentle, spiritual form of eternity, knowledge, and bliss. The final foot of Brahman was *āyatanavān*. The word *āyatana* means "place, home, or refuge." Krishna's abodes are called Vaikuntha, Goloka, and Vrindavan. The Lord of these transcendental, spiritual abodes is *āyatanavān*.

The *jñānīs* who follow the philosophical path think of Brahman as without attributes and form, as composed of pure light. Although they are taken by this concept, the devotees think of Krishna as possessing transcendental attributes and a spiritual form, name, and pastimes.

In His teachings to Sarvabhauma Bhattacharya, Sri Chaitanya Mahaprabhu quotes a verse from the *Hayaśīrṣa-pañcarātra* (as recorded in CC 2.6.142):

yā yā śrutir jalpati nirviśeṣaṁ
sā sābhidhatte sa-viśeṣam eva
vicāra-yoge sati hantu tāsāṁ
prāyo balīyaḥ sa-viśeṣam eva

Some passages in the *Upaniṣads* speak of the Lord as being without attributes, but then go on to establish Him as possessing fully spiritual attributes. If one analyzes the two kinds of texts, one will come to the conclusion that those establishing His transcendental attributes are stronger than the others.

Krishna Das Kaviraj explains this further (CC 2.6.140–41):

sarvaiśvarya paripūrṇa svayaṁ bhagavān
tāṅre nirākāra kari karaha vyākhyāna

nirviśeṣa tāṅre kahe yei śruti gaṇa
prākṛta niṣedhi kare aprākṛta sthāpana

> The Supreme Lord is complete in all divine majesty, but you describe Him as formless. Those passages in the *śruti* that say He is impersonal are simply condemning a material understanding of His form and attributes and go on to say that His form and attributes are transcendental and free of mundane characteristics.

The impersonal conception of Brahman and the partial concept of Paramatma are both included in the full understanding of the Divine Person, the result of an incomplete perception of the Truth. *Śrīmad-Bhāgavatam* (1.2.11) states:

vadanti tat tattva-vidas
tattvaṁ yaj jñānam advayam
brahmeti paramātmeti
bhagavān iti śabdyate

> Knowers of the truth have ascertained that the supreme nondual substance is named in three ways: as Brahman, as Paramatma, and as *Bhagavān*.

Srila Kaviraja Goswami states that the impersonal Brahman aspect of the Lord is only His bodily effulgence. So the idea of Brahman as full in sixteen parts, four in each of its quarters, *prakāśavān, anantavān, jyotiṣmat,* and *āyatanavān,* just as the moon is considered full when it has all its sixteen parts, is demonstrated in this story from the *Upaniṣads*.

TEMPTATION BY THE PROSTITUTE HIRA

Haridasa Thakur was born a Muslim, but in his youth he became attracted to chanting the names of Krishna. He left home to live in a simple hut in the jungle. Although still young, he had decided to live in seclusion to chant and meditate on the Holy Name. Not having been brought up a Hindu, he did not engage in any of the various kinds of devotional rituals Hindus practiced but instead concentrated exclusively on chanting a quota of three hundred thousand names a day. His only other ritual was watering a sacred tulasi plant. For food, he begged from the pious people in the nearby village of Benapole. Since all the local people saw that he was of spotless character and unshakeable in his devotion to the Holy Name, they respected him.

At that time, the principal landlord in the area was an atheist named Ramachandra Khan. Ramachandra could not stand it that people showed so much reverence for a poor hermit and so little for him, despite his riches and political influence. Out of envy and a deep-seated dislike of the Lord's devotees, Ramachandra began to look for flaws in Haridasa's character. Try as he might, however, he could not find the slightest blemish.

Finally, he decided to take action. He thought, "The infallible way to ruin a holy man's reputation is to catch him in bed with a woman. The *Purāṇas* are full of stories of the gods sending the heavenly courtesans, *Apsaras*, to seduce sages who had become too powerful or arrogant through their abstention. The gods are nearly always successful. There are many beautiful harlots in town. It is the pride of such women to be able to seduce *any* man, so it should be easy enough to find one ready to accept this challenge."

Ramachandra summoned the most accomplished prostitutes. Even among these women there were some who were pious enough to find the task he was proposing unpalatable. One of them, however, a very beautiful young woman named Laksha-hira, or Hira, stated proudly that no man could resist her charms. She would have Haridasa in the palm of her hand within three days.

Ramachandra Khan rubbed his hands together gleefully. "I will send one of my armed guards with you," he said, "to take this pretender a prisoner as soon as he has been compromised." Hira prudently refused, saying it would be better to wait until she was sure Haridasa was ready.

That night, the lovely Hira dressed and decorated herself in such a way that she was irresistible to every man she passed on the street on her way to Haridasa's hermitage. When she arrived, the saint was deeply absorbed in meditation. Hira showed reverence to the tulasi plant outside his door, and then to Haridasa. This shows the powerful influence of sacred places, for even though a prostitute had gone there with the basest motive, she still bowed down when coming into contact with a holy site suffused with the saint's devotions.

Hira went and stood near Haridasa. She played coquettishly with her sari, revealing the curve of her bosom. "You know, Thakur," she said, "you are a very handsome man. You are still young, so why are you wasting your life without a companion? No woman would be able to resist someone with your qualities. I myself have come because I am filled with desire for you."

When Haridasa remained silent, not even opening his eyes, Hira changed tactics. "I am burning with desire for you. If you don't touch me, I don't know how I will be able to remain alive."

Haridasa finally answered. "Don't worry," he said, "I will gladly fulfill your desires. The only problem is that I have only just begun chanting my regular number of Holy Names. As soon as I am finished I will do as you wish. In the meantime, please wait. You can sit here and listen to the sound of the Holy Name." So Haridasa went on chanting until morning, at which point the prostitute became impatient and left.

Hira returned to Ramachandra Khan and assured him that Haridasa had given his word and that it would not be long before he succumbed. Khan encouraged her with promises of rich rewards for her success.

That night, Hira returned to Haridasa's hut. The saint expressed his regret at having been unable to fulfill her desires the previous night and assured her that as soon as he was finished chanting his vow, he would do whatever she wished. Once again, Hira offered obeisance to tulasi and sat down. She spent another night waiting for Haridasa to finish chanting, eventually nodding off to sleep. When morning came, she expressed her disappointment at having to leave without her desires being fulfilled. Haridasa apologized and said, "I have taken a vow to chant ten million Holy Names before the end of the month. I am almost finished. As a matter of fact, the vow should be completed tonight. As soon as it is over, I shall accept you. Do not worry."

So for a third night Hira returned, again offering obeisance to the tulasi bush and sitting beside Haridasa to listen to him chant. As she continued to listen to his pure utterance of the name, the contaminations in her mind melted away and she began to regret her mission. Soon she could hold back no longer and fell at his feet, telling him all about Ramachandra Khan's wicked plans and begging for his forgiveness.

Haridasa answered, "I know all about Ramachandra Khan's evil intentions. I would have left here on the day you came, but I wanted to show you my mercy, so I stayed for these three days."

In fact, what Haridasa meant when he said he would "accept" her was that he would accept her as a disciple. When he said he would "fulfill" her desires, he meant that by giving her the Holy Name, the inner cravings of her soul would be satisfied. And when he said he would give her his association, he meant he would instruct her in devotional service, not that he would engage in sexual relations with her.

Hira asked Haridasa to instruct her so that she might be saved. He told her that whatever money she had earned by sinful means should be given in charity to the *brāhmaṇas* and that she should come and take up residence in his hut, where she was to worship tulasi and chant the Holy Names constantly.

In his *Anubhāṣya* to *Caitanya-caritāmṛta* 3.3.139, Srila Bhaktisiddhanta Saraswati Goswami Thakur comments on Haridasa Thakur's instructions to Hira:

> Even though the guru has a legitimate claim on all of his disciple's worldly possessions, he does not ask for them for his own use. Those who take *dakṣiṇā*, or alms, are opening the door to the house of Yamaraja. A Vaishnava guru is not such a person bound for the house of Yama; he is a traveler on a higher road. For this reason, there is an arrangement for giving donations of material wealth, etc., to *brāhmaṇas* on the *karma-mārga*. By not accepting his disciple's possessions, which are after all intended for sense gratification, the Vaishnava guru remains independent of his disciple and does not compromise his integrity. He renounces the disciples' possessions because he knows they will awaken in him disinterest for the service of the Lord. Haridasa Thakur's teaching here is that the guru's duty is to rid his disciple of his mundane pride and not to himself accept the material possessions the disciple renounces.

Hira did exactly as her guru instructed her and gave all her riches to the *brāhmaṇas*. Then she shaved her hair and donned a single piece of white cloth before returning to the hut. There she took up a life of devotion, chanting three *lakhs* of names just as her guru had been doing. By virtue of her service to the tulasi plant and her chanting of the Holy Name, she became very renounced, conquering her senses. Before long, she attained pure love for Krishna. Through Haridasa Thakur's mercy, the prostitute had become a great *Vaishnavi*.

This shows how a qualified guru can through compassion transform even a person with wicked intentions.

CHAPTER 6

Service to Sri Guru

On introducing the sixty-four principal types of devotional practice, Rupa Goswami says that an aspiring devotee's first business is to take shelter of a spiritual master, become initiated by him, and receive his instructions. The next item of devotional practice is to perform deeply faithful service to one's spiritual master (*guru-pādāśrayas tasmāt kṛṣṇa-dīkṣādi-śikṣaṇam, viśrambhena guroḥ sevā*). The blessings of the guru and the Lord come quickly to the fortunate person who serves the spiritual master with deep faith.

When Mahaprabhu instructed Sanatana Goswami to write a book of instructions on Vaishnava behavior and ritual (the *Hari-bhakti-vilāsa*), He gave him an outline of subjects he should discuss. This outline is given in the *Caitanya-caritāmṛta* (2.24.332). The word *guru-sevā* is explained there by Srila Prabhupada, who quotes the following series of verses in his *Anubhāṣya*:

prathamaṁ tu guruṁ pūjya
tataś caiva mamārcanam
kurvan siddhim avāpnoti
hy anyathā niṣphalaṁ bhavet

> One should first show reverence to the spiritual master and then go on to worship Me. One who worships in this way attains perfection; otherwise,

one's religious activities are useless. (*Mahārṇava*, as quoted in HBV 4.344)

gurau sannihite yas tu
pūjayed anyam agrataḥ
sa durgatim avāpnoti
pūjanaṁ tasya niṣphalam

One who worships any other person while near his spiritual master comes to misfortune. All his acts of worship are fruitless. (*Mahārṇava*, as quoted in HBV 4.345)

nāham ijyā-prajātibhyāṁ
tapasopaśamena ca
tuṣyeyaṁ sarva-bhūtātmā
guru-śuśrūṣayā yathā

I, the soul of all beings, am not as pleased by the performance of the prescribed duties of the four ashrams, i.e., sacrifices, service to the family, austerities, and renunciation, as I am by service to the guru. (ŚB 10.80.34)

guru-suśrūṣaṇaṁ nāma
sarva-dharmottamottamam
tasmād dharmāt paro dharmaḥ
pavitraṁ naiva vidyate

Service to the spiritual master is the topmost religious activity. There is no religion or piety that is more holy than this. (HBV 4.355)

Scripture usually ordains that the disciple perform the five-part *puraś-caraṇa* vow after taking initiation in order to awaken the power of the mantra. This method is prescribed in the *Hari-bhakti-vilāsa* (17.11):

pūjā traikālikī nityaṁ
japas tarpaṇam eva ca
homo brāhmaṇa-bhuktiś ca
puraścaraṇam ucyate

> There are five aspects to the *puraścaraṇa* observance: puja three times a day, constant chanting of *japa,* oblations of water, daily fire sacrifice, and feeding of the *brāhmaṇas*.

This means that if one takes the vow to chant one's mantra ten thousand times, then he must also offer one thousand oblations of water, sacrifice one hundred oblations into the fire, and feed ten *brāhmaṇas*. Of course, it is very difficult to undertake such an observance flawlessly. So for less qualified fools like myself, the scriptures have prescribed a simplified process that consists of simply serving the spiritual master. We would do better to follow the simplified process, as recommended in the *Hari-bhakti-vilāsa* (17.241–43):

athavā devatā-rūpaṁ
guruṁ dhyātvā pratoṣayet
tasya cchāyānusārī syād
bhakti-yuktena cetasā

guru-mūlam idaṁ sarvaṁ
tasmān nityaṁ guruṁ bhajet
puraścaraṇa-hīno'pi
mantrī siddhyen na saṁśayaḥ

yathā siddha-rasa-sparśāt
tāmraṁ bhavati kāñcanam

sannidhānād guror eva
śiṣyo viṣṇumayo bhavet

> Alternatively, one should satisfy the guru by meditating on him in the form of the Deity. He should think of himself as devotedly following the guru like a shadow. One should constantly worship the guru who is the basis of all of one's spiritual activities. Even if one does not perform the *puraścaraṇa,* one can attain perfection in chanting the mantra through service to the guru. Of this there can be no doubt, for it is said, "Just as copper becomes gold through the touch of specially treated mercury, so does a disciple take on the qualities of Vishnu through the association of his guru."

In his commentary on these verses, Sanatana Goswami writes: "In the following three verses, the author changes the subject by saying that the *puraścaraṇa* ritual can be perfected simply by serving the spiritual master."

In conclusion, it may be said that serving the spiritual master has unlimited benefits. All perfections can be achieved by serving the spiritual master. Krishna Himself appears as the spiritual master and gives the surrendered disciple the treasure of the disciple's heart—love for Krishna.

guru-rūpe kṛṣṇa kṛpā karena bhakta-gaṇe

> Krishna gives His blessings to the devotees through His manifestation as the spiritual master.

The disciple should therefore never let himself be distracted from serving the spiritual master in the way that the guru wishes.

guru-kṛpā-jale nibhāi viṣaya-anala
rādhā govinda bala rādhā govinda bala

Extinguish the fire of sense desire with the water of the guru's mercy. Then chant the names of Radha and Govinda! Chant the names of Radha and Govinda!

SERVICE TO SRI GURU AS *PURAŚCARAṆA*

It is said that when the two brothers, Rupa and Sanatana, became eager to join Chaitanya Mahaprabhu and dedicate themselves to a life of pure devotion, they engaged two *brāhmaṇas* to each perform a *puraścaraṇa* of the *kṛṣṇa-mantra* in order to help them achieve that goal. Krishna Das Kaviraj Goswami recounts this decision in the *Caitanya-caritāmṛta* (2.19.3–5):

śrī-rūpa sanātana rahe rāmakeli-grāme
prabhure miliyā gelā āpana bhavane
dui bhāi viṣaya-tyāgera upāya sṛjila
bahu dhana diyā dui brāhmaṇe varila
kṛṣṇa-mantre karāila dui puraścaraṇa
acirāt pāibāre caitanya caraṇa

Rupa and Sanatana remained in their own homes in Ramakeli village, where they returned after their meeting with Chaitanya Mahaprabhu. The two brothers then started thinking about how they could escape their material entanglements. They engaged two *brāhmaṇas* with a large sum of money and asked them to perform a *puraścaraṇa* of the *kṛṣṇa-mantra* so that they could quickly have Chaitanya Mahaprabhu's association.

GENERAL RULES FOR THE *PURAŚCARAṆA*

The scriptures describe *puraścaraṇa* as a five-fold penance or set of vows. This penance is considered necessary for a disciple who has received a mantra from his spiritual master at initiation and wishes to perfect the chanting of it—to attain *mantra-siddhi*. Sanatana Goswami clarifies in his commentary on *Hari-bhakti-vilāsa* 17.12:

guroḥ prasādena labdhasya mantrasya etat-pañcāṅgopāsanaṁ
puraḥ prathamaṁ vidhīyata iti puraścaraṇam ucyate

> *Puraścaraṇa* is defined as that five-part worship that is immediately put into practice in order to reach perfection in the mantra that has been received through the grace of the guru.

The *Pañcarātra Āgamas* state that one may chant one's *dīkṣā-mantra* for a hundred years, but without a *puraścaraṇa* it is impossible to achieve *mantra-siddhi*. This is further confirmed in *Hari-bhakti-vilāsa* (17.7):

puraskriyā hi mantrāṇāṁ pradhānaṁ vīryam ucyate
vīrya-hīno yathā dehī sarva-karmasu na kṣamaḥ
puraścaraṇa-hīno hi tathā mantraḥ prakīrtitaḥ

> The principal source of a mantra's power is *puraścaraṇa*. Just like a person without physical strength is unable to perform any activity, so too a mantra is said to be impotent if no *puraścaraṇa* has been performed.

The *Hari-bhakti-vilāsa* (17.11–12) continues the description of the five aspects of the *puraścaraṇa*:

pūjā traikālikī nityaṁ
japas tarpaṇam eva ca
homa brāhmaṇa-bhuktiś ca
puraścaraṇam ucyate

Puja three times a day (morning, noon, and evening), constant chanting of *japa*, oblations of water, a daily fire sacrifice, and the feeding of *brāhmaṇas*.

guror labdhasya mantrasya
prasādena yathāvidhi
pañcāṅgopāsanaṁ siddhyai
puraś caitad vidhīyate

In order to attain perfection in the mantra that was given at the time of initiation, it is enjoined that the disciple should first perform these five kinds of worship in accordance with the regulations.

Puraścaraṇa is a process by which one can cut the ropes that bind him to material life. Indeed, there is no other way to attain the desired perfection. Lord Krishna states in the Bhagavad Gita (10.25), *yajñānāṁ japa-yajño'smi*: "Of sacrifices I am the sacrifice of *japa*." This shows that *japa*, or quiet chanting of the mantra, is the best of religious practices. After one has taken one's morning bath, he should perform puja of Krishna. Then, he should continue chanting his mantra, which is an element of the puja, until midday.

In the *Sāradā-tilaka* it is said that one should chant his mantra a minimum of twenty thousand times in the course of a *puraścaraṇa*. The *Prapañca-sāra* confirms that twenty thousand is a good number for those who are incapable of doing more. The *Sanat-kumāra-saṁhitā* says that in Satya Yuga, one was obliged to complete a *puraścaraṇa* of one *lakh* (one hundred thousand mantras) in order to achieve perfection. In the Treta Yuga two *lakhs* (two hundred thousand mantras) were required. That increased to three *lakhs* in the Dvapara Yuga, and four *lakhs* in Kali Yuga. And if one wishes to achieve any special ends, one needs to complete a *puraścaraṇa* of five *lakhs* (five hundred thousand mantras).[1]

---

1 These details are given in *Hari-bhakti-vilāsa* 17.205–17.

When one has completed the requisite number of mantras, one is then required to perform a great puja and hold a festival for the Lord. In order to please the guru, one should also prepare a feast for the *brāhmaṇas* and feed the poor and helpless. It is said that one should offer one tenth as many oblations into the fire sacrifice as one has chanted mantras, one tenth that many oblations of holy water, and feed one tenth of that number of *brāhmaṇas*. In other words, if one chants the mantra twenty thousand times, he must offer two thousand oblations (*tarpaṇa*). Oblations for the fire sacrifice (*homa*) should be made of cow ghee mixed with cane sugar, whole red lotus flowers, and honey. If red lotus flowers are unavailable, then rice pudding prepared with ghee and sugar is acceptable. In this example, one would also have to offer *tarpaṇa* two hundred times.

One would then have to please the spiritual master by feeding one tenth that number of *brāhmaṇas*, in other words, twenty. One should first offer the *brāhmaṇas* a reverent reception by washing their feet and offering water to drink (*arghya*). Then one should serve them a meal including tasty foodstuffs of all four types, so they can eat to their full satisfaction. After this has been done, the performer of the *puraścaraṇa* should also distribute food to the poor, disabled, and hungry people of the neighborhood.

In this way, one must chant the fixed number of mantras on each day of the vow, followed by offering the corresponding numbers of *tarpaṇa* and *homa* and serving the requisite number of guests. If any part of the process is neglected or performed improperly, the entire *puraścaraṇa* is considered null and void. One can only correct the error by repeating that portion that was missed or improperly performed with double the quota of *japa*. If one cannot chant the required number of mantras, one can make up for that by feeding twice the usual number of *brāhmaṇas*. Elsewhere it is said that one can make up for the inability to chant the required number of mantras by doubling the amount of *tarpaṇa* or performing the same number of prostrated obeisances.[2]

SPECIFIC RULES FOR CHANTING *JAPA*

In order to chant one's mantras, one must first take from the spiritual master a *japa-mālā* made from tulasi wood. Sanatana Goswami writes in his commentary on *Hari-bhakti-vilāsa* 17.103:

> *mālāṁ ca prathamaṁ sva-guru-hastād eva grāhyā*
> *guruṁ sampūjya tad-dhastād gṛhṇīyāt sarva-siddhaye iti tantrokteḥ.*

> One should take the *mālā* from the hand of one's own guru. This is stated in the *Tantras*: "Offer proper worship to the guru and then accept the *mālā* from his hand. This will bring all success in chanting."

The *Hari-bhakti-vilāsa* (17.116, 123–26) adds: there are rules governing the use of the fingers while counting the number of times one has chanted the mantra. On the *mālā*, one normally uses the thumb and middle finger. Chanting without the thumb will not bring the results one seeks. Nor should one touch the beads with one's forefinger. Similarly, one should never touch his beads with the left hand. One should not shake or rattle one's beads or throw them down. One should not touch them while in an impure state or let them drop from one's hand.

One can also count mantras without a *mālā*. In Sanskrit, each of the fingers has a name—the thumb is *aṅguṣṭha*, the forefinger *tarjanī* (because it is used when berating someone), the middle finger *madhyamā*, the ring finger *anāmikā* (because it descends in size), and the little finger *kaniṣṭhā*, or "the smallest." Each finger has three segments. Starting

[2] *Tarpaṇa* is explained in the third chapter of *Hari-bhakti-vilāsa* (3.305): "One should pour handfuls of water over one's head using the *kumbha-mudrā* while chanting the *mūla-mantra*." A more detailed version follows in HBV 3.338. *Tarpaṇa* refers to the offering of handfuls of water onto the mantra's specific yantra while chanting the mantra (HBV 1.233). Another familiar form of *tarpaṇa* is offering handfuls of water while bathing in a holy stream. This is usually accompanied by uttering mantras to the different gods and forefathers.

from the middle segment of the ring finger, the devotee counts ten mantras by moving the thumb counterclockwise from segment to segment with each repetition of the mantra, until he arrives at the base of the forefinger. One must avoid the two bottom segments of the middle finger, which are considered to be the same as Mount Meru. It is said that Lord Brahma polluted these two segments, making them unusable for such a sacred purpose. Nor should one skip over them. Instead, one should reverse directions and count the next ten mantras by proceeding clockwise around the finger segments (HBV 17.117–119).

There are many other prohibitions that must be observed when chanting one's mantra. One should not talk with others while chanting; one should not think of anything other than Krishna; one should not chant while lying in bed, walking to and fro, or when in a frivolous, doubting, or disturbed state of mind. One should be careful not to sneeze, pass air, or yawn, for all these things disrupt one's concentration. One should neither look at nor touch dogs or cats. If one sees such unclean creatures while chanting *japa*, one should perform *ācamana* before continuing. If one touches such a creature, he should bathe before returning to chanting. In fact, one should avoid looking at anything that can distract one from meditation on the mantra. One should chant while contemplating the meaning of the mantra and on the lotus feet of the Lord. If one is attentive in this way, one will quickly attain perfection in chanting.

There are three kinds of *japa*. Their technical names are *vācika*, *upāṁśu*, and *mānasika*, audible, whispered, and mental. Each of these is considered progressively superior to the other. The kinds are defined as follows:

yad ucca-nīca-svaritaiḥ spaṣṭa-śabdavad akṣaraiḥ
mantram uccārayed vyaktaṁ japa-yajñaḥ sa vācikaḥ

> When one pronounces each letter of the mantra clearly, using the proper inflections and accents, this is called the audible (*vācika*) performance of *japa*. (HBV 17.156)

Sanatana Goswami clarifies in his commentary that *ucca-nīca-svaritaiḥ* is a reference to the different kinds of accents, specifically as they are used in pronouncing the Vedic mantras. When the chanter moves the lips and pronounces the words of the mantra only loudly enough that he himself can hear them, that is called *upāṁśu-japa*. And Srila Rupa Goswami gives a general definition of *japa* in the *Bhakti-rasāmṛta-sindu* (1.2.151), "Very soft repetition of the mantra is called *japa*" (*mantrasya sulaghūccāro japa ity abhidhīyate*). And the third kind of *japa* is mental (*mānasika*). It is considered superior to the other kinds and is considered equivalent to meditation.

FAITHFUL SERVICE TO THE GURU

The mercy of the spiritual master leads to the mercy of the Supreme Lord. Because the satisfaction of the spiritual master is so essential to the disciple's spiritual life, the scriptures—both the *śruti* and the *smṛti*—are full of instructions about the importance of serving him. The essence of all these scriptures is *Śrīmad Bhāgavatam*. In text 10.80.34, Krishna tells His fellow student Sudama:

nāham ijyā-prajātibhyāṁ
tapasopaśamena ca
tuṣyeyaṁ sarva-bhūtātmā
guru-śuśrūṣayā yathā

> I, the soul of all beings, am not as pleased by the performance of the prescribed duties of the four *āśramas*, i.e., sacrifices, service to the family, austerities and renunciation, as I am by service to the guru.

Prahlada Maharaja states something similar in *Śrīmad Bhāgavatam 7.7.30–33*: by serving the guru devotedly (*guru-śuśrūṣayā bhaktyā*), one can awaken *rati*, or come to the stage of *bhāva*:

guru-śuśrūṣayā bhaktyā sarva-labdhārpaṇena ca
saṅgena sādhu-bhaktānām īśvarārādhanena ca

> *śraddhayā tat-kathāyāṁ ca kīrtanair guṇa-karmaṇām*
> *tat-pādāmburuha-dhyānāt tal-liṅgekṣārhaṇādibhiḥ*
> *hariḥ sarveṣu bhūteṣu bhagavān āsta īśvaraḥ*
> *iti bhūtāni manasā kāmais taiḥ sādhu mānayet*
> *evaṁ nirjita-ṣaḍ-vargaiḥ kriyate bhaktir īśvare*
> *vāsudeve bhagavati yayā saṁlabhyate ratiḥ*

> One can conquer the six enemies—lust, anger, greed, intoxication, envy, and illusion—by serving the guru with devotion, by offering everything one has attained, by the association of pious devotees, and by the worship of the Lord; by having faith in topics about the Lord and by glorifying His virtues and activities, by meditating on His lotus feet and gazing on His Deity forms; and by seeing every living beings as essentially good due to knowing that the Supreme Lord is present within each of them. One who is thus purified and practices devotion to the Lord Vasudeva quickly reaches the stage of *bhāva* or *rati.*

The original meaning of the word *śuśrūṣā* is "the desire to hear." It thus means faithfully serving the spiritual master by drinking in the nectarean words he speaks through the path of the ears. Besides this, though, it has taken on wider meanings. In his commentary on these verses, Vishwanatha states that here *śuśrūṣā* means "performing personal service to the spiritual master, such as bathing him or massaging his feet."

In the *Bhakti-rasāmṛta-sindhu,* Srila Rupa Goswami lists sixty-four different kinds of devotional practices. Of these, the first three are all connected with the spiritual master:

1. Taking shelter of a guru—*guru-pādāśrayaḥ.*
2. Taking initiation and instruction about Krishna from that guru—*tasmād dīkṣādi-śikṣaṇam.*

3. Serving the guru with deep respect and faith—*viśrambhena guroḥ sevā.*

In other words, one first takes shelter of the spiritual master and then takes initiation from him. This is followed by taking instruction in the *Bhāgavata-dharma,* or the practice of devotional service. This includes hearing about the *sambandha-, abhidheya-,* and *prayojana-tattvas.* As one is learning about devotional service from the spiritual master, one should serve him with deep faith, which is the meaning of the word *viśrambha.* One's attitude toward the guru should be that he is an incarnation of the Deity we desire to attain, or our *iṣṭa-devatā.* One should serve the guru with strong faith and love, knowing that all success in our spiritual endeavor will come from satisfying him. If the disciple takes up the vow to serve the spiritual master in this consciousness, he quickly receives his blessings, through which the blessings of Krishna are quickly attained.

IS THERE A NEED FOR INITIATION OR *PURAŚCARAṆA*?

While this question has earlier been addressed, the *Caitanya-caritāmṛta* (2.15.108) elucidates further:

dīkṣā-puraścaryā-vidhi apekṣā nā kare
jihvā-sparśe ā-caṇḍāla sabāre uddhāre

> The Holy Name does not depend on initiation or the performance of *puraścaraṇa* after initiation. Everyone, including the outcastes, are delivered simply by vibrating the sound of the name on their tongues.

The *Hari-bhakti-vilāsa* (1.149) quotes the *Rāmārcana-dīpikā:*

vinaiva dīkṣāṁ viprendra
puraścaryāṁ vinaiva hi
vinaiva nyāsa-vidhinā
japa-mātreṇa siddhidāḥ

> All Vaishnava mantras are so powerful that they bestow perfection simply when being muttered, even if one has not been initiated or performed *puraścaraṇa* or engaged in purification rituals such as *nyāsa,* etc.

All these quotes indicate the all-powerful nature of the names of Krishna and Rama and their mantras. The innate power of the Holy Names means they are completely independent in giving their effects of any external ritual process, including initiation. Unfortunately, some people use texts like these to support their lack of faith in the process of taking shelter of and serving a spiritual master. Jiva Goswami argues against such a position in the *Bhakti-sandarbha* (283–84), the salient portions of which are given here for the perusal of those wanting to know his *siddhānta*:

yadyapi śrī-bhāgavata-mate pañcarātrādivad arcana-mārgasyāvaśyakatvaṁ nāsti, tad vināpi śaraṇāpatty-ādīnām ekatareṇāpi puruṣārtha-siddher abhihitatvāt, tathāpi śrī-nāradādi-vartmānusaradbhiḥ śrī-bhagavatā saha sambandha-viśeṣaṁ dīkṣā-vidhānena śrī-guru-caraṇa-sampāditaṁ cikīrṣadbhiḥ kṛtāyāṁ dīkṣāyām arcanam avaśyaṁ kriyetaiva.

> Even though, according to the opinion of the *Bhāgavatam,* there is no absolute necessity of following the path of Deity worship as prescribed in the *Pañcarātra* scriptures, since even without it any one of the devotional processes starting from surrender (*śaraṇāpatti*) is sufficient in itself to bestow the ultimate goal of life, still, those who follow the process of Sri Narada and wish to establish a specific relationship with the Lord through a spiritual master by the process of initiation, will most certainly engage in Deity worship after taking *dīkṣā*.[3]

[3] *See Bhakti-sandarbha* 237, and *Śrīmad Bhāgavatam* 7.15.25.

yadyapi svarūpato nāsti, tathāpi prāyaḥ svabhāvato dehādi-sambandhena kadar-tha-śīlānāṁ vikṣipta-cittānāṁ janānāṁ tat-tat-saṁkocīkaraṇāya śrīmad-ṛṣi-pra-bhṛtibhir atrārcana-mārge kvacit kvacit kācit kācin maryādā sthāpitāsti.

For even though there is no inherent necessity for initiation and Deity worship, since most people are by nature addicted to sinful activities and distracted in mind due to the relationship with the body, Narada and other seers have here and there established the regulations of Deity worship in order to reduce these proclivities.

In his conversations with Prakashananda Saraswati, Sri Chaitanya Mahaprabhu said:

kṛṣṇa mantra haite habe saṁsāra mocana
kṛṣṇa nāma haite pābe kṛṣṇera caraṇa

By chanting the *kṛṣṇa-mantra* one will be liberated from material existence. And by chanting Krishna's name one will attain His lotus feet. (CC 1.7.73)

Here the distinction is being made between the *dīkṣā-mantra,* which is essentially an offering of oneself to God, and the Holy Names, which are a direct calling out to the Lord. This distinction is in the grammar of the two kinds of mantras. The *dīkṣā-mantra* generally contains a seed syllable, or *bīja,* such as *oṁ* or *klim.* The name of the Lord is then placed in the dative case, indicating movement toward the Lord. The mantra is completed with a word denoting the act of offering or sacrificing to the Lord, such as *namaḥ* or *svāhā.*

The mantras of the Holy Name, such as the Hare Krishna *mahā-mantra,* on the other hand, contain nothing but Krishna's names in the vocative case, meaning that one is calling out to Him directly.

The initiation mantra is thus necessary for the processes of self-purification by which we become liberated from the material condition; the Holy Names result in the good fortune of attaining Krishna's lotus feet.

Some people point to Ajamila, who was able to attain the Lord's abode simply by chanting the Holy Name, without taking shelter of a guru. They think, like him, they can attain perfection by approaching the Lord directly, without the intercession of a spiritual master and becoming initiated. Vishwanatha Chakravarti clearly rebuts this position in his *Sārārtha-darśinī* comment on 6.2.9–10:

ye go-gardabhādaya iva viṣayeṣv evendriyāṇi sadā cārayanti, ko bhagavān, kā bhaktiḥ, ko gurur iti svapne'pi na jānanti, teṣām eva nāmābhāsādi-rītyā gṛhīta-hari-nāmnām ajāmilādīnām iva niraparādhānāṁ guruṁ vināpi bhavaty evoddhāraḥ. harir bhajanīya eva bhajanaṁ tat-prāpakam eva. tad-upadeṣṭā gurur eva. gurūpadiṣṭā bhaktā eva pūrve hariṁ prāpur iti viveka-viśeṣavattve'pi

no dīkṣāṁ na ca sat-kriyāṁ na ca puraścaryāṁ manāg īkṣate
mantro'yaṁ rasanā-spṛg eva phalati śrī-kṛṣṇanāmātmakaḥ

iti pramāṇa-dṛṣṭyā ajāmilādi-dṛṣṭāntena ca kiṁ me guru-karaṇa-śrameṇa nāma-kīrtanādibhir eva me bhagavat-prāptir bhāvinīti manyamānas tu gurv-avajñā-lakṣaṇa-mahāparādhād eva bhagavantaṁ na prāpnoti, kintu tasminn eva janmani janmāntare vā tad-aparādha-kṣaye sati śrī-guru-caraṇāśrita eva prāpnotīti.

> Those who are as ignorant as cows or mules, and like them engaged uniquely in the pursuit of bodily pleasures and comforts, who even in their dreams have absolutely no concept of who or what God is, or of devotion or the spiritual master, may be able to directly achieve the mercy of the Lord through a facsimile of the Holy Name, *nāmābhāsa*, as Ajamila did. This is because such people have not had the occasion to commit offenses. On the other hand,

> when someone comes to know that Krishna is to be worshiped, that bhakti is the process of worship, that the spiritual master is the instructor in devotional service, and that in the past, devotees who received direction from their spiritual masters attained the Lord, then even if he quotes the verse from the *Padyāvalī* (29) that states, "The mantra of the Holy Names produces results as soon as it touches the tongue, even for one who has not taken initiation or performed any other good deeds or rituals, such as the *puraścaraṇa*," and says, "What need have I of taking the trouble to find a guru and take initiation from him? I will attain perfection simply by chanting kirtan of the Holy Name," then he commits the offense to the Holy Name known as disdaining the spiritual master (*gurv-avajñā*). He will only be able to attain the Lord in this or another life when the effects of this offense have dissipated and he has taken shelter of a spiritual master.

The *Chāndogya Upaniṣad* (6.14.2) states, *ācāryavān puruṣo veda*: "One who has a spiritual master [i.e., one who has taken initiation from a spiritual master] knows God."

The *Muṇḍaka Upaniṣad* (1.2.11) states:

tad-vijñānārthaṁ sa gurum evābhigacchet
samit-pāṇiḥ śrotriyaṁ brahma-niṣṭham

> In order to realize the truth, one should take fuel for the sacrificial fire in hand and approach a spiritual master who is learned and fixed in Brahman.

In other words, in order to attain knowledge of the process of pure loving devotion, the disciple should take gifts in hand and approach a guru who knows the essence of the Vedic scriptures and has attained an understanding of Krishna.

The *Kaṭha Upaniṣad* (1.3.14) further states:

uttiṣṭhata jāgrata prāpya varān nibodhata
kṣurasya dhārā niśitā duratyayā durgaṁ pathas tat kavayo vadanti

> The Veda *puruṣa* gives the following beneficial instruction to the sages: "Rise up (*uttiṣṭhata*)! Awaken (*jāgrata*)! Seize the benefits of this human form of life (*prāpya varān*) and become conscious (*nibodhata*). This path is difficult to tread (*durgaṁ pathaḥ*), like the edge of a sharp and dangerous razor blade (*kṣurasya dhārā niśitā duratyayā*)."

In other words, "O wise ones, arise and make an effort to gain knowledge of the self. Arise and turn away from all subjects not related to Krishna. Awake! Abandon lethargy, laziness, illusion, and sleep, and awaken to your true identity as a servant of God. Seize the benefits of human life by taking shelter of a realized saint and learn from him the nature of the Lord. Learn from a realized saint, because such knowledge is subtle and the path to attaining the Lord is narrow. Furthermore, it is like the sharp blade of a razor, difficult to tread. One who swerves even slightly from the path his spiritual master gives him, whether through carelessness or inattention, will inevitably fall."

Others interpret this verse in different words: "This material world is a dangerous place—like a razor's edge. Without the guidance and mercy of a spiritual master, it is impossible to make one's way through the world. For this reason, the knowledgeable (*kavayaḥ*), those who have attained an understanding of God's nature and how to serve Him, reveal this difficult path of spiritual knowledge to us. There is no other way to cross the ocean of material existence without the mercy and help of the saintly devotees and the spiritual master."

Therefore we should pray, as the *Caitanya-caritāmṛta* (3.1.2) instructs:

durgame pathi me'ndhasya
skhalat-pāda-gater muhuḥ
sva-kṛpā-yaṣṭi-dānena
santaḥ santv avalambanam

> This path is difficult to tread, and I am blind. I am constantly slipping and falling as I advance. I pray that the saints will help me by giving me the walking stick of their mercy.

The *Śvetāśvatara Upaniṣad* (6.23) states:

yasya deve parā bhaktir
yathā deve tathā gurau
tasyaite kathitā hy arthāḥ
prakāśante mahātmanaḥ

> Only unto those great souls who have deep devotion in both the Lord and the spiritual master, who is His manifestation and not different from Him, are all the imports of Vedic knowledge automatically revealed.

In other words, if one has the same kind of pure devotion for the spiritual master that one ideally has for the Lord, then by the spiritual master's mercy, all the truths contained in the revealed scriptures are revealed to one in their essence.

The *Caitanya-caritāmṛta* (2.19.151 and 2.22.25) also says:

> *brahmāṇḍa bhramite kono bhāgyavān jīva*
> *guru kṛṣṇa prasāde pāya bhakti-latā-bīja*

> Wandering in this way through the worlds, some fortunate *jīva* receives the seed of the devotional creeper through the mercy of guru and Krishna.

> *tāte kṛṣṇa bhaje kare gurura sevana*
> *māyā jāla chuṭe pāya śrī-kṛṣṇa-caraṇa*

> Thereupon, he takes up the worship of Krishna and the service of his spiritual master. He thus escapes the net of Maya and attains Krishna's lotus feet.

The *Bhāgavatam* (11.20.17) states:

> *nṛ-deham ādyaṁ sulabhaṁ sudurlabhaṁ*
> *plavaṁ su-kalpaṁ guru-karṇa-dhāram*
> *mayānukūlena nabhasvateritaṁ*
> *pumān bhavābdhiṁ na taret sa ātma-hā*

> This human body is the root of all benefits. It seems so easily obtained yet is in fact extremely rare. It is like a boat especially designed for crossing the ocean of material existence. If one has a spiritual master to guide him like the boat's helmsman and is given the favorable winds of My mercy, but still fails to cross, then he is willingly committing suicide.

That is to say, by the blessings of the spiritual master, one gets the favorable winds of Krishna's mercy. By this combination of blessings, one can easily cross the ocean of material existence.

Sanatana Goswami quotes *Śrīmad Bhāgavatam* 11.3.21 in the *Hari-bhakti-vilāsa* (1.32), in which the nine Yogendras state:

tasmād guruṁ prapadyeta
jijñāsuḥ śreya uttamam
śābde pare ca niṣṇātaṁ
brahmaṇy upaśamāśrayam

Therefore one who is inquisitive about the ultimate good in life should surrender to a spiritual master who has thoroughly understood the purport of the scriptures, who is fixed in divine realization, and has attained peace from the impulse of the senses, and who is free from anger and greed.

The *Muṇḍaka Upaniṣad* was quoted above, in which it was said, *samit-pāṇiḥ śrotriyaṁ brahma-niṣṭham:* "One should approach the wise and learned guru with gifts in hand." The exact words used were *samit-pāṇiḥ*. Our spiritual masters have interpreted this to mean more than "carrying fuel for the sacrifice." Rather, it refers to an attitude one needs to develop when approaching the spiritual master. In fact, there are three types of fuel—or attitudes—one needs in order to fully benefit from the association of an advanced devotee. Bhagavad Gita (4.34) describes these:

tad viddhi praṇipātena
paripraśnena sevayā
upadekṣyanti te jñānaṁ
jñāninas tattva-darśinaḥ

Learn the truth by approaching a spiritual master. Inquire submissively and render service to him. Self-realized souls can impart knowledge because they are seers of the truth.

"O Arjuna, when you are in the presence of a spiritual master who knows the truth about Krishna, fall down before him like a rod (*praṇipāta*) and pray: 'O Gurudeva! Why have I become trapped in this cycle of birth and death and how can I be delivered?'" Such questions are called *paripraśna*, appropriate inquiries one should make of a spiritual master. Then one should serve (*sevā*) the spiritual master with a sincere attitude. When the spiritual master sees such real interest in the goal and means of spiritual life, as well as an open and honest attitude of service, his heart warms to the disciple and he reveals to him all the scriptural truths as well as his own realizations of them. This is true not just of initiating spiritual masters but of all advanced devotees capable of providing guidance by explaining the three facets of spiritual knowledge: *sambandha*, *abhidheya*, and *prayojana*.

Prostrate yourself before the spiritual master, please him with sincere service, and beg him to reveal the truths of spiritual life to you, saying, "O Gurudeva! How have I fallen into this material existence, where I must suffer the three kinds of miseries? How can I be delivered?" In response to your heartfelt inquiries, your spiritual master, who has direct experience of the Supreme Brahman, will divulge his understanding to you. The *Bhakti-rasāmṛta-sindhu* (1.2.101) declares:

śruti-smṛti-purāṇādi-
pañcarātra-vidhiṁ vinā
aikāntikī harer bhaktir
utpātāyaiva kalpate

> Even exclusive devotion to Lord Hari is considered to be a disruption if it ignores the rules enunciated in the *śrutis*, *smṛtis*, *Purāṇas*, and *Pañcarātra* scriptures.

In the age of Kali, the path of tantra, which is delineated in the texts known as the *Āgamas*, is dominant. Those who follow a tantrik path must first take initiation into a *kṛṣṇa-mantra*, then engage in the sacrifice of the Holy Name as described in *Śrīmad Bhāgavatam* (11.5.32): *yajñaiḥ saṅkīrtana-prāyair yajanti hi sumedhasaḥ*. This is the process Sri Chaitanya Mahaprabhu taught in his *Śikṣāṣṭakam*.

In the first of Mahaprabhu's verses, He says that seven benefits arise from chanting the Holy Name, beginning with purification of the heart. Elsewhere, the Lord says that all perfection comes from chanting the *mahā-mantra* (*ihā haite sarva-siddhi hoibe sabāra*). The *dīkṣā-mantra* is an invocation of self-surrender, which leads to liberation from material entanglement. Chanting the *mahā-mantra* leads one to Krishna's lotus feet. Therefore the two processes—chanting the *dīkṣā-mantra* and chanting the Holy Name—have to be combined. By serving the spiritual master's lotus feet with sincere faith through chanting and meditating on the Holy Name, one attains perfection in the mantra along with all spiritual success. The mercy of the spiritual master is everything. Therefore, service to him is the principal type of *puraścaraṇa*.

CHAPTER 7

The Necessity of Initiation

The *Hari-bhakti-vilāsa* (2.3–4) expands on the necessity of taking initiation:

> *dvijānām anupetānāṁ sva-karmādhyayanādiṣu*
> *yathādhikāro nāstīha syāc copanayanād anu*
> *tathātrādīkṣitānāṁ tu mantra-devārcanādiṣu*
> *nādhikāro'sty ataḥ kuryād ātmānaṁ śiva-saṁstutam*

> Just as one born in a *brāhmaṇa* family cannot engage in the Vedic rituals without first being invested with the sacred thread, similarly, no person has the right to engage in chanting the mantra or worshiping the Deity without first being initiated. Therefore one should become praised by Shiva himself by taking initiation.

In his commentary on this verse, Srila Sanatana Goswami states that since no one is permitted to eat without first offering his food to the Deity, and since initiation is a necessary prerequisite to Deity worship, it is clear that initiation is absolutely necessary (*dīkṣāyā nityatvaṁ sidhyati*). But Sanatana goes on to say that even though worship of the *śālagrāma-śilā* is what is being specified here, initiation is in fact a necessary prerequisite for all kinds of service to Krishna and not simply for worship of His Deity form.[1]

[1] *śālagrāma-śilādhiṣṭhānaṁ vargeṣu mukhyatvāt sarvāṇy eva bhagavad-anuṣṭhānāny upalakṣayati.*

Therefore, the next verse of the *Hari-bhakti-vilāsa* (2.5) states that the ordinary person is transformed by initiation through a kind of alchemical process:

yathā kāñcanatāṁ yāti
kāṁsyaṁ rasa-vidhānataḥ
tathā dīkṣā-vidhānena
dvijatvaṁ jāyate nṛṇām

> Just as it is possible to transform base metal into gold through an alchemical process, so an ordinary human being becomes twice-born by taking initiation.

In Jagannath Puri, Sri Chaitanya Mahaprabhu told Srila Sanatana Goswami:

dīkṣā kāle bhakta kare ātma samarpaṇa
sei kāle kṛṣṇa tāre kare ātma sama
sei deha kare tāra cid ānanda maya
aprākṛta dehe tāṅra caraṇa bhajaya

> At the time of initiation, when a devotee surrenders to the spiritual master, Krishna makes him equal to Himself. He transforms the devotee's body into spiritual substance; the devotee then worships the Lord in that spiritualized body. (CC 3.4.192–93)

In the delineation of *bhāgavata-dharma* in *Śrīmad Bhāgavatam*'s Seventh Canto, Prahlada states (in text 7.7.31) that by serving the spiritual master and offering everything to him, one can quickly attain *rati*, or *prema*.

There are many, many statements in the Vedic scriptures that stress the importance of taking a spiritual master, and that only a person who has taken shelter of a spiritual master can be said to know the Supreme

Truth. Numerous such verses have been quoted in the *Hari-bhakti-vilāsa*. Without becoming initiated by a *sad-guru*, one is not authorized to worship the Lord's Deity form.

The *Viṣṇu-yāmala* (as quoted in HBV 2.9) glorifies initiation:

divyaṁ jñānaṁ yato dadyāt
kuryāt pāpasya saṅkṣayam
tasmād dīkṣeti sā proktā
deśikais tattva kovidaiḥ

> Those who are expert in the study of the revealed scriptures consider *dīkṣā* the process that gives one transcendental knowledge and causes one's sinful reactions to be destroyed.

As mentioned, the *Hari-bhakti-vilāsa* (2.12) quotes the *Tattva-sāgara*:

yathā kāñcanatāṁ yāti
kāṁsyaṁ rasa vidhānataḥ
tathā dīkṣā vidhānena
dvijatvaṁ jāyate nṛṇām

> Just as bell metal turns into gold when touched by mercury, a person becomes twice-born through the process of initiation.

Just as an alchemical process transforms bell metal into gold by combining it with mercury, so initiation turns every human being (*sarveṣām eva*) into a twice-born (*dvijatva*) *brāhmaṇa*. The analogy indicates that just as an alchemist knows the alchemical processes that allow him to transform brass into gold, so a realized spiritual master has the requisite knowledge of the alchemy of devotion and can therefore transform a disciple into a *brāhmaṇa* through initiation.

The *Hari-bhakti-vilāsa* is the king of Vaishnava scriptures dealing with the rules for behavior. At the very beginning of this book, the rules for *dīkṣā* are given based on the *Krama-dīpikā*, a work by Keshavacharya. The *Hari-bhakti-vilāsa* (2.2) quotes this work as saying:

vinā dīkṣāṁ hi pūjāyāṁ
nādhikāro'sti karhicit

> Without being initiated, no one has the right to engage in Deity worship.

In the *Āgamas* it is said that just as a *brāhmaṇa* cannot study the Vedas or perform other duties related to a *brāhmaṇa's* dharma before receiving the sacred thread, so a person who has not been initiated has no right to engage in Deity worship. For this reason, the expression *śiva-saṁstuta* ("praised by Lord Shiva" or "auspiciously praised.") is used to describe those who are initiated. Both the *Hari-bhakti-vilāsa* (2.3–4) and the *Bhakti-sandarbha* (283) state:

tathātrādīkṣitānāṁ tu
mantra devārcanādiṣu
nādhikāro'sty ataḥ kuryād
ātmānaṁ śiva saṁstutam

> A person who has not received Vaishnava initiation has no authority to chant the mantra or worship the Deity form of the Lord. Therefore one should take initiation, by which he will become praised even by Lord Śiva.

The words *śiva-saṁstutam* indicate that anyone who takes initiation becomes a Vaishnava and an object of praise to the best of Vaishnavas, Shiva himself. This is because worship of Vishnu is superior even even to the worship of Shiva.

There is a verse that states: "Anyone who eats without having first offered his food to the *śālagrāma-śilā* will for eons be repeatedly born as a worm in the stool of outcastes and other lower human beings." Texts such as this indicate that worship of the Deity is absolutely necessary, and since one cannot engage in Deity worship without first having been initiated, they also establish the absolute necessity of initiation. Since worship of the *śālagrāma-śilā* is given a prominent place among the various types of service offered to the Lord, all other types of devotional activities are indicated by extension. In other words, initiation is necessary for one to become eligible for all devotional practices.[2]

The need for initiation is further supported by the *Skanda Purāṇa*, (quoted in HBV 2.5) in the conversation between Rukmangada and Mohini:

te narāḥ paśavo loke
kiṁ teṣāṁ jīvane phalam
yair na labdhā harer dīkṣā
nārcito vā janārdanaḥ

> Those human beings who have not been initiated into the service of Lord Hari and have never worshiped Him are comparable to animals. What is the value of their lives?

This verse also confirms that without first being initiated, one cannot possibly engage in worship of the Deity. The *Brahma-yāmala* (quoted in HBV 2.6) adds:

---

[2] *śiva-saṁstutaṁ dīkṣitam ity arthaḥ. pradhānatvena śrī-viṣṇu-dīkṣā-grahaṇāt śrī-śivasyāpi samyak-stuti-viṣayam iti bhāvaḥ. evaṁ ca dīkṣāṁ vinā pūjāyām anadhikārāt, tathā —śālagrāma-śilā-pūjāṁ vinā yo'śnāti kiñcana | sa cāṇḍālādi-viṣṭhāyām ākalpaṁ jāyate kṛmiḥ || ity ādi vacanair pūjāyāś cāvaśyakatvād dīkṣāyā nityatvaṁ sidhyati. śrī-śālagrām-śilādhiṣṭhānaṁ vargeṣu mukhyatvāt sarvāṇy eva bhagavad-adhiṣṭhānāny upalakṣayati. nityatvam eva brahma-vacanena ca sādhayati te narā iti. janārdano yair nārcita iti dīkṣāṁ vinārcanāsiddheḥ.* (Sanatana Goswami, Dig-darśanī)

adikṣitasya vāmoru
kṛtaṁ sarvaṁ nirarthakam
paśu-yonim avāpnoti
dīkṣā-virahito janaḥ

> All the activities of the noninitiated are in vain. One who is not properly initiated will be reborn as an animal.

The *Viṣṇu-yāmala* (quoted in HBV 2.7) further specifies:

snehād vā lobhato vāpi
yo gṛhṇīyād adīkṣayā
tasmin gurau sa-śiṣye tu
devatā-śāpa āpatet

> If out of affection or greed one takes a disciple without following the initiation rituals, then both he and his disciple are subjected to the curses of all the gods.

Sanatana Goswami writes in his commentary that *devatā-śāpaḥ* can mean either the curses of all the gods or the curse of the specific Deity of one's mantra. He then discusses, again, the need for initiation.

The question is sometimes asked, "Scriptures glorify Deity worship by saying that even careless or minimal performance of it yields great benefits. If this is so, why then do we have all this enthusiasm for initiation? Why is it necessary?" The *Hari-bhakti-vilāsa* (2.8) responds:[3]

avijñāya vidhānoktāṁ
hari-pūjā-vidhi-kriyām
kurvan bhaktyā samāpnoti
śata-bhāgaṁ vidhānataḥ

---

[3] *nanu, yathā kathañcid bhagavad-arcanena mahā-phalaṁ śrūyate, ato guroḥ sakāśād dīkṣā-grahaṇe ko'yam āgrahaḥ? tatrāha—avijñāyeti.*

> Even if one engages in Deity worship with devotion, if one does not know the rules for such worship, he will only get one-hundredth a part of the results.

Sanatana Goswami comments:

> One who does not learn, or take care to learn, from the guru the methods of worshiping Lord Hari as they have been handed down by previous instructors, and simply follows the general instruction to worship the Deity with devotion will only get a hundredth part of the benefits that would come to one who did so in following the guru and his directives. The meaning is that if one shows indifference to the spiritual master and the path shown by the previous *ācāryas,* he will not get the full results of his puja.[4]

For this reason, the *Viṣṇu-yāmala* (quoted in HBV 2.12) goes on to describe the glories of *dīkṣā,* as previously mentioned:

> *yathā kāñcanatāṁ yāti*
> *kāṁsyaṁ rasa vidhānataḥ*
> *tathā dīkṣā vidhānena*
> *dvijatvaṁ jāyate nṛṇām*

> Just as bell metal turns into gold through the correct alchemical process (by touching it with pure mercury), so a person becomes twice-born through the process of initiation.

[4] *haripūjā-vidheḥ kriyānuṣṭhānaṁ vidhānoktāṁ pūrva-pūrvair upadeṣṭṛbhir yathā-vidhy evopadiṣṭāṁ śrī-guru-mukhād avijñāya viśeṣeṇājñātvā, vidhānato bhaktyā kurvann api, śatāṁśānām ekam aṁśaṁ labhate. gurv-anapekṣayā pūrva-pūrva-śiṣṭa-darśita-mārgānādareṇa pūjā-phalaṁ na samyag bhavatīti bhāvaḥ.*

Here, Sanatana Goswami writes: "In this verse, 'a person' (*nṛṇām*) means everyone without restriction (*sarveṣām eva*), and 'twice-born' (*dvijatvam*) means 'a *brāhmaṇa*' (*vipratā*)." This latter equation of *dvijatva* with the status of becoming a *brāhmaṇa* means that it is not like the sacred thread rite, which bestows the status of twice-born not just on *brāhmaṇas* but on *vaiśyas* and *kṣatriyas* as well.

For this reason, in his commentary on *Hari-bhakti-vilāsa* 5.454, Sanatana Goswami states that even persons of the lower castes can engage in the worship of the *śālagram-śilā* as long as they have been initiated properly by a guru into a *kṛṣṇa-mantra* and have adopted the spiritual practices of *Vaishnavism*.

In the verse on which Sanatana is commenting, Vishnu says:

strī-śūdra-kara-saṁsparśo
vajra-pāta-samo mama

> The touch of a woman or a *śūdra*'s hand is the same as a thunderbolt to Me.

But, Sanatana says, "Through the power of initiation into a *viṣṇu-mantra*, *śūdras* and other lowborn humans attain the same status as *brāhmaṇas*."[5] Therefore the above verse is only applicable to uninitiated women and *śūdras*. "Those among the *śūdras* or outcastes who have become Vaishnavas are not to be named according to their mundane caste, for Lord Krishna said to Uddhava, 'Devotion fixed on Me purifies even a dog-eater of the flaws associated with his birth'" (ŚB 11.14.20).[6]

Sanatana further states, "Therefore, the Vaishnavas are considered to be on the same platform [of purity] as the *brāhmaṇas*."[7] As a result, after taking initiation into a *viṣṇu-mantra*, even *śūdras* or other lowborn per-

---

[5] *bhagavad-dīkṣā-prabhāvena śūdrādīnām api vipra-sāmyaṁ siddham eva.*

[6] *śūdreṣv antyajeṣv api madhye ye vaiṣṇavās te śūdrādayo na kilocyante. bhaktiḥ punāti man-niṣṭhā śvapākān api sambhavāt.*

[7] *ata eva vipraiḥ saha vaiṣṇavānām ekatraiva gaṇanā.*

sons are eligible to worship the *śālagrāma-śilā*. This has been pointed out with great clarity in the scriptures. The essential qualification is devotion. This is why it is said that a lowborn devotee is still better than a *brāhmaṇa* who, although learned in the Vedas and experienced in all the Vedic sacrifices, has no devotion for the Lord. All his learning does not make him better than the lowest *śūdra* in the eyes of the Lord. Sri Chaitanya Mahaprabhu says:

nīca-jāti nahe kṛṣṇa-bhajanera ayogya
sat-kula-vipra nahe bhajanera yogya
je bhaje se baṛa abhakta hīna chāra
kṛṣṇa-bhajane nāhi jāti-kulādi vicāra

> Someone born in a low caste is not disqualified from worshiping Krishna; someone born as a pious *brāhmaṇa* is not especially qualified to worship Him. The person who worships is superior, whereas one who does not is lowly. There is no consideration of birth or background in serving Krishna. (CC 3.4.66–7)

jāti kula saba nirarthaka bujhāite
janmilena haridāsa adhama kulete

> In order to prove to the world that one's caste or family background have no relevance to one's spiritual life, Haridasa took birth in a lowly family. (C.Bh. 1.16.237)

Advaita Acharya told Haridasa Thakur, "Anyone who gives you something to eat does the equivalent of feeding a million *brāhmaṇas*" (*tomāke khāoāile hoy koṭi brāhmaṇa bhojana*)."

To return to the glories of *dīkṣā*: a few more things need to be said. It is generally seen in Indian society that those of the *brāhmaṇa* caste worship the *śālagrāma-śilā* after receiving the sacred thread but without taking

Vaishnavas *dīkṣā*. It is clear that such people do not accept the edicts of the scriptures cited above. Those who have not received a *viṣṇu-mantra* are not eligible to even prepare food for the Deity. Those who act according to their own concocted ideas rather than following the scriptural injunctions are engaged in activities outside their jurisdiction.

Another custom can be observed in *brāhmaṇa* society: even those who have been initiated into something other than one of the *viṣṇu-mantras* claim the right to worship the various forms of Lord Viṣṇu. In fact, one only has the right to worship the particular Deity into whose mantra one has been initiated. That is one's *iṣṭa-devatā*, worshipable object, and one should remain faithful to that Deity.

By way of contrast, since Lord Vishnu is the source of every other god or universal power, His devotees are within their rights to offer the remnants of *viṣṇu-pūjā* to these gods, who are His devotees. Even so, *Śrīmad Bhāgavatam* teaches that just as watering the root of a tree means it is unnecessary to water the leaves and branches, and just as by feeding the stomach one satisfies all the limbs and organs of the body, so one who focuses his attention on bringing pleasure to God will bring satisfaction to the entire world.

mūlete siñcile jala śākhā pallavera bala
śire vāri nahe kāryakārī

> If one waters the root of a plant, the leaves and branches remain healthy. Pouring water on the head of the plant brings it no benefit.[8]

tat tad evācaret karma
hariḥ prīṇāti yena hi
tasmiṁs tuṣṭe jagat tuṣṭaṁ
prīṇite prīṇitaṁ jagat

---

[8] *yathā taror mūla-niṣecanena*
tṛpyanti tat-skandha-bhujopaśākhāḥ
prāṇopahārāc ca yathendriyāṇāṁ
tathaiva sarvārhaṇam acyutejyā (ŚB 4.31.14).

> Engage in those activities that will bring pleasure to Lord Hari. If He is pleased, the whole world is pleased. If He is satisfied, the whole world is satisfied. (*Padma Purāna* 3.61.43)

Krishna is the life of our life and the root of our root, so by seeking to please Him, we bring pleasure to all creatures in the universe from the tiniest bacterium to the creator god, Brahma.

And there is another surprising development in brahminical society that gives cause for lamentation. It has become a general rule for members of the *brāhmaṇa* caste to eat meat, fish, eggs, garlic, onions, and other non-*sattvik* foods, or to smoke cigarettes. Yet still they claim they are fit to worship the Deity. Intoxicants, the slaughterhouse, gambling den, and house of prostitution are the haunts of Kali, the presiding Deity of this fallen age. How can the touch of those who frequent these haunts be felt by the Deity as anything other than a thunderbolt?

Even among the Vaishnavas we see individuals who are engaged in impious activities who continue to wear tulasi beads around their necks and *tilaka* on their foreheads. They even play the *mṛdaṅga* and *kartals* and sing *līlā-kīrtana* or twenty-four-hour *nāma-yajñas*, often showing great enthusiasm for the chanting. Many among them even challenge, "What do any regulations have to do with worshiping the Lord?"

In response, we ask them to kindly examine the following text from the *Chāndogya Upaniṣad* (7.26.2):

āhāra-śuddhau sattva-śuddhiḥ
sattva-śuddhau dhruvā smṛtiḥ

> By purifying our eating habits our existence is purified. When our existence is purified it becomes possible to concentrate the mind.

Meditating on these words from the *śruti*, we conclude that it is necessary to follow the guidelines for *sad-ācāra*, especially in dietary matters, for by purifying our eating habits, our minds will be sanctified, and when the mind is sanctified, it is possible to fix our thoughts on God. But it must be remembered that every sense has its particular object. If Krishna is not somehow connected to each sense activity, we cannot consider that activity fully purified. For instance, *haviṣyānna* is considered a very pure food, but if it is not offered to the Lord, it is impure and unfit for consumption. A Vaishnava follows the scriptural injunctions by only offering Krishna the foods recommended in scripture and taking His remnants as *prasāda*. As Bhaktivinoda Thakur states:

prasāda-sevā karite hoy
sakala prapañca jaya

> By honoring Krishna *prasāda,* one can vanquish the material energy completely.

The worship of the Lord's Deity is one of the essential aspects of devotional practice and should be conducted according to the directives found in scripture. When food has been transformed into *prasāda* by performing the rituals of *arcana*, then it becomes auspicious for everyone to eat.

Therefore we must accept that it is absolutely necessary to take shelter of a guide who is familiar with the injunctions established by the previous saints so that we can learn the standards that are found in the Vaishnava scriptures. The spiritual master who takes pleasure in practicing and in explaining the Vaishnava religion will reveal all the deep secrets of the Lord's worship to his affectionate disciples, clarifying fzzor them what association to avoid, which persons are worthy of association, and the sequence in which to study the devotional texts.

CHAPTER 8

Mantra vs. Holy Name

THE POTENCY OF THE *VIṢṆU-MANTRAS*

The Supreme Lord's *Śaktyāveśa-avatāra*, Vedavyasa, hinted at potency of the Lord's names many centuries ago in the *Padma Purāṇa*:

arcye viṣṇau śilā dhīr guruṣu nara matir
vaiṣṇave jāti buddhir
viṣṇor vā vaiṣṇavānāṁ kali mala mathane
pāda tīrthe'mbu buddhiḥ
śrī viṣṇor nāmni mantre sakala kaluṣa he
śabda sāmānya buddhir
viṣṇau sarveśvareśe tad itara sama dhīr
yasya vā nārakī saḥ

One who thinks the Deity in the temple to be made of wood or stone, who thinks of the spiritual master in the disciplic succession as an ordinary man, who thinks a Vaishnava of the infallible Lord's own clan to belong to a certain caste or creed, or who thinks of *caraṇāmṛta* or Ganges water as ordinary water; one who considers the mantra composed of the Lord's names, which destroys all sins, to be made of ordinary words or considers the Supreme Lord of all lords, Viṣhṇu, equal to an ordinary human being, is taken to be a resident of hell.

Any mantra that reveals the Supreme Lord in His aspect of Vraja sweetness is to be considered superior because the Lord's Vrindavan form is superior to all His other forms, such as those He reveals in *Dwaraka* or *Mathura*. The eighteen-syllable mantra, which is called *sammohana*, is precisely such a mantra and is considered the king of mantras. The *Hari-bhakti-vilāsa* cites a number of scriptures, including the *Gopāla-tāpanī Upaniṣad*, the *Trailokya-sammohana-tantra*, the *Sanat-kumāra-kalpa*, and others, all of which attest to the superiority of this eighteen-syllable mantra.

Śrīmad Bhāgavatam states that all the different portions and plenary portions of the Lord emanate from Krishna, the Supreme Lord. Just as Krishna is clearly the Supreme Person above all other manifestations of God, so too is His mantra supreme above all other mantras. Since Krishna's *līlā* in *Vrindavan*, with its qualities of sweetness and munificence, is superior to the Lord's other pastimes, the mantra, which contains and reveals that *līlā*, is supreme among all mantras.

In the *Trailokya-sammohana-tantra* (quoted in HBV 1.185–86), Mahadeva glorifies the eighteen-syllable mantra to his consort Bhagavati Devi:

yathā cintāmaṇiḥ śreṣṭho yathā gauś ca yathā satī
yathā dvijo yathā gaṅgā tathāsau mantra uttamaḥ
yathāvad akhila-śreṣṭhaṁ yathā śāstraṁ tu vaiṣṇavam
yathā susaṁskṛtā vāṇī tathāsau mantra uttamaḥ
ato mayā sureśāni pratyahaṁ japyate manuḥ
naitena sadṛśaḥ kaścij jagaty asmin carācara

> Just as the philosopher's stone is the best of jewels, just as the cow is the best of beasts, just as Sati is the best among women, just as the *brāhmaṇa* is the best of human beings, and just as the Ganges is the best of rivers, so too is this mantra the best of mantras. Just as the *Vaishnnava* scriptures are the best of all spiritual teachings, and just as Sanskrit is

> supreme among languages, so too is this the best of all mantras. Therefore, O queen of the goddesses, I daily chant this mantra. There is nothing like it in the entire universe.

The *Hari-bhakti-vilāsa* (1.190–91) also quotes the *Sanat-kumāra-kalpa,* which states: "By the grace of this mantra, Indra easily attained his position as king of the demigods. Due to his bad luck, Indra was cursed by Durvasa, but again, through the power of this mantra, he was reinstated to his position."

This mantra is so powerful that it does not need the *puraścaraṇa* or any other customary ritual performance to enhance it. Simply by reciting the mantra, one can attain the desired result. The *Sanat-kumāra-kalpa* (quoted in HBV 1.192) states:

bahunā kim ihoktena puraścaraṇa-sādhanaiḥ
vināpi japa-mātreṇa labhate sarvam īpsitam

> What is the use of all these instructions? Simply by chanting this mantra, even without the strict restrictions of the *puraścaraṇa-vrata,* one can obtain everything one wishes.

PURAŚCARAṆA IN MORE DEPTH

Ordinarily, there are various purifying procedures (*samskaras*) that are prescribed before an initiation in order to purify the mantra and fully invest it with power. According to *Hari-bhakti-vilāsa,* these are ten in number: *janana, jīvana, tāḍana, rodhana, abhiṣeka, vimalīkaraṇa, āpyāyana, tarpaṇa, dīpana,* and *gopana.*[1] However, *kṛṣṇa-mantras* in general are so powerful that there is no need for any of these *saṁskāras*: *balitvāt kṛṣṇa-mantrāṇāṁ saṁskārāpekṣaṇaṁ na hi.*

However, even though the *saṁskāras* are deemed unnecessary, the *Hari-bhakti-vilāsa* does give an extensive description of the *puraś-*

[1] These *saṁskāras* are explained at length in HBV 1.228ff.

caraṇa observance in its seventeeth chapter. The *Agastya-saṁhitā* (as quoted in HBV 17.11) defines *puraścaraṇa*: There are five aspects to the *puraścaraṇa* observance: puja three times a day, constant chanting of *japa*, oblations of water, a daily fire sacrifice, and feeding of *brāhmaṇas*.

According to these directions, one should surrender to guru, Gauranga, and Radha- Krishna, performing a puja with sixteen ingredients. Then, taking the guru's permission, at an auspicious moment one should begin to recite his mantra. There is a specific mantra (*saṅkalpa*) a devotee should utter as a promise to see his vow to completion:

adyāṣṭādaśākṣara-saṁmohana-mantrasya siddhi-kāma iyat-sāṅkhya -japa-tad-daśāṁśāmukadravyaka-homa[2]*-tad-daśāṁśāṁśāmuka-tarpaṇa-tad-daśāṁśa-brāhmaṇa-bhojanātmaka-puraścaraṇaṁ kariṣye.*

> Starting today, I will perform a *puraścaraṇa* for the sake of achieving perfection in my chanting of the eighteen-syllabled *sammohana-mantra*. Each day, I will chant [number] of mantras. I will offer one-tenth that many oblations of [object to be specified] into the fire sacrifice. I will perform one-tenth that many oblations of holy water, and will feed one-tenth that number of *brāhmaṇas*.

THE SHORTER VERSION OF *PURAŚCARAṆA*

To perform the *puraścaraṇa* fully and conscientiously is not easy for people like ourselves whose minds are flickering, so the *Hari-bhakti-vilāsa* offers a shorter version of the *puraścaraṇa*: faithful service to the guru. I have reproduced these verses of the *Hari-bhakti-vilāsa* (17.241–43) here for the special attention of the *sādhaka*:

[2] The words *amuka-dravyaka* ("this certain item") are to be replaced by the items one will be offering into the fire. Similarly, the word *iyat* should be replaced by the exact number of mantras one intends to chant each day.

tato mantra-prasiddhy-arthaṁ
guruṁ sampūjya toṣayet
evaṁ ca mantra-siddhiḥ syāt
devatā ca prasīdati

In order to achieve the perfection of the mantra, one should satisfy the guru with appropriate acts of worship. By so doing, not only will one achieve the goal of perfecting the mantra, but the Deity will also be pleased with him. (HBV 17.238)

athavā devatā-rūpaṁ guruṁ dhyātvā pratoṣayet
tasya cchāyānusārī syād bhakti-yuktena cetasā
guru-mūlam idaṁ sarvaṁ tasmān nityaṁ guruṁ bhajet
puraścaraṇa-hīno'pi mantrī siddhyen na saṁśayaḥ

On the other hand, one may satisfy the guru by meditating on him as a form of the Deity. The disciple should follow the guru like a shadow, his thoughts filled with devotion. One should constantly worship the guru in the consciousness that he is the basis of all one's spiritual activities. Even if the initiated devotee does not perform the *puraścaraṇa* according to the detailed rules described above, he can still attain perfection through service to the guru. Of this there can be no doubt.

yathā siddha-rasa-sparśāt tāmraṁ bhavati kāñcanam
sannidhānād guror eva śiṣyo viṣṇumayo bhavet

Just as copper becomes gold through the touch of specially treated mercury, so does a disciple take on the qualities of Vishnu through the association of his guru.

In his commentaries to these verses, Srila Sanatana Goswami writes, "By pleasing the guru alone one can attain all the benefits of *puraścaraṇa* (*kevalaṁ śrī-guru-prasādenaiva puraścaraṇa-siddhiḥ syāt*)."

According to the *Hari-bhakti-vilāsa*, one should chant the mantra after worshiping the Deity with puja three times a day. Failing that, one should do it twice a day, or at least once. If the *sādhaka* lives in the same village as the guru, he should go daily to pay homage to him. One should always associate with devotees, etc.

yasya deve ca mantre ca
gurau triṣv api niścalā
na vyavacchidyate buddhis
tasya siddhir adūrataḥ

mantrātmā devatā jñeyā
devatā guru-rūpiṇī
teṣāṁ bhedo na kartavyo
yadīcched iṣṭam ātmanaḥ

> One is not far from perfection if his intelligence is fixed unwaveringly in the Deity, the mantra, and the guru. The soul of the mantra is the Deity. The Deity is manifest in the form of the guru. One should not make a distinction between these three if he wishes to obtain his heart's desire. (HBV 17.65-66)

In the *Seventh Canto* of the *Śrīmad Bhāgavatam*, it is similarly stated that one obtains the grace of the Lord through faithful and devoted service to the guru. Krishna said the same thing to his friend Sudama Vipra.

nāham ijyā-prajātibhyāṁ
tapasopaśamena ca
tuṣyeyaṁ sarva-bhūtātmā
guru-śuśrūṣayā yathā

> I, the soul of all beings, am not as pleased by the performance of the prescribed duties of the four *āśramas*, i.e., sacrifices, service to the family, austerities and renunciation, as I am by service to the guru. (ŚB 10.80.34)

Even though we have obtained such a powerful mantra from Sri Gurudeva, due to the lack of constancy and the mercy of the spiritual master, we are not able to perceive the great potency that lies dormant in the mantra. We saw that even a non-*brāhmaṇa* who did not follow the fundamental regulative principles of spiritual life was still able to recite a mantra with such potency that a snake's body was forced out of a dense jungle and made to return to the house where it had bitten a child, making it counteract its own bite. Should those who have received the mantra in a pure disciplic succession be unable to perceive the power that lies within it? Of course not.

Devotion has the power to attract Sri Krishna. By the grace of Krishna's internal potency, Srimati Radharani, one can expect to receive the grace of the goddess of devotion. The guru is nondifferent from Srimati Radharani, so by his grace one can directly experience the Lord's statements, which tell us that one can know Him only by devotion (*bhaktyāham ekayā grāhyaḥ, bhaktyā mām abhijānāti*).

THE DISTINCTION BETWEEN THE MANTRA AND THE HOLY NAME

In His instructions to Prakashananda Saraswati, Mahaprabhu made the following distinction between the mantra (by which I mean the initiation mantra) and the Holy Name (which I am defining here as the *mahā-mantra*):

kṛṣṇa mantra haite habe saṁsāra mocana
kṛṣṇa nāma haite pābe kṛṣṇera caraṇa

> By chanting the *kṛṣṇa-mantra* one will be liberated from material existence. And by chanting Krishna's name, one will attain His lotus feet. (CC 1.7.73)

This world is based on the principle of accepting and rejecting sense objects. One who fixes his mind on his mantra is liberated from such entanglement. Then, by chanting the Holy Names in *saṅkīrtana,* one attains direct service to the Lord's lotus feet.

kṛṣṇa nāma-mahā-mantrera ei ta svabhāva
je jape tāra kṛṣṇe upajaya bhāva

> The nature of the *mahā-mantra* of Krishna's names is such that whoever chants it develops feelings for Krishna. (CC 1.7.83)

kṛṣṇa nāmera phala premā sarva śāstre kaya

> All scriptures say that the fruit of chanting the Holy Names is to develop love for Krishna. (CC 1.7.86)

The Lord Himself states that all perfections come by the grace of the Holy Name (*ihā haite sarva siddhi haibe sabāra*). But most importantly, the fifth and ultimate goal of human life, love for Krishna, arises from the chanting of the Lord's names:

kṛṣṇa-viṣayaka prema parama puruṣārtha
jāra āge tṛṇa-tulya cāri puruṣārtha
pañcama puruṣārtha premānandāmṛtasindhu
mokṣādi ānanda jāra nahe eka bindu

> Love for Krishna is the supreme goal of human life or *puruṣārtha*. The other four goals of life are insignificant in comparison to it. This fifth goal of life, *prema,* is like an ocean of ecstatic nectar. In comparison, the

> joys derived from dharma, *artha, kāma,* and *mokṣa* are nothing more than a drop of water. (CC 1.7.84–5)

All these scriptural quotations show that the ultimate achievement of a devotee who takes shelter of the Holy Name is love for Krishna, or *kṛṣṇa-prema*. In their heart of hearts, saintly persons constantly behold the inconceivably beautiful blackish form of the son of Yashoda and His inconceivable, innumerable attributes with the eye of devotion tinged with the salve of love.[3]

PAÑCARĀTRIKA AND *BHĀGAVATA* APPROACHES TO DEVOTIONAL SERVICE

The Supreme Lord, the son of the king of Vraja, is influenced only by the love of pure devotees—by those whose only desire is to bring pleasure to His transcendental senses. Most people engage in sinful activities, pushed by their material bodies, and so their minds are disturbed. In the *Pañcarātra* school, importance is given to Deity worship, preceded by initiation into the mantra, because Deity worship helps diminish the focus on the body and mind and fix it on Krishna. However, both the *Pañcarātra* and the *Bhāgavatam* describe the ultimate goal as pure devotional service. The essence of the *Bhāgavatam* is summarized by Rupa Goswami in the *Bhakti-rasāmṛta-sindhu* (1.1.11, quoted in CC 2.19.167):

anyābhilāṣitā śūnyaṁ
jñāna karmādy anāvṛtam
ānukūlyena kṛṣṇānu-
śīlanaṁ bhaktir uttamā

[3] *premāñjana cchurita bhakti vilocanena*
santaḥ sadaiva hṛdayeṣu vilokayanti
yaṁ śyāmasundaram acintya guṇa svarūpaṁ
govindam ādi puruṣaṁ tam ahaṁ bhajāmi

> The highest category of devotion is defined as the culture of a favorable attitude toward Krishna devoid of all material desires and without adulteration by monistic philosophy or fruitive action.

Krishna Das Kaviraj Goswami explains in the next verse (2.19.168) of the *Caitanya-caritāmṛta*:

> *anya vāñchā anya pūjā chāṛi jñāna karma*
> *ānukūlye sarvendriye kṛṣṇānuśīlana*

> A devotee must engage all his senses in the cultivation of favorable Krishna consciousness. He must give up all other desires, the worship of other gods, the cultivation of monistic knowledge, and fruitive activities.

But Rupa goes on to support this definition of bhakti with a verse from the *Nārada Pañcarātra* (given in BRS 1.1.12 and quoted in CC 2.19.170):

> *sarvopādhi vinirmuktaṁ*
> *tat paratvena nirmalam*
> *hṛṣīkeṇa hṛṣīkeśa*
> *sevanaṁ bhaktir ucyate*

> Bhakti is defined as the engagement of the senses in the service of the proprietor of the senses. This service has to be free from any contamination from identification with the body and pure by being exclusively fixed on Him.

Here the primary characteristic of devotion is the engagement of the senses in the service of the Lord of the senses. This devotion has two characteristics, both of which are considered secondary—that is, contingent on its proper execution. The first is that bhakti should be free from *upādhi* (identification with selfish interests), and the second is that it become pure by one becoming absolutely fixed on the Lord alone. Thus the two definitions are parallel to one another. From this practice of the *abhidheya*, or devotional service, one arrives at the ultimate goal, the *prayojana* of *prema*.

ei śuddha-bhakti ihā haite premā haya
pañcarātre bhāgavate ei lakṣaṇa kaya

> These activities are called *śuddha-bhakti*, pure devotional service. If one renders pure devotional service, he develops his original love for Krishna in due course of time. The characteristics of that love have been described in the *Pañcarātras* and in *Śrīmad Bhāgavatam*. (CC 2.19.169)

Thus although the characteristics of pure devotional service are identical according to both those on the *Pañcarātra* and the *Bhāgavata* paths, there is some difference in the main practices of each. Here, the chanting of the mantra and Deity worship are associated with the *Pañcarātra* system and *Dvapara Yuga*, while the chanting of the Holy Names is an ecstatic practice associated with the *bhāgavatas* and is particularly appropriate to the age of Kali. This is confirmed by Madhvacharya in a verse found in his commentary on the *Maṇḍūkya Upaniṣad*:

dvāparīyair janair viṣṇuḥ
pañcarātraiś ca kevalam
kalau tu nāma-mātreṇa
pūjyate bhagavān hariḥ

> The Supreme Lord Vishnu was worshiped according to the *Pañcarātra* method alone in the *Dvapara Yuga*; in the Age of Kali, He is worshiped exclusively by the chanting of the Holy Name.

THE IMPORTANCE OF CHANTING THE HOLY NAMES

There are many verses in the *Bhāgavatam* that attest to the preeminence of the three principal devotional activities, hearing, chanting, and remembering:

tasmād ekena manasā
bhagavān sātvatāṁ patiḥ
śrotavyaḥ kīrtitavyaś ca
dhyeyaḥ pūjyaś ca nityadā

Therefore, one should constantly hear about, glorify, meditate on, and worship the Supreme Lord, the protector of the devotees, with single-minded concentration. (ŚB 1.12.14)

tasmāt sarvātmanā rājan
hariḥ sarvatra sarvadā
śrotavyaḥ kīrtitavyaś ca
smartavyo bhagavān nṛṇām

Therefore, O King, wherever one may be, the Supreme Lord Hari should always be talked about, glorified, and remembered with full concentration. (ŚB 2.2.36)

tasmād bhārata sarvātmā
bhagavān īśvaro hariḥ
śrotavyaḥ kīrtitavyaś ca
smartavyaś cecchatābhayam

O scion of the Bharata dynasty! One who desires fearlessness should hear about, glorify, and remember the Supreme Lord Hari, the soul of all beings and the Supreme Controller, for He alone steals away all one's miseries. (ŚB 2.1.5)

In the final analysis, despite this emphasis on all three types of devotional activity, the *Bhāgavatam* singles out kirtan, glorifying the Lord by chanting His names, as supreme.

etan nirvidyamānānām
icchatām akuto-bhayam
yogināṁ nṛpa nirṇītaṁ
harer nāmānukīrtanam

> O King, it has been ascertained that for those yogis who are indifferent to material pleasures and who desire complete fearlessness, the best path is constant chanting of the Holy Name of the Lord. (ŚB 2.1.11)

nāma-saṅkīrtanaṁ yasya
sarva-pāpa-praṇāśanaṁ
praṇāmo duḥkha-śamanas
taṁ namāmi hariṁ param

> I bow down to the Supreme Lord Hari, the chanting of whose name results in the destruction of all sin and by paying homage to whom all miseries are quieted. (ŚB 12.13.23)

Sri Chaitanya Mahaprabhu confirms these statements from the *Bhāgavatam*:

bhajanera madhye śreṣṭha nava-vidhā bhakti
kṛṣṇa-prema, kṛṣṇa dite dhare mahā-śakti
tāra madhye sarva śreṣṭha nāma-saṅkīrtana
niraparādhe nāma laile pāya prema-dhana

> Of the many ways to execute devotional service, there are nine varieties that are considered the best,

> for they possess a great capacity to deliver love for Krishna and thus Krishna Himself. Of these nine processes of devotional service, the most important is the chanting of the Lord's Holy Name, for if one chants without committing offenses he will obtain the treasure of love for the Lord. (CC 3.4.70–1)

> *eka kṛṣṇanāme kare sarvapāpa kṣaya*
> *navavidhā bhakti pūrṇa nāma haite haya*

> Simply by chanting the Holy Name of Krishna, one is relieved from all the reactions of a sinful life. One can complete the nine processes of devotional service simply by chanting the Holy Name. (CC 2.15.107)

In the twelfth chapter of the Bhagavad Gita, it is said that remembering, contemplating, and meditating on the Lord are dependent on inner purification and thus not easily perfected by ordinary people. On the other hand, since *saṅkīrtana* is an activity executed by the external senses, success is within any practitioner's grasp, even the disturbed, persons living in this Kali age.

Śrīmad Bhāgavatam (6.3.22) states that bhakti is primarily executed in the form of *saṅkīrtana*:

> *etāvān eva loke'smin*
> *puṁsāṁ dharmaḥ paraḥ smṛtaḥ*
> *bhakti-yogo bhagavati*
> *tan-nāma-grahaṇādibhiḥ*

> Therefore, the supreme religious activity for people in this world is devotional service to the Lord, performed by such acts as repeating His divine names.

The definition of kirtan has been given in the *Bhakti-rasāmṛta-sindhu* (1.2.145) as "the audible glorification of the Lord's names, attributes, and activities, etc." (*nāma-līlā-guṇādīnām uccair bhāṣaṇaṁ tu kīrtanam).* Moreover, the best type of kirtan, also spoken of in the *Bhāgavatam* and taught by the Goswamis, such as Sri Sanatana, Sri Rupa, and Sri Jiva, is the chanting of the Holy Name.

THE CHANTING OF THE HOLY NAMES IS THE RELIGIOUS PRINCIPLE FOR THIS AGE

Mahaprabhu and all His associates clearly state that among all the devotional practices, the chanting of the Holy Names is the most important. *Harināma-saṅkīrtana* has nothing other than love for Krishna as its goal. Religiosity, material prosperity, sense enjoyment, and liberation are not to be achieved through the chanting of the Holy Name. In the age of Kali, the Holy Name is the essence of all religious activities and the essence of all mantras. There are many statements in the scriptures that support this truth:

nāma vinā kali-kāle nāhi āra dharma
sarva-mantra-sāra nāma ei śāstra marma

> In the age of Kali, there is no religious activity other than the chanting of the Holy Names. The Holy Name is the essence of all mantras. (CC 1.7.74)

A number of verses from the *Twelfth Canto* of *Śrīmad Bhāgavatam* emphasize the chanting of the Holy Names in this Age of Kali.

kaler doṣanidhe rājann
asti hy eko mahān guṇaḥ
kīrtanād eva kṛṣṇasya
muktasaṅgaḥ paraṁ vrajet

> O King! The age of Kali is an ocean of faults, but it contains one great virtue: simply by chanting the

names of Krishna one becomes liberated and goes to the supreme abode. (ŚB 12.3.51)

kṛte yad dhyāyato viṣṇuṁ
tretāyāṁ yajato makhaiḥ
dvāpare paricaryāyāṁ
kalau tadd harikīrtanāt

That which is achieved in Satya Yuga by meditation on Vishnu, in Treta Yuga by performing fire sacrifices, and in Dvapara Yuga by Deity worship, is attained in Kali Yuga by chanting the name and glories of Hari. (ŚB 12.3.52)

Narada Muni, the seer of the gods, clearly states that in the age of Kali there is no other means of attaining perfection:

harer nāma harer nāma
harer nāmaiva kevalam
kalau nāsty eva nāsty eva
nāsty eva gatir anyathā

In this age of quarrel and hypocrisy the only means of deliverance is the chanting of the Holy Names of the Lord. There is no other way, there is no other way, there is no other way. (*Bṛhan-nāradīya Purāṇa,* quoted in CC 1.7.76)

Mahaprabhu explains this verse to Prakashananda Saraswati:

kalikāle nāmarūpe kṛṣṇaavatāra
nāma haite haya sarvajagatnistāra
dārḍhya lāgi harer nāmaukti tinavāra
jaḍa loka bujhāite punaḥ evakāra
kevalaśabde punarapi niścayakaraṇa

jñāna yoga tapa karmādi nivāraṇa
anyathā je māne tāra nāhika nistāra
nāhi nāhi nāhi e tina evakāra

> In this Age of Kali, Krishna has incarnated in the form of His Holy Name (the Hare Krishna *mahā-mantra*). The whole world will be delivered through the grace of the Holy Name. In order to vigorously affirm this, Narada's verse repeats the words *harer nāma* three times. Then, just to make it clear for the really dull, it stresses the same words with *eva,* "certainly." This assertion is further strengthened by the use of the word *kevala,* "alone," which prohibits all other processes, such as cultivation of knowledge, practice of mystic yoga, performance of austerities, and fruitive activities. Then, just to make sure that it is clear that no one who disregards this teaching will achieve salvation, the words "there is no other way" are repeated thrice. (CC 1.17.22–5)

The importance of the *mahā-mantra* for the age of Kali has been emphasized in the *Kali-santarana Upaniṣad*:

hare kṛṣṇa hare kṛṣṇa
kṛṣṇa kṛṣṇa hare hare
hare rāma hare rāma
rāma rāma hare hare

iti ṣoḍaśakaṁ nāmnāṁ
kalikalmaṣanāśanam
nātaḥ paratаropāyaḥ
sarvavedeṣu dṛśyate

> The sixteen names of the *mahā-mantra* destroy the pollution of this age of Kali. Throughout the entire

body of Vedic literature one cannot find a more sublime means of spiritual religion.

MAHAPRABHU APPEARED TO PREACH THE CHANTING OF THE HOLY NAMES

Sri Chaitanya Mahaprabhu, the incarnation of the Lord in Kali Yuga, came primarily to teach the process of devotional service:

avatari caitanya kaila dharmapracāraṇa
kalikāle dharma kṛṣṇanāmasaṅkīrtana
saṅkīrtanayajñe tāṅre kare ārādhana
sei ta sumedhā āra kalihatajana

Sri Chaitanya Mahaprabhu descended to preach religious principles. In the age of Kali, the only religious principle is the chanting of the Holy Names of Lord Krishna. Anyone who worships the Lord by the sacrifice of the Holy Name is most intelligent. As for the rest, they have been defeated by the spirit of the age of quarrel. (CC 2.11.98–9)

The significance of His appearance to teach the Holy Names is further underlined by *Śrīmad Bhāgavatam* (11.5.32):

kṛṣṇa-varṇaṁ tviṣā kṛṣṇaṁ
sāṅgopāṅgāstra-pārṣadam
yajñaiḥ saṅkīrtana-prāyair
yajanti hi sumedhasaḥ

In the age of Kali, the golden Lord, on whose lips the name of Krishna always remains, appears in the company of His expansions, portions, weapons, and associates. Those who are very intelligent will worship Him through the sacrifice of congregational glorification (*saṅkīrtana-yajña*).

Mahaprabhu had the further purpose of bestowing the most elevated and effulgent kind of spiritual experience on the entire world. One day, as He was thinking how the living beings of the world could be made eligible to enter this experience, He put His arms around Swarupa Damodara and Ramananda Ray, His closest companions, and said with great jubilation:

harṣe prabhu kahena śuna svarūparāmarāya
nāma-saṅkīrtana kalau parama upāya
saṅkīrtana-yajñe kalau kṛṣṇa-ārādhana
sei ta sumedhā pāya kṛṣṇera caraṇa
nāma-saṅkīrtana haite sarvānartha-nāśa
sarva-śubhodaya, kṛṣṇa-premera ullāsa

> My dear Swarupa Damodara and Ramananda Ray, know from Me that chanting of the Holy Names is the most feasible means of salvation in this age of Kali. In this age of Kali, the process of worshiping Krishna is to perform sacrifice by chanting the Holy Name of the Lord. One who does so is certainly very intelligent, and he attains shelter at the lotus feet of Krishna. Simply by chanting the Holy Name of Lord Krishna, one can be freed from all undesirable habits. This is the means of awakening all good fortune and initiating the flow of waves of love for Krishna. (CC 3.20.8–9, 11)

From this statement we can easily understand that the Lord invested some special powers in the chanting of His Holy Names in this particularly fortunate age of Kali. This special power is its capacity to awaken affectionate attachment, *rāga*, for the Lord. This is thus the best process by which one can develop *rāga-bhakti*, or devotional service in spontaneous affection.

The scriptures ordinarily describe three styles of chanting a mantra: the *vācika*, or vocal chanting; the *upāṁśu*, in which one whispers the mantra in such a way that only oneself can hear it; the *mānasika*, in which one chants mentally. Each of these is said to be superior to the one that precedes it. Nevertheless, a mantra is *japa*, that is, to be muttered or recited silently, only when one tries to fulfill the obligation of chanting it a certain number of times. Generally, there is no scriptural injunction to chant a mantra without counting the number of times one chants it. In the case of the *mahā-mantra*, however, this particular distinction is not made. One can chant both within the constraints of a daily vowed quota or outside such constraints. There are no restrictions in this matter, just as there are none concerning the times of day when one may chant or one's state of purification. Mahaprabhu said this in His *Śikṣāṣṭaka*: *niyamitaḥ smaraṇe na kālaḥ*.

ki bhojane ki śayane kibā jāgaraṇe
aharniśa cinta kṛṣṇa balaha vadane

> Think of Krishna and utter His names both day and night, whether you are eating, lying down, or engaged in your waking activities.

sarva kṣaṇa bala ithe vidhi nāhi āra

> The only rule is to chant the Holy Name always. There is no other requirement.

Elsewhere it is said:

na deśa-niyamas tatra na kāla-niyamas tathā
nocchiṣṭādau nimeṣo'sti śrī-harer nāmni lubdhaka

> O hunter! There are no rules governing the time or place where one may chant the Holy Name of the Lord. Nor is it necessary for one to be in a state of

> ritual purity. One can chant even if one's hands or mouth are unwashed after eating, sleeping, or going to the toilet.

We must remember that the sixteen names and thirty-two syllables of the Hare Krishna mantra are called the *mahā-mantra* and their power is special.

> *kṛṣṇa-nāma mahā-mantrera ei ta svabhāva*
> *jei jape tāra kṛṣṇe upajaye bhāva*

> This is the nature of the *mahā-mantra* consisting of Krishna's names. Whoever recites it develops ecstatic feeling for Krishna. (CC 1.7.83)

In the *Anubhāṣya* on this verse, Srila Prabhupada writes:

> Some foolish people do not understand that the formula consisting of sixteen names and thirty-two syllables is the *mahā-mantra*. Taking it to be another, ordinary mantra that should be muttered silently or mentally, they artificially claim that it should not be chanted aloud or sung. Those who have attained love for Krishna engage in loud chanting of these names in the company of other devotees. By such singing of the *mahā-mantra*, everyone in the world is initiated into the Holy Name. Anyone who sings the names aloud will simultaneously hear and remember the name. Because Krishna and His name are not different from each other, a tendency to serve the Lord will awaken in anyone who recites His names in *japa*. Someone who has attained the stage of *bhāva* is no longer polluted by the contaminations resulting from bondage within ignorance. Rather, his personal relationship with the Lord has been awakened within him and he relishes the combination of ingredients which make up the composition of divine mellows (*rasa*). As this stage of ecstatic feeling, *bhāva*, intensifies, it becomes *prema*. The sixteen names

> and thirty-two-syllable formula consisting of Krishna's names is the great formula. All the other mantras listed in the *Pañcarātra* literature are considered to be just mantras. The Holy Names of the Lord are known as the *mahā-mantra*.

The *Caitanya-caritāmṛta* (2.15.108) states:

dīkṣā puraścaryā vidhi apekṣā nā kare
jihvā sparśe ācaṇḍāle sabāre uddhāre

> All perfections come from the Holy Name. It does not require initiation into it or an observance of *puraścaraṇa*. As soon as the Holy Name touches the tongue of even the lowest class of human, it delivers him immediately.

These statements show that the *mahā-mantra* of the Holy Names is more potent than any other mantra, including the eighteen-syllable *Gopala mantra*. One who received initiation into the Gopala mantra is given the right to practice the *vidhi-mārga*, whereas someone who chants the *mahā-mantra*, whether initiated or not, is given the qualifications for all situations in life. In particular, a practitioner of the *rāgānugā* path quickly attains his desired goal in Vraja by taking shelter of the worship of the Holy Name. For one on the *vidhi-mārga* or *arcana-mārga*, the ecstatic mood of Vraja is vague and distant. Spiritual practices on the *vidhi-mārga* have no power to bestow this mood: *Vidhi-mārge vraja-bhāva pāite nāhi śakti.*

IF THE NAME IS SO POWERFUL, WHY DO WE NEED INITIATION?

Jiva Goswami responds to the question of why the *dīkṣā-mantra* and initiation are both necessary if the Holy Name has such great purificatory power and so many other advantages. The *Bhakti-sandarbha* (285) states:

> Now if you say, "The *dīkṣā-mantra* itself consists of names of the Lord. Added to that are words indicating submission, such

> as *namaḥ* or *svāhā*, etc., through which Narada and other seers, by the desire of the Lord, have endowed the mantra with some special potency. Furthermore, they are capable of awakening a specific personal relationship with the Lord. [Of all these ingredients] in the mantra, the names of the Lord alone are capable of independently giving the mantra's reciter the supreme goal of life [i.e., *prema*]. Thus we find that in the mantra there is an even greater power than can be found in the name. In view of all these considerations, why is there a necessity for initiation?"
>
> The answer is that there is no fundamental necessity for initiation. Nevertheless, because people are by nature generally caught up in bad habits and are unable to concentrate due to bodily associations, etc., the great seers, such as Narada and others, have on occasion established some fundamental regulations here and there calling for the performance of Deity worship (*arcana-mārga*) in order to reduce such bad habits and lack of concentration. For this reason, the scriptures call for the performance of penances as atonement for the nonperformance of Deity worship. Where neither of these faults (of the bodily and mental aberrations) are prominent, there is no need for initiation.[4]

Srila Prabhupada elaborates in his *Anubhāṣya* (1.7.72–4): "The conditioned soul absolutely must achieve perfection in the mantra in order to rid himself of his material ego and his tendency for sense gratification. The word *namaḥ* is interpreted as follows: ma means *ahaṅkāra*; *na* negates egoism. Thus, by perfecting the chanting of the mantra (*mantra-siddhi*), one gains a direct experience of the transcendent reality. Sri Rupa Goswami sings in his *Nāmāṣṭaka*, addressing the Holy Name: *ayi*

---

[4] *nanu bhagavannāmātmakā eva mantrāḥ. tatra viśeṣeṇa namaḥśabdādyalaṁkṛtāḥ śrī-bhagavatā śrīmadṛṣibhiś cāhitaśaktiviśeṣāḥ śrī-bhagavatā samam ātmasambandha viśeṣapratipādakāś ca. tatra kevalāni śrībhagavannāmāny api nirapekṣāṇy eva paramapuruṣārthaphalaparyantadānasamarthāni. tato mantreṣu nāmato'py adhikasāmarthye labdhe kathaṁ dīkṣādyapekṣā. ucyate. yadyapi svarūpato nāsti tathāpi prāyaḥ svabhāvato dehādisambandhena kadarthaśīlānāṁ vikṣiptacittānāṁ janānāṁ tattatsaṁkocīkaraṇāya śrīmadṛṣiprabhṛtibhir atrārcanamārge kvacit kvacit kācit kācin maryādā sthāpitāsti.*

mukta-kulair upāsyamānam: 'O Holy Name! You are worshiped by the liberated souls.'"

THE MANTRA BRINGS PURIFICATION, THE HOLY NAME BRINGS ECSTATIC LOVE

We have already seen that Mahaprabhu was in Kashi, He instructed Prakashananda Saraswati about the Holy Name and the mantra. Prakashananda criticized the Lord, saying that chanting the Holy Name was not a suitable activity for a person in the renounced order of life. In response, the Lord said:

prabhu kahe śuna śrīpāda ihāra kāraṇa
guru more mūrkha dekhi karila śāsana
mūrkha tumi, tomāra nāhika vedāntādhikāra
kṛṣṇa-mantra japa sadā ei mantra-sāra
kṛṣṇa-mantra haite habe saṁsāra-mocana
kṛṣṇa-nāma haite pābe kṛṣṇera caraṇa

> Venerable sir, please hear from Me the reason why I chant. My spiritual master considered Me a fool and therefore chastised Me. "You are a fool," he said, "and have no qualification to study Vedānta philosophy. Go and chant the *kṛṣṇa-mantra* constantly, for it is the essence of all mantras. By chanting the *kṛṣṇa-mantra* You will be liberated from material existence. And by chanting Krishna's name, You will attain His lotus feet." (CC 1.7.71–3)

The sum and substance of these statements is as follows: when a submissive disciple approaches the spiritual master with questions and a service attitude, the guru awards him initiation into a mantra that contains within it the divine knowledge of a specific relationship with Krishna. From that moment, having received the divine mercy of the guru, the disciple starts to cast off his absorption in everything that is not Krishna. He is engaged in Krishna's service and, as he develops affection for the

Lord, he begins to feel a preference for calling out His Lord's names. By this practice he reaches fulfillment, finding pure love for the Lord's lotus feet. Srila Prabhupada Bhaktisiddhanta Saraswati Thakur summarized this process in his *Anubhāṣya* to *Chaitanya-charitamrita* 1.7.73:

> By chanting the *kṛṣṇa-mantra*, the *jīva* begins to have experience of the supra-mundane realm. This results in his faith in external material perception based on sense gratification gradually being eliminated. Then taking shelter in one of the five relationships, he begins to relish the divine mellows through the combinations of all the ingredients that go into their composition: the *vibhāvas*, *anubhāvas*, *vyabhicārī-bhāvas*, and *sāttvikas*. The heart, which has been purified by the influence of such relish, becomes illuminated in pure goodness, and in such a state, the living being can experience the object of his worship. This process cannot be identified with the enjoyments of the *jīva's* gross or subtle coverings.
>
> The name and the one who is named are not distinct entities. This is the divine knowledge (*divya-jñāna*) that is achieved through initiation. One who is factually situated in the regular practice of spiritual life with the object of having this realization attains direct service to Krishna. In this state, one loses interest in the grammatical formalism of the mantra, with its *bīja-mantra* (*oṁ*, *klīṁ*, etc.), dative case endings (*-āya*, *-ave*, *-āyai*, *ābhyāṁ*, *-ebhyaḥ*, etc.), and words indicating relationships (*svāhā*, *namaḥ*, etc.). He rather favors a direct expression of his relationship with the Lord by calling out to Him in the vocative case. This takes place naturally in the heart that has been illuminated by the mode of pure goodness.[5] In this state, the devotee gains the ability to unrestrictedly serve the Holy Name in the vocative form. All scriptures and all mantras that contain *divya-jñāna* liberate the *jīva* completely and then engage him directly in the service of the Lord.

---

[5] Bhaktisiddhanta Saraswati Thakur's language in this section is based on BRS 2.1.7–10. These verses trace the development of a devotee's capacity to relish transcendental mellows.

In his comments on the subsequent verse, Saraswati Thakur continues:

> The name and the named are not different from one another. Therefore, just as Lord Krishna is the absolute reality, eternal, pure, complete, liberated, the embodiment of pure consciousness, a transcendental philosopher's stone, so too is His name . . . . Only through the worship of the Holy Name (*nāma-bhajana*) can both one's gross and subtle misidentifications be destroyed . . . . The *Vaikuntha* name alone can save the living being from absorption in thoughts of material sense gratification. Because it alone is powerful enough to do this, it is called the *mantra-sāra*, the essence of all mantras. Every material thing has its name, form, attributes, characteristics, and functions, all of which are subject to argument and experimental empiricism. The same is not true for the *Vaikuntha* name; the name, form, attributes, and associates, etc., of the Lord are all situated in nonduality.

THE GLORIES OF THE HOLY NAMES

The chanting of the Holy Names in *harināma-saṅkīrtana* has everywhere been designated as the religious principle for the age of Kali—in the Vedas (*oṁ āsya jānanto nāma cid vivaktan mahas te viṣṇo sumatiṁ bhajāmahe*), in the *Upaniṣads*, such as in the *Kali-santarana Upaniṣad*, in the *śmṛtis*, such as the Bhagavad Gita, in the *Purāṇas*, such as the *Bhāgavata Purāṇa* and lesser *Purāṇas*, as well as in the histories, such as in the *Mahābhārata*. Even so, the Supreme Lord Sri Chaitanya Mahaprabhu descended in this age to show by His own example that the loud chanting and singing of the great formula of sixteen names and thirty-two syllables stands above all other religious activities. In His *Śikṣāṣṭaka*, He announces the glorious victory of *harināma-saṅkīrtana* in a booming voice, and He taught the same through His *nāmācārya*, Srila Haridasa Thakur, who unfailingly chanted three hundred thousand names aloud every day. After being flogged in twenty-two market places on the orders of the governor of Ambika Kalna, Haridasa showed his allegiance to the Holy Name when he said:

khaṇḍa khaṇḍa deha mora jāya yadi prāṇa
tathāpiha vadane nā chāṛi harināma

> Although my body may be torn to bits and my life may leave it, even so I will never give up chanting the Holy Names. (*Caitanya-bhagavata* 1.14.135)

Mahaprabhu's other dear associates showed similar incomparable allegiance to the Holy Name. When we consider the way in which the Lord and His devotees revealed the power of the *mahā-mantra,* we are thrilled with joy and astonishment.

Then why are we so unfortunate? Why do we not immediately receive the fruits of chanting? The reason is clear: we offend the Holy Name. The *Padma Purāṇa* (as quoted in both HBV 11.527 and CC 3.3.60) states:

nāmaikaṁ yasya vāci smaraṇa-patha-gataṁ śrotra-mūlaṁ gataṁ vā
śuddhaṁ vāśuddha-varṇaṁ vyavahita-rahitaṁ tārayaty eva satyam
tac ced deha-draviṇa-janatā lobha-pāṣaṇḍa-madhye
nikṣiptaṁ syān na phala-janakaṁ śīghram evātra vipra

> Should someone utter the Holy Name of the Lord even once, or should he merely remember it or hear it in passing, it will certainly deliver him from material bondage, whether it is correctly or incorrectly pronounced, properly joined or vibrated in separate parts. O *brāhmaṇa,* if one uses the Holy Name for the benefit of the material body, to gain material wealth and followers, or under the influence of greed or atheism—in other words, if one utters the name with offenses—such chanting will not produce the desired result with the same rapidity.

Even so, if we continue to chant diligently, as our offensives are eliminated we will be able to experience the benefit of the chanting, love for

Krishna. By chanting the mantra received at initiation, one minimizes his material attachments and one's taste for chanting the Holy Names increases. By chanting the Holy Name, one experiences the awakening of one's love for Krishna by the grace of the Holy Name.

Bhaktivinoda Thakur writes in *Śri Nāma-Māhātmya*, song 1, of *Śaraṇāgati*:

īṣat vikaśi punaḥ dekhāya nija-rūpa-guṇa
citta hari laya kṛṣṇa pāśa
pūrṇa vikaśita hañā vraje more jāya lañā
dekhāya nija svarūpa vilāsa

> When the name is even slightly revealed, it shows me my own spiritual form and characteristics. It steals my mind and takes it to Krishna. When the name is fully revealed, it takes me directly to Vraja, where it shows me my personal role in the eternal pastimes.

By the grace of the Holy Name, we too will come to a state where we will say with Chaitanya Mahaprabhu:

kibā mantra dile gosāñi kibā tāra bala
japite japite mantra karila pāgala

> What mantra have you given me, O Gurudeva! What powers does it possess? As I chant this mantra, I feel that it is turning me into a madman. (CC 1.7.81)

When we come to this point, we will begin to understand the power of the Holy Name.

CHAPTER 9

Sampradāya

The institution of the *sampradāya* has existed in the holy land of Bharata since time immemorial. The word *sampradāya* is a passive nominal formation from the Sanskrit verb root, *sam-pra-dā*, "to hand down." Lexicographers define it as "the instruction that is passed down in a line of spiritual masters." This is also called disciplic succession or *guru-paramparā*, and implies that instruction in spiritual truth is passed down personally from one teacher directly to his disciples in a chain (*śrauta-paramparā*). Although the word *sampradāya* is commonly used in Bengali and other Indian languages to refer to a number of social institutions—religions, groups, and associations—its fundamental meaning is "the teachings received in a line of spiritual masters."

Other synonyms for this concept include *āmnāya, nigama,* and Veda. The great sage, Vyasadeva, uses the term *āmnāya* in *Śrīmad Bhāgavatam* (1.4.29):

bhārata-vyapadeśena
āmnāyārthaḥ pradarśitaḥ

> By means of the *Mahābhārata,* I revealed the ancient knowledge of the Vedas as I received it through disciplic succession.

The word *āmnāya* is derived from the verb root *mnā* combined with the prefix *ā*. Two definitions are given for this term: "that by which religious instruction is given" and "that by which religious teachings are repeated over and over again."

The same word is sometimes found prefixed by *sam*, as in *samāmnāya*.[1] Our most worshipable Srila Prabhupada explains this term in his *Gauḍīya-bhāṣya* to *Chaitanya-bhagavata* 2.1.255[2]:

"Srila Sridhar Swami explains the word *samāmnāya* in his commentary on *Bhāgavatam* 10.47.33 as meaning the Veda. The most perfect teaching is the one that directs us to the supreme abode of Vishnu. It is that which the sages have repeated over and over again, and that by which the supreme religious teaching is given."

Vishwanatha Chakravarti has defined *samāmnāya* as complete knowledge (*sampūrṇo vedaḥ*). The word *veda* is defined as that scripture that gives us knowledge of God and religion. It is explained in the Vedānta: "That divine instruction or word of God that brings knowledge of dharma and Brahman into human society is called Veda."[3] Something similar is stated in the *Purāṇas*: "The *Veda* is the scripture that was spoken by Lord Brahma and explains dharma."[4]

The root of the word *nigama* means "emanation"—because the four Vedas emanated from Lord Brahma's four mouths. Another definition breaks the word down into two parts: the prefix *ni*, meaning *nitarām*, or "forever," and *gama*, meaning "explain" (from the causative form of the verb "to go"). Thus the scripture that forever explains the supreme truth of Brahman is called *nigama*, or *Veda*.

Gaudiya Vedanta *ācārya* Baladeva Vidyabhushana writes in his *Prameya-ratnāvali* (1.4):

---

[1] *āmnāyate samyag abhyasyate athavā āmnāyate upadiśyate dharmo'neneti āmnāyaḥ*

[2] *kṛṣṇera bhajana kahi samyag āmnāya | ādi-madhya-ante kṛṣṇa-bhajana-bujhāya:* "The most perfect strands of the Vedic literature as passed down in disciplic succession direct us to worship Krishna. From beginning to middle to end, they explain only the worship of Krishna."

[3] *dharma-brahma-pratipādakāpauruṣeya-vākyaṁ vedaḥ.*

[4] *brahma-mukha-nirgata-dharma-jñāpaka-śāstraṁ vedaḥ.*

bhavati vicintyā viduṣāṁ niravakarā guru-paramparā nityam
ekāntitvaṁ siddhyati yayodayati yena hari-toṣaḥ

> Learned Vaishnavas should constantly remember the pure line of spiritual masters, for by so doing, they will perfect the single-minded devotion that brings satisfaction to Lord Hari.

A disciple can attain a pure heart by discussing the pure character and activities of his spiritual masters. This is how his material ego is replaced with identification as a servant of the servants of the Lord. This makes it possible for him to receive the mercy of the Lord. The Lord's exclusive devotees are very dear to him, so service to such devotees is the surest way of achieving His pleasure and attracting His blessings.

Baladeva follows his *Prameya-ratnāvali* verse with three others (1.5–7) taken from the *Padma Purāṇa*, in which he introduces the four *sampradāyas* of *Kali Yuga*:

sampradāya-vihīnā ye mantrās te niṣphalā matāḥ
ataḥ kalau bhaviṣyanti catvāraḥ sampradāyinaḥ
śrī-brahma-rudra-sanakāḥ vaiṣṇavāḥ kṣiti-pāvanāḥ
catvāras te kalau bhāvyā hy utkale puruṣottamāt

> Any mantra that does not come in disciplic succession is considered fruitless. Therefore, in the age of Kali, four divine individuals will found disciplic schools. These four Vaishnava *sampradāyas* are the Sri, Brahma, Rudra, and Sanaka *sampradāyas*. All of them will preach out of the city of Purushottam, in Orissa.

rāmānujaṁ śrīḥ svīcakre madhvācāryaṁ caturmukhaḥ
śrī-viṣṇu-svāminaṁ rudro nimbādityaṁ catuḥsanaḥ

> Lakshmi Devi accepted Ramanuja as her representative, Lord Brahma took Madhvacharya, Rudra took Vishnuswami, and the four Kumaras (Sanandana, Sanatana, Sanaka, and Sanat Kumara) accepted Nimbaditya as their representative in establishing their disciplic lines.

Baladeva Vidyabhushana quotes these verses in his book, *Prameya-ratnāvalī*, citing the *Padma Purāṇa* as their source. In the 1927 edition of the *Prameya-ratnāvalī*, two commentaries were published: *Kānti-mālā*, by Krishnadeva Vedanta-vagisha and *Prabhā*, by Akshaya Kumar Shastri.[5] Both these commentaries confirm that the verses come from the *Padma Purāṇa*. Narahari Chakravarti (also known as Ghanashyama Das), the son of Jagannatha Chakravarti, a disciple of Vishwanatha Chakravarti Thakur, also quoted these two verses in his *Bhakti-ratnākara* (5.2111–2) and attributed them to the *Padma Purāṇa*.

Finally, there is the testimony of Kavi Karnapura, also known as Puri Das,[6] the youngest son of Mahaprabhu's intimate associate Shivananda Sena. Puri Das offered obeisance to Mahaprabhu, calling him the "the family's worshipable Deity" (*kulādhidaivata*[7]). In his *Gaura-gaṇoddeśa-dīpikā* (21–22), Karnapura quotes a portion of these verses and attributes it to the *Padma Purāṇa*:

prādurbhūtāḥ kali-yuge
catvāraḥ sampradāyikāḥ

---

[5] Calcutta (Shyam Bazar): Sanskrit Sahitya Parishad, 1927.

[6] Shivananda Sena had three sons, Chaitanya Das, Sri Rama Das, and Sri Puri Das. Puri Das was given the name Kavi Karnapura by Lord Chaitanya Himself when at the age of seven, he recited a Sanskrit poem he had written (CC 3.16.65–75). It is said that this extraordinary ability came as the result of sucking Mahaprabhu's toes when Puri Das was a baby (CC 3.12.50). Karnapura's guru was Srinatha Chakravarti. Karnapura wrote ten books, including *Caitanya-carita-mahā-kāvya, Caitanya-candrodaya, Ānanda-vṛndāvana-campū, Alaṅkāra-kaustubha, Gaura-gaṇoddeśa-dīpikā, Bṛhad-gaṇoddeśa-dīipikā, Ārya-śataka, Caitanya-sahasra-nāma, Śrī-keśavāṣṭaka* and a commentary on the Tenth Canto of *Śrīmad Bhāgavatam.*

[7] *devo naḥ kula-daivataṁ vijayatāṁ caitanya-kṛṣṇo hariḥ* (*Ānanda-vṛndāvana-campū* 1.3).

śrī-brahma-rudra-sanakā-
hvayāḥ pādme yathā smṛtāḥ

ataḥ kalau bhaviṣyanti
catvāraḥ sampradāyinaḥ
śrī-brahma-rudra-sanakā
vaiṣṇavāḥ kṣiti-pāvanāḥ

> The founders of four *sampradāyas* appeared in Kali Yuga. According to the *Padma Purāṇa,* they were Sri, Brahma, Rudra, and Sanaka Rishi. There it is said, "Therefore the Vaishnava, Sri, Brahma, Rudra, and Sanaka Rishi, will appear in the Age of Kali to purify the world by establishing the four Vaishnava *sampradāyas.*"

Gopal Guru Goswami, an associate of Mahaprabhu and disciple of Vakreshwara Pandita, also accepted this concept of disciplic line and the principle of four distinct Vaishnava *sampradāyas*.

In his translation and commentary on the *Prameya-ratnāvalī,* our most worshipable Srila Prabhupada speaks these verses: "The four Vaishnava disciplic lines trace their origins to these original spiritual masters: Lakshmi, Brahma, Rudra, and the four Kumaras (Sanaka, Sanatana, Sanandana, and Sanat Kumara). In the Age of Kali, four great founder-*ācāryas* attached themselves to these original spiritual masters and spread their teachings. Each of them began their preaching task out of Purushottam Kshetra in Orissa. *Maṭhas* representing each of the four *sampradāyas* had a strong presence in Puri as recently as a century ago. At certain times, one or the other of them becomes stronger and takes the lead in doing spiritual welfare work for the conditioned souls of this world."

Without following the directives given by spiritual masters in the *sampradāya*, the mantra one receives cannot be perfected. The divine founders of the disciplic successions knew this, so they appointed Ramanuja, Madhva, Vishnuswami, and Nimbarkacharya as their representatives to teach the four Vaishnava versions of Vedanta. Ramanuja taught the *Viśiṣṭādvaita* doctrine, Madhvacharya taught the Dvaitavada, Vishnuswami taught the Shuddhadvaita, and Nimbarka the Dvaitadvaita.

Ramanuja's birthplace was in a village named Perembedar, some forty kilometers from the current metropolis of Chennai. Born in 938 CE, he lived a long life of 120 years, during which he preached worship of the Lord in His form as Lakshmi-Narayana. Madhvacharya, the promulgator of the doctrine of pure duality, appeared in 1119 CE in Udipi, in the area known as Parashuram Kshetra. He worshiped Krishna exclusively. The preacher of purified monism (Shuddhadvaita), Vishnuswami, was also from Tamil Nadu, and like Nimbarka he taught the worship of Radha-Krishna. Nimbarka was from Munger Pattanam in Andhra Pradesh, born to Aruni Rishi and Jayanti Devi.

According to their respective traditions, Vishnuswami and Nimbarka appeared long before Ramanuja and Madhva. There are differing opinions about the actual dates of Ramanuja and Madhvacharya. According to some, there have been a number of teachers named Vishnuswami besides the one from Andhra Pradesh. There is also some disagreement about Vallabhacharya's role in the Vishnuswami *sampradāya*. There is no need to go into these controversies here. Suffice it to say that these four founders of the pure Vaishnava disciplic lines all spent time in Jagannath Puri, Purushottam Kshetra, in order to begin their work of preaching devotion to Lord Vishnu according to their specific visions. There is a *maṭha* in Jagannath Puri known as the Chari-sampradaya Matha. Krishnadeva Vedanta-vagisha, who wrote the *Kānti-mālā* commentary on Baladeva's *Prameya-ratnāvalī*, states: *śiṣṭānuśiṣṭa-gurūpadiṣṭo mārgaḥ sampradāyaḥ, tad-upadiṣṭena pathā vinā mantra-śāstrād upalabdhā viṣṇu-mantrā muktidā na bhavanti*: "A *sampradāya* is the path of succession of disciples instructed by preceding gurus. Unless one follows in such a path, all the *viṣṇu-mantras* one chants will not bring one liberation." This is why it is absolutely necessary to accept allegiance to one of the lineages of pure devotees.

Gauḍiya Vedanta ācārya Baladeva Vidyabhushana continues by giving the detailed list of his own disciplic succession:

śrī-kṛṣṇa-brahma-devarṣi-bādarāyaṇa-saṁjñakān
śrī-mādhva-śrī-padmanābha-śrīman-narahari-mādhavān
akṣobhya-jayatīrtha-jñānasindhu-dayānidhīn
śrī-vidyānidhi-rājendra-jayadharmān kramād vayam
puruṣottama-brahmaṇya-vyāsatīrthāṁś ca saṁstumaḥ
tato lakṣmīpatiṁ mādhavendraṁ ca bhaktitaḥ
tac-chiṣyān śrīśvarādvaita-nityānandān jagad-gurūn
devam īśvara-śiṣyaṁ śrī-caitanyaṁ ca bhajāmahe
śrī-kṛṣṇa-prema-dānena yena nistāritaṁ jagat

Our most worshipable spiritual master, Srila Prabhupada Bhaktisiddhanta Saraswati Thakur explains these verses in his *Gauḍīya-bhāṣya* (2.1.255) commentary to the *Chaitanya-bhagavata*:

> The author here lists his own disciplic succession, or chain of gurus in the Brahma *sampradāya*. He is a Vaishnava in the Gaudiya family and a teacher of the Vedanta. Krishna is for him the ultimate worshipable object and the original spiritual master. His disciple is Lord Brahma. Brahma's disciple is Devarshi Narada. Narada's disciple was Badarayana Vyasa, whose disciple was Madhvacharya. Madhva's disciple was Padmanabha, who was followed by Narahari, who was in turn followed by Madhava. Madhava's disciple was Akshobhya. Akshobhya's disciple was Jayatirtha. Jayatirtha's disciple was Jnanasindhu, his disciple was Dayanidhi, his disciple was Rajendra, his disciple was Jayadharma. We Gaudiya Vaishnavas are disciples who follow in this lineage.
>
> Jayadharma's disciple was Brahmanya Tirtha, whose disciple was Vyasa Tirtha. We wholeheartedly praise all these gurus. Vyasa Tirtha's disciple was Lakshmipati, whose disciple was Madhavendra Puri. I bow down to Madhavendra Puri's disciples, the world teachers Ishwara Puri, Advaita Acharya, and Nityananda Prabhu. Ishwara Puri's disciple was Lord Chaitanya Mahaprabhu, who delivered the world by freely distributing

love for Krishna. This is the disciplic succession of the Gaudiya Vaishnavas.

The spiritual masters in the line of Madhvacharya were sannyāsīs who carried the single staff (*eka-daṇḍi*). Most were given the *sannyāsa* title "Tirtha." Madhavendra Puri did not have the title Tirtha but was a "Puri." It therefore stands to reason that he received *Pañcarātrika* initiation from someone in the Madhva line, but later took *sannyāsa* from a spiritual master with the title Puri. The *Bhakti-ratnākara* states that Nityananda Prabhu took initiation from Lakshmipati Tirtha.

The main center of the *Tattvavadis*, or the Madhva *sampradāya*, is found in Uttaradhi. Its sannyāsīs all go by the name Tirtha. Today, some of the leaders of the *sahajiyā* sect express doubts about the Gaudiya *sampradāya*'s connection to the Madhva line because of this. These doubts come from their ignorance and can be corrected by looking at the disciplic successions given in the Gaura-*gaṇoddeśa-dīpikā*, Gopal Guru Goswami's *Arcanā-paddhati*, and *Bhakti-ratnākara*, all of which agree substantially.

The *Gopāla-pūrva-tāpinī Upaniṣad* gives a thorough explanation of how Lord Brahma was Sri Krishna's disciple. Legends of Madhva Muni's taking shelter of Vedavyasa are long-established. It is told that once, Madhva and Shankaracharya were engaged in debate in Manikarnika before an audience of a thousand erudite sages. From the sky, the blue-skinned Vedavyasa appeared to everyone and publicly rejected Shankara's interpretation of his writings while accepting those of Madhva.

Baladeva Vidyabhushana goes on to say (*Prameya-ratnāvalī* 1.10) that Chaitanya Mahaprabhu accepted the nine principal points (*prameya*) of Madhva's philosophy, all of which can be demonstrated by reference to the Vedic scriptures.

śrī-madhvaḥ prāha viṣṇuṁ paratamam akhilāmnāya-vedyaṁ ca viśvaṁ
satyaṁ bhedaṁ ca jīvān hari-caraṇa-juṣas tāratamyaṁ ca teṣām

mokṣaṁ viṣṇv-aṅghri-lābhaṁ tad amala-bhajanaṁ tasya hetuṁ pramāṇaṁ
pratyakṣādi-trayaṁ cety upadiśati hariḥ kṛṣṇa-caitanya-candraḥ

> Lord Chaitanya Mahaprabhu taught that Madhva said: (1) Lord Vishnu is the Supreme Truth; (2) He is the goal of all the sacred texts; (3) the world is real; (4) the living beings are different from the Lord; (5) their constitutional position is to serve the Lord's lotus feet; (6) there is a hierarchy among living beings—some are liberated and some are in bondage; (7) the *jīva* attains liberation on attaining the Lord's lotus feet; (8) this comes about by means of untainted worship of the Lord; and (9) all this is known by three kinds of evidence—direct perception (*pratyakṣa*), inference (*anumāna*), and revealed authority (*śabda*).

In the *Prameya-ratnāvalī*, Baladeva has set out to demonstrate how the Vedic revelations do in fact support Madhva's nine propositions. He did not himself invent Madhva's doctrine but followed the tradition, which summarized these teachings in the following verse, also quoted at the conclusion of *Prameya-ratnāvalī*:

śrī-madhva-mate hariḥ paratamaḥ satyaṁ jagat tattvato
bhedo jīva-gaṇā harer anucarā nīcocca-bhāvaṁ gatāḥ
muktir naija-sukhānubhūtir amalā bhaktiś ca tat-sādhanam
akṣādi-tritayaṁ pramāṇam akhilāmnāyaika-vedyo hariḥ

> According to Madhva's teachings, Lord Hari is the Supreme Truth and the subject of all sacred texts; the world is real, but different from the Lord, in other words, a transformation of his external energy; living beings are many and are all eternal servants of the Lord; according to the extent of their spiritual practice, there is a hierarchy among

> them—some are closer to the Lord, others farther away; forgetfulness of service to the Lord is ignorance, the entry of which is the cause of the *jīva's* deformity; this deformity results in taking birth as humans or gods; the *jīva* attains liberation by casting off this deformity, becoming situated in its spiritual nature, and enjoying the joys of service to the Lord. The means of attaining correct knowledge about the Lord is threefold: direct perception, the use of reason, and revelation.

The earlier statement that liberation is attainment of Lord Vishnu's lotus feet (*mokṣaṁ viṣṇv-aṅghri-lābhaṁ*) does not contradict what is stated here, for if the *jīva* is by nature the Lord's eternal servant, then there can be no other means of attaining Him than by worshiping Him. *Amalā-bhakti* means devotion untainted by other desires or processes, such as karma or *jñāna*. Only such pure devotion can lead the soul to the joys of direct service to the Lord.

From these writings by Baladeva, we learn that Sri Chaitanya Mahaprabhu accepted Sri Madhvacharya's theological position as true and in line with Vedanta. However, we see in the ninth chapter of the *Caitanya-caritāmṛta's Madhya-līlā* a description of Mahaprabhu's visit to Udipi, the seat of the *Tattvavadi* school (followers of Madhvacharya) and His conversation with the then *ācārya* of that school, Raghuvarya Tirtha, about the means and end of spiritual life. From Krishna Das's description we learn that the *Tattvavadis* held that the best means of spiritual practice is to follow one's prescribed duties according to the *varṇāśrama* system, and the topmost attainment is the five kinds of liberation in the Lord's abode of *Vaikuntha*. Mahaprabhu contradicted him by saying that the nine kinds of devotional practice beginning with *śravaṇa* and kirtan are topmost, because they are the means by which one can attain the supreme goal of love for Krishna. Mahaprabhu told Raghuvarya Tirtha:

The nine types of devotional practice beginning with *śravaṇa* and kirtan lead to the attainment of the fifth and most perfect achievement of human life, namely *prema-bhakti*. The other four goals of human life—the perfection of duty, gaining wealth, enjoying sense pleasure, and salvation—are all adulterated and ultimately deceptive. Only *prema* is free from any element of self-deception. Engaging in religious works or sacrificing the results of one's activities can never result in *prema*. These practices may result in some self-purification and, if the mind is pure, one may develop faith in the life of devotion when in the association of devotees. Such faith leads to engagement in hearing and chanting about Krishna, which in turn frees the heart of all impurities and leads to the attainment of *prema*. Nevertheless, there is no direct or necessary correlation between engaging in works or renouncing them and loving devotion to the Lord. *Prema-bhakti* depends entirely on faith, manifested in acts of self-surrender.

ācārya kahe—tumi je koho, sei satya hoy
sarva-śāstre vaiṣṇavera ei suniścaya
tathāpi madhvācārya aiche kariyāche nirbandha
sei ācariye sabe sampradāya sambandha

> What you say is true. The Vaishnava scriptures all say this. Even so, Madhvacharya set down principles, which we who belong to his succession follow. (CC 2.9.274–5)

In other words, the *Tattvavadi ācārya* accepted that Mahaprabhu's conclusions were in line with the devotional scriptures. Nevertheless, he admitted that he was bound to accept the teachings of his own disciplic line's founder. Sri Chaitanya Mahaprabhu answered:

prabhu kohe karmī jñānī dui bhakti-hīna
tomāra sampradāye dekhi sei dui cihna

sabe eka guṇa dekhi tomāra sampradāye
satya vigraha īśvare karaho niścaye

> Both the fruitive worker and the speculative philosopher are considered nondevotees, yet we see both these elements present in your *sampradāya*. The only merit I can see in your *sampradāya* is that you accept that God possesses an eternal form. (CC 2.9.276–7)

Srila Jiva Goswami mentions Madhvacharya in his *Tattva-sandarbha* (section 24), using the honorific plural *śrī-madhvācārya-caraṇaiḥ*. Baladeva Vidyabhushana comments:

> Madhva Muni also considered *Śrīmad Bhāgavatam* the most worshipable scripture. He saw that Shankaracharya had not commented on the *Bhāgavatam*, even though he too had great respect for it [and had shown his proclivity for devotion to Krishna in other works, such as the *Govindāṣṭakam*, *Sahasra-nāma-bhāṣya*, etc.]. Shankara's disciples, such as Purnaranya, had commented on the *Bhāgavatam*, but their presentation led to impersonalist conclusions. Fearing that devotees who read these commentaries would be misled about the *Bhagavatam*'s purport and think it taught that the ultimate truth is formless and nothing but pure consciousness, Madhva wrote his own commentary, which he called *Bhāgavata-tātparya*, in which he showed that the object of the *Bhāgavatam* was the personal God, *Bhagavan*. In this way he showed the true path to the Vaishnava.
>
> By using the plural *madhvācārya-caraṇaiḥ*, Sri Jiva shows the greatest respect. This indicates that he honors Jiva as a previous *ācārya* in his disciplic succession. Madhva was an incarnation of the wind god, Vayu. He was omniscient and extremely courageous. He once defeated a great scholar, a conqueror of the ten directions, who had mastered fourteen different fields of knowl-

edge in a mere fourteen moments[8] and thus inherited from him his fourteen ashrams. That *digvijayi* then became his disciple and was known by the name Padmanabha.

Jiva refers to Madhva again later in the *Tattva-sandarbha* (section 28), using the title *tattva-vāda-gurūṇām*. Baladeva glosses this epithet, "Madhvacharya is the teacher of Tattvavada, which is the philosophy that the phenomenal world and the personal God are real" (*sarvaṁ vastu satyam iti vādas tattva-vādas tad-upadeṣṭīṇām ity arthaḥ*). Shankaracharya taught that this world is false (*jagan mithyā*) and that only Brahman is true (*brahma satyam*). Madhvacharya objected to this doctrine and said *sarvaṁ vastu satyam*, all things are true. Indeed, this world we perceive may be temporary and ultimately prone to destruction, but it is still a product of God's eternal energies, and He is the Supreme Truth. Since the world has this connection to the Supreme Truth, it cannot be written off as false or illusory. One need not accept that it is in itself the ultimate or eternal truth, but it nevertheless has an immediate truth or meaning for us.

Sri Jiva Prabhu further refers to some of Madhvacharya's principal works, like the *Bhāgavata-tātparya, Bhārata-tātparya*, and *Brahma-sūtra-bhāṣya* (commentaries on the *Bhāgavatam, Mahābhārata*, and *Vedānta*-sutras, respectively). He makes reference to the various rare *śruti, śmṛti*, and *Purāṇic* texts that he quotes in these books, such as the *Caturveda-śikhā*, rare or lost portions of the *Garuḍa Purāṇa, Saṁhitās* like the *Mahā-saṁhitā*, and Tantras like the *Tantra-bhāgavata, Brahma-tarka*, etc. Jiva states that these works may have been extant during Madhva's time, but they have either become very rare or completely lost. Madhva collected these quotes in his wide travels, but few people have been able to find those works today. Madhvacharya established the dualist position; nevertheless, his citations from the *Brahma-tarka*, a work written by Vedavyasa that is completely unheard of today, support the *acintya-bhedābheda* doctrine. For example, the following two examples have been cited by Nishkinchan Maharaj in his commentary on section 28 of the *Tattva-sandarbha:*

---

[8] The word *kṣaṇa* is used, meaning somewhere around four minutes. In other words, in fifty-six minutes.

viśeṣasya viśiṣṭāsyāpy abhedas tad eva tu
sarvaṁ cācintya-śaktitvād yujyate parameśvare
tac-chaktyaiva tu jīveṣu cid-rūpa-prakṛtāv api
bhedābhedau tad anyatra hy ubhayor api darśanāt

The attribute (*viśeṣa*) and the one possessing the attribute (*viśiṣṭa*) are always nondifferent. All things are possible in the Supreme Lord due to His inconceivable potencies. Similarly, the simultaneous oneness and difference of the Lord from both the *jīvas* and the spiritual nature (*cid-rūpa-prakṛti*) are also possible by the same inconceivable potency.

The concept of simultaneous oneness and difference is the basis of all Gaudiya theology. As this concept was approved by Madhvacharya, one must accept that there is an unbreakable link between his *sampradāya* and the one that follows the teachings of Sri Chaitanya Mahaprabhu. Sri Jiva Goswami acknowledged his dependence on Madhvacharya for quotes more than on any other Vaishnava *ācārya*.

Madhva was a member of the Shankara *sampradāya* in name only. When he was only twelve years old (according to some sources, nine), he took *sannyāsa* from a Shankara sannyasi named Acyutapreksha Tirtha and was given the name Purnaprajna Tirtha. Even so, he never accepted the nondual philosophy taught by Shankara. In fact, Acyutapreksha eventually took initiation from his own disciple and became a Vaishnava.

Madhva traveled to Badarikashram, where he met Vyasadeva and received instruction from him along with eighteen *śālagrāma* stones to worship. Once, Madhva was bathing in the ocean when he found a Deity of young Krishna encased in a large piece of *gopichandan* clay. This Krishna Deity and the eighteen *śālagrāmas* are worshiped to this day in Udipi.

Just as Madhva was the disciple of Vyasadeva, Vyasa was the disciple of Narada Muni (see *Bhāgavatam*, Canto 1, chapter 4–7). The *Bhāgavatam* also shows how Narada was Lord Brahma's disciple (ŚB 2.7.51). And in the *Brahma-saṁhitā, Gopāla-tāpinī Upaniṣad,* and *Śrīmad Bhāgavatam* it is stated that Lord Krishna appeared to Brahma and initiated him. In the *Bhāgavatam* (11.14.3) Lord Krishna tells Uddhava:

kālena naṣṭā pralaye
vāṇīyaṁ veda-saṁjñitā
mayādau brahmaṇe proktā
dharmo yasyāṁ mad-ātmakaḥ

> In the course of time, the Vedic message was lost in the great flood of universal destruction. Then I once again spoke this religious knowledge about Myself to Brahma.

The *Muṇḍaka Upaniṣad* (1.1.1) states:

brahmā devānāṁ prathamaḥ sambabhūva
viśvasya kartā bhuvanasya goptā
sa brahma-vidyāṁ sarva-vidyā-pratiṣṭhām
atharvāya jyeṣṭha-putrāya prāha

> Brahma appeared as the first of all the gods. He created the universe and continues to protect the earth. He taught the knowledge of Brahman [which he had received from the Lord], which is the basis of all learning, to his oldest son Atharva.

What is this "knowledge of Brahman" (*brahma-vidyā*)? The *Ṛgveda-saṁhitā* (1.22.20) states:

tad viṣṇoḥ paramaṁ padaṁ
sadā paśyanti sūrayaḥ
divīva cakṣur ātatam

> The godly always see that supreme abode of Vishnu, which is like the sun expanding through the infinite sky.

These same words appear in the *Kaṭha Upaniṣad* (1.3.9). The *Śvetāśvatara Upaniṣad* (5.4) says:

sarvā diśa ūrdhvam adhaś ca tiryak
prakāśayan bhrājate yadvanaḍvān
evaṁ sa devo bhagavān vareṇyo
yoni-svabhāvān adhitiṣṭhaty ekaḥ

> As the radiance of the sun shines everywhere in space, so does the glory of God rule over all His creation.

Another verse from the *Muṇḍaka Upaniṣad* (1.2.13) states:

tasmai sa vidvān upasannāya samyak
praśānta-cittāya śamānvitāya
yenākṣaraṁ puruṣaṁ veda satyaṁ
provāca tāṁ tattvato brahma-vidyām

> The learned spiritual master who has realized Krishna should properly instruct the peaceful and self-controlled disciple in the knowledge of Brahman (*brahma-vidyā*), i.e., knowledge combined with love for Krishna, by which He can be attained. (*Muṇḍaka Upaniṣad* 1.2.13)

All these different *śruti* texts make it clear that the Brahma *sampradāya* is the oldest of all. Brahma was the first to be instructed in *brahma-vidyā* by the Lord. The instruction Lord Brahma gave his disciples continues to be handed down to this day, where it still flourishes.

In *Jaiva Dharma*, chapter 13, Srila Bhaktivinoda Thakur asks, "Why is there such a thing as a *sampradāya*?" He writes:

> In this world, there are many people who are misled by the *Mayavada* doctrine. If there were no *sampradāya* of devotees free from the flaws of *Mayavada*, it would be exceedingly difficult to get the association of saintly people. This is why it is said in the *Padma Purāṇa*, "Any mantra that does not come in disciplic succession is considered fruitless. Vaishnavas following the Sri, Brahma, Rudra, and Sanaka *sampradāyas* purify the world." Among these four *sampradāyas*, the one following Lord Brahma is the oldest. This line of disciplic succession comes down to the present day. . . . The institution of *sampradāya* is exceedingly important. This is why the pure disciplic succession is current among the saintly."

In the *Gaura-gaṇoddeśa-dīpikā*, Kavi Karnapura has listed the names of the *ācāryas* in the Brahma *sampradāya*:

> *paravyomeśvarasyāsīc chiṣyo brahmā jagat-patiḥ*
> *tasya śiṣyo nārado'bhūt vyāsas tasyāpa śiṣyatām*
> *śuko vyāsasya śiṣyatvaṁ prāpto jñānāvarodhanāt*[9]
>
> Brahma, the master of this universe, was the disciple of Narayana, the Lord of *Vaikuntha*. His disciple was Narada, and Vyasa became the disciple of Narada. Suka became the disciple of Vyasa after his tendencies for *brahma-jñāna* were disrupted.

In the *Brahma-vaivarta Purāṇa*, a story is told about how this flow of knowledge was interrupted: after Srila Vedavyasa had written *Śrīmad*

[9] Some readings have *avabodhanāt*, which gives the meaning "by awakening his spiritual knowledge."

Bhāgavatam, he had some people recite some of its verses to his son, Sukadeva, who was absorbed in meditation in a secluded part of the forest. The sweetness of these verses, which described the Lord's beauty and virtues, broke Sukadeva's trance. Being omniscient, Sukadeva was able to recognize the verses as his father's compositions, so he ran home in order to hear and study the entire work. This shows how pure consciousness of Brahman, *jñāna*, is disrupted by bhakti.[10]

vyāsāl labdha-kṛṣṇa-dīkṣo madhvācāryo mahāyaśaḥ
tasya śiṣyo'bhavat padmanābhācāryo mahāśayaḥ
tasya śiṣyo naraharis tacchiṣyo mādhava-dvijaḥ
akṣobhyas tasya śiṣyo'bhūt tac-chiṣyo jayatīrthakaḥ
tasya śiṣyo jñāna-sindhus tasya śiṣyo mahānidhiḥ
vidyānidhis tasya śiṣyo rājendras tasya sevakaḥ
jayadharmā munis tasya śiṣyo yad-gaṇa-madhyataḥ
śrīmad-viṣṇu-purī yas tu bhaktiratnāvalī-kṛtiḥ
jayadharmasya śiṣyo'bhūd brahmaṇyaḥ puruṣottamaḥ
vyāsatīrthas tasya śiṣyo yaś cakre viṣṇusaṁhitām
śrīmān lakṣmīpatis tasya śiṣyo bhaktirasāśrayaḥ
tasya śiṣyo mādhavendro yad-dharmo'yaṁ pravartitaḥ
tasya śiṣyo'bhavat śrīmān īśvarākhya-purī-yatiḥ
kalayāmāsa śṛṅgāraṁ yaḥ śṛṅgāra-phalātmakaḥ
advaitaṁ kalayāmāsa dāsya-sākhye phale ubhe
īśvarākhya-purīṁ gaura urarīkṛtya gaurave
jagad āplāvayāmāsa prākṛtāprākṛtātmakam

Madhvacharya took initiation into a *kṛṣṇa-mantra* from Vyasa. His disciple was Padmanabhacharya, whose disciple was Narahari, who was followed by Madhava Dvija. Akshobhya was his disciple, then Jayatirtha, Jnanasindhu, Mahanidhi, Vidyanidhi, and Rajendra followed. Jayadharma Muni was one of Rajendra's many disciples and Vishnu Puri, the author of *Bhakti-ratnāvalī*, and Brahmanya

[10] See ŚB 1.7.11 and 2.1.9.

> Purushottama, became his disciples. Vyasa Tirtha, the author of the *Viṣṇu-saṁhitā* was the disciple of Puruṣhottama. Lakshmipati Tirtha, a reservoir of ecstatic devotion, was the disciple of Vyasa Tirtha. Madhavendra Puri became the disciple of Lakshmipati, and it is through him that this religion of pure devotion was established. His disciple, the sannyāsī Ishwara Puri, took up the mood of conjugal devotion, while Advaita Acharya [also a disciple of Madhavendra] took up the moods of servitude and friendship. Gaura accepted Ishwara Puri as His guru, and then flooded the material and spiritual worlds with *prema*. (*Gaura-gaṇoddeśa-dīpikā* 23–32)[11]

Vakreshwara Pandita's disciple was Gopal Guru Goswami. Gopal Guru also accepted this disciplic succession. Narahari Chakravarti was the son of Vishwanatha Chakravarti Thakur's disciple Jagannatha. He was also known as Ghanashyama Das. In his *Bhakti-ratnākara,* he also accepted the version of the *sampradāya* given by Karnapura and Gopal Guru.

Our worshipable gurus Bhaktivinoda Thakur and Bhaktisiddhanta Saraswati Thakur both showed that they accepted this disciplic succession. Bhaktivinoda Thakur wrote in *Sri Mahāprabhura śikṣā*:

> The Brahma *sampradāya* is the disciplic chain of the servants of Lord Chaitanya Mahaprabhu. Kavi Karnapura has confirmed this in his *Gaura-gaṇoddeśa-dīpikā*, where he gives the names of all the members of this disciplic succession. Baladeva Vidyabhushana, who is our Vedanta *ācārya,* also supported this same disciplic succession. Is there any doubt that those who reject this connection are Sri Krishna Chaitanya's followers' greatest enemies?

Bhaktivinoda Thakur continues in *Mahāprabhura-śikṣā* to show how Chaitanya Mahaprabhu accepted the Brahma-Madhva *sampradāya*:

---

[11] These verses are also quoted in *Bhakti-ratnākara* 5.2149-2162.

> Nimbarka's doctrine, known as *dvaitādvaita-vāda*, did not achieve completion. With the coming of Chaitanya Mahaprabhu, this doctrine was perfected in the Vaishnava world as *acintya-bhedābheda*. Sri Chaitanya Mahaprabhu accepted the Madhva *sampradāya* because the teaching of *acintya-bhedābheda* is implicit in their approval of the Lord's eternal form. Studied scientifically, some distinctions are recognizable in the theologies of the different Vaishnava *ācāryas*, and this is why distinct schools grew around each of them. The Supreme Truth Sri Chaitanya Mahaprabhu, through His omniscience, was able to make up the gap in each of the *sampradāya's* doctrines. He accepted the flawlessness of Madhva's concept of the Lord's eternal, blissful, spiritual body, Ramanuja's idea of the Lord's potencies, Vishnuswami's pure nonduality (*śuddhādvaita*), and Nimbarka's "conceivable" duality and nonduality, but He made up their deficiencies by presenting a fully scientific theology called *acintya-bhedābheda*, "the inconceivable oneness and difference" of God and creation. It will not be long before only one Vaishnava *sampradāya* remains in existence, whose name will be the Brahma *sampradāya*, for all the other Vaishnava schools will be resolved in it.

Our disciplic channel, or *āmnāya*, is thus the Sri Brahma-Madhva-Gaudiya *sampradāya*. Srila Prabhupada gave the disciplic succession in Bengali at the beginning of his edition of the *Caitanya-caritāmṛta*:

kṛṣṇa hoite catur-mukha, hoy kṛṣṇa-sevonmukha
brahmā hoite nāradera mati
nārada hoite vyāsa, madhva kohe vyāsa-dāsa
pūrṇaprajña padmanābha gati (1)

> The four-headed Brahma came to know about devotional service through Lord Krishna Himself, and Narada received his understanding of this divine service from Brahma. After Narada came Vyasa in the disciplic succession. His servant was known as

Madhva, or Purnaprajna Tirtha, who was in turn the sole refuge of Padmanabha Tirtha.

nṛhari mādhava baṁśe, akṣobhya paramahaṁse
śiṣya boli aṅgīkāra kore
akṣobhyera śiṣya jaya- tīrtha nāma paricaya
tāra dāsye jñānasindhu tore (2)

Madhva's line was continued by Narahari Tirtha and Madhava Tirtha, who made Paramahaṁsa Akshobhya his disciple. Akshobhya's follower was the great servant Jaya Tirtha, who in turn delivered Jnanasindhu.

tāha hoite dayānidhi, tāra dāsa vidyānidhi
rājendra hoilo tāha ha'te
tāhāra kiṅkora jaya-dharma nāme paricaya
paramparā jāno bhālo mate (3)

Through him came Dayanidhi, whose servant was Vidyanidhi [Vidyadhiraja Tirtha]. Rajendra Tirtha became a disciple of Vidyadhiraja Tirtha. Rajendra Tirtha's servant in turn was known as Jayadharma. In this way you should properly understand this disciplic succession.

jayadharma-dāsye khyāti, śrī-puruṣottama-jati
tā ha'te brahmaṇya-tīrtha sūri
vyāsatīrtha tāra dāsa, lakṣmīpati vyāsa-dāsa
tāhā ha'te mādhavendra purī (4)

The sannyasi Sri Purushottama Tirtha is known as the servant of Jayadharma. After him came Subrahmanya Tirtha, whose servant was the great Vyasa Tirtha. Vyasa Tirtha's servant was Lakshmipati

Tirtha, whose disciple was Madhavendra Puri Goswami.

mādhavendra purī-bara, śiṣya-bara śrī-īśvara
nityānanda śrī-advaita vibhu
īśvara-purīke dhanya, korilen śrī-caitanya
jagad-guru gaura mahāprabhu (5)

The chief disciple of the great Madhavendra Puri was the great Ishwara Puri, and two of his other disciples were the renowned incarnations of the Godhead, Sri Nityananda and Advaita Acharya. Sri Chaitanya Mahaprabhu, the spiritual preceptor of all the worlds, made Ishwara Puri greatly fortunate [by accepting him as His spiritual master].

mahāprabhu śrī-caitanya, rādhā-kṛṣṇa nahe anya
rūpānuga-janera jīvana
viśvambhara priyaṅkara, śrī-svarūpa dāmodara
śrī gosvāmī rūpa-sanātana (6)

Sri Chaitanya Mahaprabhu is no one else than Radha and Krishna combined, the heart and soul of the followers of Rupa. Sri Swarupa Damodara Goswami, Rupa Goswami, and Sanatana Goswami were the dear associates of Vishwambhara [Sri Chaitanya].

rūpa-priya mahājana, jīva raghunātha hana
tāra priya kavi-kṛṣṇadāsa
kṛṣṇadāsa-priya-bara, narottama sevā-para
jāra pade viśvanātha-āśa (7)

The great souls Jiva Goswami and Raghunatha Das Goswami were very dear to Rupa Goswami.

> To them the great poet Krishna Das was most dear, and to him in turn the great servant Narottama Das, whose feet were the sole refuge of Srila Vishwanatha Chakravarti.
>
> *viśvanātha-bhakta-sātha, baladeva jagannātha*
> *tāra priya śrī-bhaktivinoda*
> *mahā-bhāgavata-bara, śrī-gaurakiśora-bara*
> *hari-bhajanete jā'ra moda* (8)
>
> Among Vishwanatha's *bhaktas* were Baladeva Vidyabhushana and Jagannatha Das Babaji, to whom Bhaktivinoda was dear. Among Bhaktivinoda's associates was the illustrious *mahā-bhāgavata* Gaura Kishora Das Babaji, whose joy lay in *hari-bhajana*.
>
> *śrī-vārṣabhānavī barā, sadā sevya-sevā-parā,*
> *tāhāra dayita-dāsa nāma*
> *ei saba harijana, gaurāṅgera nija-jana*
> *tāṅdera ucchiṣṭa mora kāma*[12]
>
> Srimati Radharani is totally devoted to loving service to Krishna, the supreme object of devotional life. Srila Prabhupada was known as "the servant of the beloved of the daughter of King Vrishbhanu." All of these great souls are Gauranga's intimate associates. It is my desire to take their remnants.

When he was just a boy of five, Advaita Acharya's son Achyutananda heard his father say that Keshava Bharati was Chaitanya Mahaprabhu's guru. This made the child sad, and so he told his father, who was an incarnation of Mahavishnu:

[12] This line is sometimes given as *ihārā paramahaṁsa, gaurāṅgera nija-vaṁśa*, "These saints are all *paramahaṁsas* and are Gauranga Mahaprabhu's own family."

jagad guru tumi kara aiche upadeśa
tomāra ei upadeśe naṣṭa hailo deśa
caudda bhuvanera guru caitanya gosāñi
tāṅra guru anya ei kono śāstre nāi

> You are a teacher to the world, and yet you are teaching such things! Your instructions will destroy the country. Lord Chaitanya Mahaprabhu is the teacher of the fourteen worlds, but you say that someone else is His spiritual master! No scripture will ever say such a thing. (CC 1.12.15–16)

All the devotees, headed by Advaita, were overjoyed to hear such realization coming from a five-year-old child. However, some people used this same logic to establish Mahaprabhu as the founder of the Gaudiya Vaishnava disciplic succession and reject any connection they may have had to Madhvacharya. We ask them, what is gained from such a proposition? Does Mahaprabhu gain in glory if He becomes the founder of His own *sampradāya*? Can Mahaprabhu not share His power with His devotees so that they can do the work of spreading the chanting of the Holy Name? Lord Chaitanya is Krishna Himself, the original Supreme Person, the source of all *avatāras*; He is the cause of all causes and the creator of all religious principles for all human beings everywhere. He is not just the guru of the fourteen worlds but of the unlimited millions of worlds! However, when He appeared as Chaitanya Mahaprabhu, He came as a devotee in order to preach the religion of the age through His example. For this reason, even though He is the spiritual master to the universe, in order to show others how to act, He adopted the *sampradāya* that accepted the philosophy of inconceivable, simultaneous oneness and difference, the Madhva *sampradāya*, and set the important example of how to take shelter of and serve a spiritual master in disciplic succession.

When the Lord appeared as Krishna, possessing a body that embodies the Vedic revelation, He set the same example by engaging in the pastime of studying the Vedas with Sandipani Muni. He and His friend

Sudama showed the world how to serve the spiritual master. Serving the guru in this way did not diminish the Lord's supreme status.

> Furthermore, Krishna instructed Brahma, who took Devarshi Narada as his disciple, who in turn instructed Vyasa. Madhvacharya is Vyasadeva's direct disciple, so situated firmly in his succession. When Sri Chaitanya Mahaprabhu took initiation in the line of Madhva, He taught us all the absolute necessity of being a member of a particular *sampradāya*. Of course, some of Madhva's *siddhāntas*, such as his understanding of the *Vraja gopīs* and Maha-Lakshmi, do not appear particularly favorable to the followers of Chaitanya Mahaprabhu, but the fact is that simply by recognizing that Mahaprabhu's teachings represent the essence of what Madhva taught and then fully adhering to them, we show sufficient and appropriate respect for Madhvacharya and those who follow him.

dharmasya tattvaṁ nihitaṁ guhāyāṁ
mahājano yena gataḥ sa panthā

The truths of religion are hidden away. Therefore,
the path to follow is the one taken by the great souls.

Srila Jiva Goswami Prabhu showed particular gratitude to Madhvacharya and displayed toward him the respect due an *ācārya*. Even more telling is the testimony of Kavi Karnapura, the son of Shivananda Sen. When he was a baby, Karnapura had the good fortune to suck Mahaprabhu's toe, and this is credited with giving him such poetic talent that at the age of only seven, he extemporaneously wrote and recited Sanskrit verses to the Lord that brought Him great joy and amazed the Lord's associates. One verse, found in Karnapura's *Ārya-śataka* (and quoted in CC 3.16.74), goes like this:

śravasoḥ kuvalayam akṣṇor
añjanam uraso mahendra-maṇi-dāma

vṛndāvana-ramaṇīnāṁ
maṇḍanam akhilaṁ harir jayati

All glories to Hari, the ornament for all the beauties of Vrindavan—He is a blue lotus for their ears, black collyrium for their eyes, and a necklace of blue sapphires to decorate their breast.

It was through this feat of poetic skill at such a young age that he earned the title *kavi-karṇapūra*, "flower ornament for the poets' ears," by which he is still best known. His many works of devotional poetry—*Ānanda-vṛndāvana-campū, Gaura-gaṇoddeśa-dīpikā, Caitanya-candrodaya-nāṭaka, Caitanya-carita-mahā-kāvya, Alaṅkāra-kaustubha*, to name a few—are still loved and honored by all devotees of Chaitanya Mahaprabhu. This Kavi Karnapura listed the names of all the members of the Madhva *sampradāya* in his *Gaura-gaṇoddeśa-dīpikā.*

Furthermore, Baladeva Vidyabhushana, our Gaudiya Vedanta *ācārya*, took initiation in a line that began with Gauri Das Pandita of Ambika Kalna. His disciple was Hridaya Chaitanya, who was followed by Shyamananda, Rasikananda, and Nayanananda. Nayanananda's disciple was Radha-Damodara of Kanyakubja. It was from this Radha-Damodara Goswami that Baladeva took initiation. Then he later took *veśa* and was known as Ekanti Govinda Das Babaji. He wrote the explanation of the *Vedānta-sūtras* known as the *Govinda-bhāṣya,* and thus preserved the honor of the Gaudiya Vaishnava *sampradāya,* the group of followers of Sri Chaitanya Mahaprabhu, which had been seriously compromised. And, at the very beginning of his *Bhāṣya*, he proudly acknowledges the connection to the Brahma-Madhva *sampradāya*. Those who show an excess of zeal for glorifying Sri Chaitanya Mahaprabhu reject this connection, which has been accepted by the aforementioned great souls. Such contempt for the standards set by these great souls can only be seen as the offense of *mahad-atikrama* ("transgressing the great souls").

āyuḥ śriyaṁ yaśo dharmaṁ
lokān āśiṣa eva ca
hanti śreyāṁsi sarvāṇi
puṁso mahad-atikramaḥ

> My dear King, the result of transgressions against great souls is the destruction of life, fortune, reputation, duty, and blessings to the world—in short, all benedictions. (ŚB 10.4.46)

Sri Kavi Karnapura, Baladeva, Gopal Guru, and other great souls revealed the path to be followed. But there are those who not only do not follow these souls but who show them disdain, committing the offence of *gurv-avajñā*.

In the *Caitanya-caritāmṛta* (1.9.10), Krishna Das Kaviraj glorifies Madhavendra Puri:

jaya śrī-mādhava purī kṛṣṇa prema pūra
bhakti-kalpa-tarura teṅho prathama aṅkura

> All glories to Madhavendra Puri, who is full of the love of Krishna. He was the first shoot of the desire tree of devotion.

He took shelter of Lakshmipati Tirtha, thus becoming part of the Madhva *sampradāya*. Ishwara Puripada followed Madhavendra, as everyone knows. Therefore we really have no other option but to accept this connection.

Srila Bhaktivinoda Thakur has bequeathed to us a short text of ten verses called *Daśa-mūla-niryāsa*, which summarizes the doctrines of Chaitanya Mahaprabhu in ten verses. The first of these verses gives an overview of the ten themes:

āmnāyaḥ prāha tattvaṁ harim iha paramaṁ sarva-śaktiṁ rasābdhiṁ
tad-bhinnāṁśāṁś ca jīvān prakṛti-kavalitāṁs tad-vimuktāṁś ca bhāvāt
bhedābheda-prakāśaṁ sakalam api hareḥ sādhanaṁ śuddha-bhaktiṁ
sādhyaṁ tat-prītim evety upadiśati harir gauracandro bhaje tam

According to Sri Chaitanya Mahaprabhu, the Vedas teach us nine principal doctrines (*Gaurāṅga-smaraṇa-stotra* 75):

1. Hari, the Almighty, is one without a second.
2. He is always invested with infinite power.
3. He is the ocean of *rasa* (the transcendental bliss that forms the essence of any relationship).
4. The soul is His *vibhinnāṁśa*, or separated part.
5. Certain souls are engrossed by *prakṛti*, his illusory energy.
6. Certain souls are released from the grasp of *prakṛti*.
7. All spiritual and material phenomena are Hari's *bhedābheda-prakāśa*, being simultaneously one with and different from the Lord.
8. Bhakti, devotional service, is the only means of attaining the final object of spiritual existence.
9. *Prema,* pure love of Krishna, is alone the final object of spiritual existence.

Madhvacharya taught that the differences (*bheda*) between God and the individual soul, between different *jīvas*, between God and material nature, between the *jīvas* and material nature, and between different phenomena of nature, are real and permanent. This is why his philosophy is called dualistic (*bheda-vāda*). Mahaprabhu gave priority to the doctrine called *acintya-bhedābheda*, but in fact this doctrine simply completes that of Madhva. In fact, Madhvacharya, in his commentary on *Śrīmad Bhāgavatam* 11.7.51, cites an ancient scripture called *Brahma-tarka*, which demonstrates clearly although indirectly that the inconceivable simultaneous oneness and difference was the doctrine he held in his heart.

viśeṣasya viśiṣṭāsyāpy abhedas tadvad eva tu
sarvaṁ cācintya-śaktitvād yujyate parameśvare
tac-chaktyaiva tu jīveṣu cid-rūpa-prakṛtāv api
bhedābhedau tad anyatra hy ubhayor api darśanāt

> The attribute (*viśeṣa*) and the one possessing the attribute (*viśiṣṭa*) are always nondifferent. All things are possible in the Supreme Lord due to his inconceivable potencies. Similarly, the simultaneous oneness and difference of the Lord from both the *jīvas* and the spiritual nature (*cid-rūpa-prakṛti*) are also possible by the same inconceivable potency.

Kavi Karnapura, Baladeva Vidyabhushana, Gopal Guru, and others sensed this about Madhva, and so testified to the deep relationship that exists between the Gaudiya Vaishnava line and the Madhvas. Thus our *sampradāya* is widely known as the Brahma-Madhva-Gaudiya *sampradāya*.

Some modern researchers have not been able to find the verses attributed to the *Padma Purāṇa* that have been quoted above and conclude that they are interpolations. No doubt motivated by envy of the Vaishnava religion, they thus minimize the necessity for a disciplic succession instructed in these verses. But this is completely illogical.

Our beloved spiritual master, who has now entered the eternal pastimes of the Lord, accepted the disciplic line given by Baladeva and the concept of the *bhāgavata paramparā*. This is the disciplic succession that we meditate on every single day. Some people do not wish to admit that Madhavendra Puri was ever a member of the Madhva *sampradāya*. On this matter, Srila Prabhupada said: "The disciplic succession of the Gaudiya Vaishnavas is the one given by Baladeva Vidyabhushana. The spiritual masters of the Madhva line are sannyasis in the single-staff (*eka-daṇḍī*) tradition, most of whom take the title 'Tirtha.' They are generally given the name Sri Madhva, followed by their *sannyāsa* name, and then the title, Tirtha. Madhavendra Puri was a sannyasi, but his title was 'Puri.' However, this does not mean that he could not have taken *sannyāsa* in the Puri line of sannyasis and still have received *Pañcarātrika-dīkṣā* in the Madhva line.

Lakshmipati Tirtha was the thirteenth guru in descent from Madhva, otherwise known as Ananda Tirtha. In the *Bhakti-ratnākara*, Nityananda Prabhu is said to have been his disciple, whereas the *Prameya-ratnāvalī* says that Nityananda Prabhu took initiation from Madhavendra Puri. The one or two other discrepancies in these guru lists are of this type.

Baladeva Vidyabhushana's lineage is further given as it follows on after Nityananda Prabhu: one of Nityananda Prabhu's followers was Gauri Das Pandita of Kalna, who in *kṛṣṇa-līlā* was one of the twelve *gopālas*, Subala Sakha. Gauri Das had a disciple named Hrdaya Chaitanya, who in turn initiated Duhkhi Krishna Das (who became Shyamananda Das), who was given instruction by Jiva Goswami in Vrindavan. Shyamananda's disciple was Rasikananda Murari, whose grandson and disciple was Nayanananda Deva Goswami. His disciple was Radha-Damodara, a great scholar born in Kanyakubja (Kanauj) who wrote the well-reputed text, *Vedānta-syamantaka*.[13] Baladeva, who won renown as the *Bhāṣyakāra* for his elaborate exposition of the *Vedānta-sūtra* according to the Gaudiya understanding, was initiated by Radha-Damodara Goswami.

Srila Prabhupada adds, "Sri Uddhava Das, or Uddhara Das, was the follower of the author of the *Govinda-bhāṣya*, Baladeva Vidyabhushana. Uddhava Das, Madhusudana Das, and Jagannatha Das Babaji, all of whom adopted the lifestyle of the *paramahaṁsa*, followed him in preaching the path of pure devotion through their example. In the Gaudiya Vaishnava *sampradāya*, these saints are the objects of the greatest faith and reverence."

---

[13] Published with notes and appendices by Umesh Chandra Banerjee. Lahore; Motilal Banarsidass (Punjab Sanskrit Book Depot), 1930.

This Jagannatha Das Babaji, who was known widely as Vaishnava Sarvabhauma, or "universal monarch of the Vaishnavas," is our predecessor *ācārya*, who gave direction to Bhaktivinoda Thakur.

Sri Chaitanya Mahaprabhu recognized the *Bhāgavatam* as the genuine commentary on the Vedanta and thus considered it unnecessary to write a separate explanation of the *Brahma-sūtras*. The *Garuḍa Purāṇa* in particular states that the *Bhāgavatam* is the explanation of the *Vedānta-sutra*, the *Mahābhārata*, and other historical epics; it gives the meaning of the Gayatri-mantra and all the Vedic literature. However, there came a time when, by the wish of the Lord, the *ācāryas* of the Ramanuja *sampradāya* in the Galta village of Jaipur created a lot of trouble by denying the validity of the Gaudiya school, which managed the service to the Govindaji Deity in Jaipur, saying that it had no historical basis. They accused the Gaudiyas of not having a tie to any one of the four Vaishnava disciplic successions.

Although the king of Jaipur was a Gaudiya Vaishnava, he was troubled by their arguments. Word came to Vishwanatha Chakravarti in Vrindavan, who was the most prominent *ācārya* of the Gaudiya school at the time. Due to his advanced age, however, Vishwanatha was unable to defend the *sampradāya's* reputation, so he sent his dear student, Baladeva Vidyabhushana, and a disciple, Krishnadeva Sarvabhauma, in his place.

When the king saw these two poverty-stricken monks arrive, he doubted they would be able to debate with the learned scholars of the Ramanuja *sampradāya*. However, his anxiety was soon dispelled when he witnessed the profound scholarship of the two ascetics. Nevertheless, it was decided that until the Gaudiya school had a Vedanta commentary of its own based on the three reliable sources (*prasthāna-traya*) of scripture (*śruti*, *smṛti*, and the *Sūtras*), it would not be accepted as a legitimate *sampradāya*.

Baladeva asked the accusers for some time—seven days according to some, three months according to others—to write a Gaudiya commentary on the Vedanta. He then went to the Govindaji temple and prayed earnestly to the Lord, "O Lord Govindaji! I am a follower of Your dear companions, Swarupa Damodara and Rupa Goswami. Please preserve their spiritual descendants and the honor of their line."

On the first two nights, Baladeva received only minimal direction from the Lord and was not satisfied with what he heard. On the third night, however, the Supreme Lord gave him His full mercy and assured him that he would be able to achieve his goal. In a very short time, Baladeva completed his commentaries on the *Upaniṣads*, *Vedānta-sūtra*, Bhagavad Gita, and *Śrīmad Bhāgavatam*. He named his exposition of the *Vedānta-sūtra* the *Govinda-bhāṣya*. This seems appropriate, because it was by Lord Govindaji's blessings and inspiration that Baladeva was able to accomplish his task.

The scholars of the other *sampradāyas* were astonished by the quality of Baladeva's commentary and were mollified by it. As a result, all opposition to the Gaudiyas as a separate *sampradāya* stopped. This was playful Lord Hari's tricky way of bringing into existence a commentary on the *Vedānta-sūtras* that would give joy to the Gaudiya Vaishnavas. It is said that whenever the Lord does anything, He accomplishes many purposes by it.[14]

We believe that Baladeva Vidyabhushana, who was so blessed and dear to Lord Govinda, is a sufficient authority to make an official statement on the disciplic succession; his word should satisfy any honest and intelligent person that the Gaudiya *sampradāya* is genuine.

[14] *eka līlāya karen prabhu kāryya pāñca-sāt* (CC 3.2.169).

CHAPTER 10

The Worship of Sri Guru

One should first worship the spiritual master and pray for his mercy before commencing the worship of Lord Chaitanya Mahaprabhu and His associates. Then one should take his permission to worship Radha and Krishna along with Their entourage.

This injunction in the *Hari-bhakti-vilāsa* (4.344) quotes Krishna on this point:

prathamaṁ tu guruṁ pūjya
tataś caiva mamārcanam
kurvan siddhim avāpnoti
hy anyathā niṣphalaṁ bhavet

> One should first worship the spiritual master and only then Me. One who proceeds in this fashion will attain success; if not, his puja of the Deity will be fruitless.

In the same book (4.345), Narada Muni says:

gurau sannihite yas tu
pūjayed anyam agrataḥ
sa durgatim avāpnoti
pūjanaṁ tasya niṣphalam

> One who worships anyone else in the presence of the guru is destined for misfortune. His worship of the Deity is without benefit.

The *Smṛti-mahārṇava* (quoted in HBV 4.343) says:

> *rikta-pāṇir na paśyeta*
> *rājānaṁ bhiṣajaṁ gurum*
> *nopāyana-karaḥ putraṁ*
> *śiṣyaṁ bhṛtyaṁ nirīkṣayet*

> One should never go empty-handed to see a king, a doctor, or a teacher. One should not look upon a son, disciple, or servant while bearing gifts.

The *Śvetāśvatara Upaniṣad* (6.23) states the importance of the spiritual master:

> *yasya deve parā bhaktiḥ*
> *yathā deve tathā gurau*
> *tasyaite kathitā hy arthāḥ*
> *prakāśante mahātmanaḥ*

> Only unto those great souls who have implicit faith in both the Lord and the spiritual master, who is His manifestation and not different from Him, is the meaning of His teachings revealed.

This means that one should have deep faith in the Supreme Lord, but above that, one must have equal faith in the spiritual master, understanding him to be the Supreme Lord's *prakāśa-vigraha* and nondifferent from Him. Only then will the master reveal the truths he has realized. In his commentary, Sanatana Goswami says that these meanings (*arthāḥ*) are *puruṣārthāḥ*, the objectives of human life up to and including the fifth and ultimate goal, love of God. In other words, without such devotion to both the spiritual master and the Supreme Lord, the ultimate goal of the revealed scriptures, love of God, will never be attained.

The *Hari-bhakti-vilāsa* then cites three important verses from the *Bhāgavatam* that stress the worship of the spiritual master. The first (ŚB 7.15.26) is spoken by Narada Muni:

yasya sākṣād bhagavati
jñāna dīpaprade gurau
martyāsaddhīḥ śrutaṁ tasya
sarvaṁ kuñjaraśaucavat

> O King! The spiritual master, the giver of transcendental knowledge, is the Supreme Lord Himself, His manifest form or *prakāśa-vigraha.* If someone has the false idea that he is an ordinary human being, a mere mortal, then all his study of scripture is as useless as the bathing of an elephant.

It is essential to note that even though someone engages in intense devotional practices, they are useless if he thinks of the spiritual master as an ordinary man. This is the point of this verse. The words *sākṣād bhagavati* clearly indicate that one must think of the guru as the Supreme Lord Himself and not as His partial expansion. The Supreme Lord is the source of all expansions, the object of all devotional service, and the one who has incarnated in the form of a servant to Himself. This is expressed by Vishwanatha Chakravarti in his *Gurvāṣṭaka: kintu prabhor yaḥ priya eva tasya*—"his 'identification' with Krishna is due to his being most dear to Him."

Since it is the Lord, the supreme object of worship, who is personally present as the spiritual master, if one has the deranged idea to think of him as an ordinary mortal, then whatever he has heard from him—whether it is the mantras received at the time of initiation or instructions in the scripture and devotional practice—ceases to have any effect.

The second verse is from the *Tenth Canto* (80.34), where Krishna speaks to His friend Sudama, who was a student together with Him at the home of His spiritual master Sandipani Muni in Avantipura:

nāham ijyā-prajātibhyāṁ
tapasopaśamena ca
tuṣyeyaṁ sarva-bhūtātmā
guru-śuśrūṣayā yathā

> I, the soul of all beings, am not as pleased by the performance of the prescribed duties of the four ashrams as I am by service to the guru.

The word *ijyā* refers to the four duties of the ashramas, which in turn refer to sacrifice. According to Sridhar Swami, this is a reference to the prescribed religious duties of the householder, while Vishwanatha Chakravarti takes it to mean the duties of the *brahmacārī*. *Prajāti* is interpreted by Sridhar Swami to mean *prakṛṣṭā-janma*, the second birth that comes with the investiture of the sacred thread at the beginning of student (*brahmacārī*) life. Vishwanatha, however, sees the word as meaning *putrotpādanam*, having children, which is householder dharma. *Tapasā*, austerity, is the essence of retired life (*vānaprastha*), while *upaśama*, complete renunciation, is the essence of *sannyāsa*. Vishwanatha and Sridhar agree on these two.

In *Śrīmad-Bhāgavatam* (11.17.27), Krishna tells Uddhava:

ācāryaṁ māṁ vijānīyān
nāvamanyeta karhicit
na martya buddhyāsūyeta
sarva deva mayo guruḥ

> O Uddhava! Know verily that I am the preceptor, so never disrespect him in any way. One should not envy the preceptor, thinking him to be an ordinary man, for he is the sum total of all the demigods.

In his comment on this verse, Sanatana Goswami states that "envy" (*asūyā*) refers to faultfinding (*doṣa-dṛṣṭi*). The *Hari-bhakti-vilāsa* (4.350) then quotes from another source:

sādhakasya gurau bhaktiṁ
mandīkurvanti devatāḥ
yan no'tītya vrajed viṣṇuṁ
śiṣyo bhaktyā gurau dhruvam

> The gods do everything they can to diminish a disciple's devotion to his spiritual master because they are afraid that through such bhakti, the disciple will pass them by and attain Vishnu before them.

And the following verse (HBV 4.351) confirms the worshipable nature of the guru:

gurur brahmā gurur viṣṇur
gurur devo maheśvaraḥ
gurur eva paraṁ brahma
tasmāt sampūjayet sadā

> The spiritual master is Brahma, he is Vishnu, he is Shiva. The spiritual master is the Supreme Brahman, so one should always worship him.

This verse is frequently recited as a *praṇāma-mantra*, with *tasmai śrī-gurave namaḥ* in the last quarter.

At this point it might be worthwhile citing the seventh verse of Vishwanatha Chakravarti Thakur's *Gurvāṣṭakam*:

sākṣād-dharitvena samasta-śāstrair
uktas tathā bhāvyata eva sadbhiḥ

kintu prabhor yaḥ priya eva tasya
vande guroḥ śrī-caraṇāravindam

> I worship the lotus feet of my spiritual master, who has been declared by the scriptures as Lord Hari Himself, and is indeed thought of that way by all the saints, due to his being very dear to the Lord.

The Supreme Lord, the *Param-Brahma*, Sri Krishna is the supreme object of devotion or the *viṣaya-vigraha*. He has appeared in this world as the *āśraya-vigraha*, or reservoir of devotion for Krishna. He does so in order to show me by his personal example the path of devotional service. He is Krishna's dearmost personal associate. He is none other than Krishna Himself appearing to me as guru.

This is the way we should understand the *tattva* of the spiritual master. Otherwise, one may fall into the trap of equating guru with God in every respect, and thus give exclusive precedence to the worship of the spiritual master and neglect the worship of Krishna or of His *avatāras*, thinking They have no importance.

CHAPTER 11

The Avadhuta's Twenty-Four Gurus

Once upon a time, Lord Krishna's forefather, King Yadu, saw a young *brāhmaṇa* who had taken up the life of an *avadhuta*, someone so renounced that he had reached the highest stage of indifference to the world. Although he had no possessions, the holy man was effulgent with health and joy. Yadu approached the *avadhuta*, whose name was Dattatreya, and asked him the secret of his ecstatic condition, to which he replied that he had received instructions from twenty-four gurus. Blessed with the knowledge he had received from them, he was able to wander the earth in a liberated state. He then explained to Yadu what he had learned. *Śrīmad-Bhāgavatam* (11.7.32) states:

santi me guravo rājan
bahavo buddhy-upāśritāḥ
yato buddhim upādāya
mukto 'ṭāmīha tān śṛṇu

I have many teachers, all of whom have taken up residence in my intelligence. By making use of this intelligence, I am able to wander through this world in complete liberty.

Srila Bhaktisiddhanta Saraswati comments:

> The *avadhuta* is saying, "Unlike others in this world, I do not look on the things of this world as objects for enjoyment but as teachers. Other people are deprived of service to guru because they are on the mental platform. Taking shelter of fixed intelligence, I wander through this world. Being situated in yoga and always seeking the goal of loving devotional service, I endeavor to overcome all obstacles by the use of my intelligence, and it is through this intelligence that I have found the twenty-four gurus I will now describe."

Srila Saraswati Thakur tells us that we must learn to see even natural phenomena as manifestations of the spiritual master. Nature itself is a manifestation of the supreme soul, who teaches us lessons about ultimate truth through nature. In fact, only one who sees the guru in all things can truly function himself as a guru (*Vivṛti* to ŚB 11.8.2).

The first five of the *avadhuta's* gurus are the principal elements: earth, air, sky, water, and fire.

1. THE EARTH

The *avadhuta* said, "From the earth I learned that when one is overcome by the elements of material nature through one's destiny, one should not swerve from the spiritual path. From the earth's trees and mountains I have also learned to be selfless, and so I am ready to act for the benefit of others, like the trees."

These qualities were also given special attention by Sri Chaitanya Mahaprabhu, who wrote:

tṛṇād api sunīcena
taror iva sahiṣṇunā

amāninā mānadena
kīrtanīyaḥ sadā hariḥ

> One can chant the Holy Names of the Lord constantly if one is more humble than grass, more tolerant than the tree, without pride, and ready to honor all others.

In the *Bhāgavatam* Krishna glorifies the generosity and tolerance of trees. One hot summer's day, Krishna was out grazing the cows with His friends. Sitting under a broad-leafed shade tree, He said, "Just look at these trees. You can tell they are the most fortunate souls because they have given their lives for the benefit of others. They subject themselves to the weather—blustering winds, blistering heat, torrential rain, frost—and throughout it all they offer us shelter. What is more, they have made a success of their lives by providing for so many other creatures. They are like the most generous benefactors, who turn no one in need away. They satisfy all with their leaves, flowers, fruit, shade, roots, bark, wood, scents, sap, branches, and even their ashes."

Krishna concludes His lesson by saying:

etāvaj janma sāphalyaṁ
dehinām iha dehiṣu
prāṇair arthair dhiyā
vācā śreya evācaret sadā

> This then is the ultimate success of human life—to behave in such a way with one's actions, possessions, intellect, and speech, so that others are benefited. (ŚB 10.22.35)

Remembering these verses, Mahaprabhu tells His followers to act for the benefit of others:

bhārata-bhūmite haila manuṣya janma yāra
janma sārthaka kariñ kara para-upakāra

Those who have taken birth as human beings in the land of Bharata varsha should make their lives successful and work for the benefit of others. (CC 1.9.41)

2. THE AIR

The *avadhuta's* second guru was the air. In the yogic worldview, there are two kinds of air—the air that flows around us and the air in the body. The latter is called praṇa, or life-airs. Praṇa does not need us to eat excessively rich or particularly tasty foods in order to remain in the body, so the *avadhuta* learned that one should eat only as much as one needs to keep one's intelligence awake and one's mind and speech sharp. The object of our sense activities should not be the pleasure of the senses alone.

Similarly, from the all-pervading air that surrounds us, the *avadhuta* learned another lesson: detachment. A yogi, he said, interacts with sense objects just as air does and, like air, does not become attached. Sometimes the air takes on the odors of objects on the earth over which it passes, and so one of the names for "wind" in Sanskrit is *gandha-vāha*, "carrier of fragrances." However, the wind carries these odors while remaining distinct from them. The yogi knows his spiritual identity, so he is unaffected by the world around him, even when it appears to others that he has taken on worldly qualities. The yogi knows that he is ultimately transcendental to the world.

3. THE SKY

The *avadhuta* named his third guru, the sky, from which he learned about the all-pervasive nature of the soul and its transcendence. On the one hand, the all-pervading sky makes no distinctions as to moving or nonmoving, conscious or unconscious beings: it is present in all equally. Similarly, the yogi recognizes that God is present in all beings equally and makes no distinction between them.

In the Bhagavad Gita, Krishna compares His relationship to creation with the sky: "All things are within Me," He says, "yet I am not in them. Then again, the creation is not in Me, because I am beyond it. Just as the wind blows in the sky but does not affect it, so the creation is within Me but does not affect Me."

4. WATER

The *avadhuta brāhmaṇa's* fourth guru was the water, from which he learned about natural purity. In its natural state water is clear, refreshing, and sweet. Saintly persons are similar to water in that they are simple, pure, and kind. Moreover, the *brāhmaṇa* said, they transform and sanctify every place they go, just as the holy rivers purify the lands through which they flow. The Sanskrit word for "holy place" is *tīrtha*, which means "crossing." India's many holy rivers were considered places where one "crossed over" to the spiritual realm. In the *Bhāgavatam* (1.13.10), King Yudhishthira says to his saintly uncle Vidura:

bhavad-vidhā bhāgavatās
tīrthī-bhūtāḥ svayaṁ vibho
tīrthīkurvanti tirthāni
svāntaḥ-sthena gadā-bhṛtaḥ

> Great devotees like you are places of pilgrimage in yourselves. Indeed, you are what makes the places of pilgrimage truly holy, for you carry the Lord in your heart.

Water in a brook gurgles. The waves breaking on the ocean shore make a sweet, regular, soothing sound. Even a crashing waterfall's constant roar soothes the soul. Similarly, although the sage purifies the world by his presence alone, his most powerful tool for benefiting others is his voice, for either through song or speech he changes the hearts of those who suffer from a lack of God consciousness. As Krishna says in the *Bhāgavatam* (11.26.26):

tato duḥsaṅgam utsṛjya
satsu sajjeta buddhimān
santa evāsya chindanti
mano-vyāsaṅgam uktibhiḥ

> An intelligent person should therefore abandon all bad association and stay in the company of devotees. Only such holy persons can cut through one's unhealthy mental attachments through the use of their powerful words.

5. FIRE

From fire, the *brāhmaṇa* said, he learned not to allow himself to be affected by what he consumes. *Śrīmad-Bhāgavatam* (11.7.45) states:

tejasvī tapasā dīpto
durdharṣodara-bhājanaḥ
sarva-bhakṣyo'pi yuktātmā
nādatte malam agnivat

> A sage who, by the practice of austerities, has been made spiritually effulgent like fire, develops infallible powers of digestion. Even if he eats inedible things he is not negatively affected.

The yogis have known since ancient times that we are what we eat and have always advised a diet that purifies existence and keeps the spirit strong. There are many things—meat, fish, eggs, alcohol, and psychotropic drugs—that increase the modes of passion and ignorance and have a negative influence on one's spiritual life.

However, even in the Bhagavad Gita Krishna says that someone who is rightly situated and acts according to his prescribed duty is not adversely affected by whatever sins he may commit. In the case of Arjuna, this referred to his having to kill members of his own family during the

Kurukshetra war. In the Bhagavad Gita (18.17) Krishna says:

yasya nāhaṅkṛtir bhāvo
yasya buddhir na lipyate
hatvāpi sa imāṁl lokān
na hanti na nibadhyate

> He who is free from egotism (arising from aversion to the Absolute), and whose intelligence is not implicated (in worldly activities)—even if he kills every living being in the whole world does not kill at all, nor does he suffer a murderer's consequences.

This applies both to Krishna and the perfected saint. After hearing about the *rāsa-līlā*, Maharaja Parikshit asks how Krishna can dance with the *gopīs*, who are the wives of other men. Sukadeva responds that Krishna could dance with them because of His unique position, and that in general, unless one has similar power, he should not transgress moral codes. *Śrīmad Bhāgavatam* (10.33.30) states:

dharma-vyatikramo dṛṣṭa
īśvarāṇāṁ ca sāhasam
tejīyasāṁ na doṣāya
vahneḥ sarva-bhujo yathā

> Whenever we see an infringement of the moral law in very powerful persons, we should not think that they are negatively affected, or that it is a fault, any more than fire is at fault because it consumes everything.

Sukadeva gives two examples, one of Shiva, who could drink an ocean of poison without ill effects, and the other of fire, which burns even flesh and poison without becoming affected. These are things that ordinary mortals cannot do, so one should know one's limits and act accordingly.

Another lesson the *brāhmaṇa* learned from fire was neither to accumulate anything nor to be greedy, but to take only what he needed. Moreover, from the sacrificial fire, the *brāhmaṇa* learned another lesson. In the Vedic sacrificial system, the *yajaman*, or patron of the sacrifice, engages *brāhmaṇa* priests to offer many things into the fire. In the earliest days, this may have included animals, a custom that ceased after the rise of Jainism and Buddhism. The *brāhmaṇa* explains that by offering things into the fire, the *yajaman* was benefited, for the fire would burn away his sinful reactions. In the same way, the saintly person may accept gifts from the faithful, but does so with detachment, conscious of offering benefit to others. In so doing, he also remains unaffected by his accepting the wealth of others.

Bhaktisiddhanta Saraswati Thakur here reminds us of one of Rupa Goswami's great teachings by quoting the *Bhakti-rasāmṛta-sindhu* (1.2.127):

anāsaktasya viṣayān
yathārham upayuñjataḥ
nirbandhaḥ kṛṣṇa-sambandhe
yuktaṁ vairāgyam ucyate

> A person who wishes to advance in devotional service should be detached from the objects of the senses, using them only inasmuch as they have utility in the service of Lord Krishna. This is called engaged detachment, or *yukta-vairāgya*.

The *brāhmaṇa* learned yet another lesson from fire—a more philosophical one about the nature of God. God is present in all things just as fire is present in wood. However, one needs a spark in order to see fire come from fuel. The *Bhāgavatam* (1.2.24) teaches:

pārthivād dāruṇo dhūmas
tasmād agnis trayī-mayaḥ

tamasas tu rajas tasmāt
sattvaṁ yad brahma-darśanam

> Firewood is a transformation of earth. Smoke is better than the raw wood. But fire is better still, for fire can be used in sacrifice and lead to many benefits. Similarly, the mode of passion is somewhat better than ignorance, but the mode of goodness is better than either of these other two qualities of nature, for only in this state can one attain knowledge of Brahman.

Of course, Vishwanatha Chakravarti points out that the state of goodness (*sattva*) is not sufficient in itself to attain direct knowledge of God. One needs to be filled with the spirit of loving devotion.

Fire is sometimes covered by ash. Although hidden, the fire is still present. If we sprinkle oil or butter on the ashes, they will burst into flames again. Similarly, the truly saintly do not like to advertise themselves. However, when a seeker approaches them with faith and an inquiry, the saints' qualities ignite and they spread the light and heat of their knowledge to others.

With a similar example, elsewhere in the *Bhāgavatam* (11.10.12), Krishna says:

ācāryo'raṇir ādyaḥ syād
ante-vāsy uttarāraṇiḥ
tat-sandhānaṁ pravacanaṁ
vidyā-sandhiḥ sukhāvahaḥ

> The teacher is like the upper piece of wood, the student like the lower. The rubbing of the upper stick on the lower is the speech of the teacher, and the fire that is produced is knowledge, which brings all happiness.

6. THE MOON

The *avadhuta's* sixth guru was the moon. The moon goes through various phases during its monthly cycle, but the fullness or darkness of the moon at the beginning and end of each fortnight are only appearances—the moon itself remains unchanged. Similarly, each of us is a spiritual being that essentially remains unchanged despite the changes in the body.

As an afterthought, the *avadhuta* added, "We could learn the same lesson from the fire as well. The fire's flames appear and disappear at every moment, and yet an ordinary observer does not notice this creation and destruction. Similarly, the mighty waves of time flow constantly, like the powerful currents of a river, creating the incessant changes in the body as it goes through birth, growth, death, and rebirth. Yet the soul, which is constantly undergoing these changes, does not realize that time is having these effects."

Krishna says the same thing in the Bhagavad Gita (2.13):

dehino'smin yathā dehe
kaumāraṁ yauvanaṁ jarā
tathā dehāntara-prāptir
dhīras tatra na muhyati

> Just as in this body we all pass first through childhood, then youth, and then old age, so at death we simply take another body. Such a change does not disturb the minds of those who know the truth.

7. THE SUN

The sun evaporates large quantities of water with its potent rays, but then releases the water back toward the earth in the form of rain. In the same way, a yogi may take possession of all types of material objects, but he redistributes them when he encounters a person in need. Thus, both in accepting objects and giving them up, the yogi is not entangled.

Even when reflected in various objects the sun is never divided; nor does it merge into its reflection. Similarly, although the soul is reflected through different material bodies, the soul remains undivided and non-material.

Lying on his bed of arrows after the battle of Kurukshetra, awaiting the propitious moment to leave his body, Bhishma offered his prayers to Lord Krishna, who stood before him. The last verse of his prayer is given in *Śrīmad Bhāgavatam* (1.9.42):

taṁ imam ahaṁ ajaṁ śarīra-bhājāṁ
hṛdi hṛdi dhiṣṭhitam ātma-kalpitānām
pratidṛśam iva naikadhārkam ekaṁ
samadhigato'smi vidhūta-bheda-mohaḥ

> Just as the one sun appears differently to those with different vantage points, so do You, the one unborn Lord, appear in the hearts of every embodied being according to their individual perspective. But I have been freed of my illusion and see You here, standing before me in Your original form.

8. THE PIGEON

Once upon a time, there was a pigeon that lived in a forest with his wife. He built a nest in a tree and lived with her there for several years. The hearts of the two pigeons were bound together with great affection. They had eyes only for each other, and their every thought was for the beloved. Naïvely trusting in the future, they enjoyed their lives as a loving couple among the trees. The pigeon was so devoted to his wife that he fulfilled her every desire, no matter how demanding.

Then the female pigeon experienced her first pregnancy. When the time came, she filled their nest with eggs and sat on them until they hatched. The two pigeons became most affectionate to their chicks, with their tender limbs and feathers, and took great pleasure in listening to their chirping, which, though still unformed, sounded sweet to them. They raised them lovingly, taking joy in the happiness of their brood.

One day, the two pigeons went out to find food for the children. During their absence, a hunter caught sight of the fledglings as they moved about near the nest. He spread out his net and captured them all.

When the adult pigeons returned, they saw the empty nest and soon caught sight of their children, trapped in the hunter's net. Overwhelmed with anguish, the mother pigeon burst into tears and rushed toward her young as they cried out to her for help. Her judgment clouded by despair, as she rushed toward the net in a desperate attempt to free her children, the hunter trapped her as well.

Seeing both his children and wife, as dear to him as life itself, fatally bound in the hunter's net, the father pigeon began to lament wretchedly. "What a fool I've been! My family life has been destroyed, leaving me unsatisfied and unfulfilled. I must have done something truly wicked for this to have happened to me. My wife was perfect for me. She loved me and was always devoted and faithful. Now she has gone with our children, leaving me behind to grieve in an empty nest."

His grief was so great that the father pigeon lost all will to live. Mesmerized by the sight of his family struggling in the net and dying, he fainted and also fell into the cruel hunter's clutches. The hunter, considering his day's work a success, went home.

The lesson the *avadhuta* drew from this drama, which he had himself witnessed, was that too much attachment to material pleasure results in pain and disappointment. He uses the word *kṛpaṇa*, "miser," to describe the father pigeon's attitude, recalling the words of the *Bṛhad-āraṇyaka Upaniṣad* (3.8.10):

> *yo vā etad akṣaram aviditvā'smāl lokāt praiti, sa kṛpaṇaḥ.*
> *atha ya etad akṣaraṁ gārgi viditvā'asmāl lokāt praiti, sa brāhmaṇaḥ.*

> O Gargi, one who goes through life and dies without coming to know the imperishable Supreme Truth is truly a miser. But one who goes through life and dies after coming to know the imperishable Supreme Truth is truly a *brāhmaṇa*.

The doors of liberation are opened wide to those who have attained the human form of life. But any human being who sees life's only goal in worldly happiness and sense gratification, even within a devoted family life, is considered a miser.

The *avadhuta* also uses the expression *ārūḍha-cyuta*, "one who has fallen after climbing a mountain." In other words, the human form of life is in itself a great attainment for the soul who wanders from one body to another, never having the intellectual equipment or awareness to seek higher truths. If after coming to this human form of life one chooses to use it for perfecting pleasures that are already available in animal species, he squanders a great opportunity that may not soon come again. Thus it is said:

nidrāhāra-bhaya-maithunaṁ ca
samānam etat paśubhir narāṇām
jñānaṁ hi teṣām adhiko viśeṣo
jñāna-vihīnaḥ paśubhiḥ samānaḥ

> Both the lower creatures and humans must sleep, eat, defend themselves, and reproduce. Human beings have a higher awareness, however. So the human being whose life is nothing more than eating, sleeping, defending, and mating, no matter how sophisticated his tastes, is nothing more than an animal.

9. THE PYTHON

The *avadhuta's* ninth guru was the python. This great snake lies quietly for great lengths of time without searching for food, preferring to wait for its prey to come to it. If nothing comes, it is capable of tolerating hunger. Bhaktisiddhanta Saraswati states, "Most of us are furtive in our eagerness to satisfy our ever-demanding senses. We should learn to tolerate these demands without giving in to them."

10. THE OCEAN

The *avadhuta's* tenth guru was the sea, from which he learned that one should not be disturbed by the thoughts and desires that constantly enter the mind. In the rainy season, the rivers constantly enter the ocean in great floods and torrents without raising its level at all. On the other hand, in the dry season, the rivers are reduced to a trickle, yet the ocean's level is not diminished in the slightest. So too does the self-realized sage remain levelheaded in all circumstances, because of his deep realization of his eternal spiritual identity.

Krishna imparts this same lesson in the Bhagavad Gita (2.70):

āpūryamāṇam acala-pratiṣṭhaṁ
samudram āpaḥ praviśanti yadvat
tadvat kāmā yaṁ praviśanti sarve
sa śāntim āpnoti na kāma-kāmī

> The ocean is constantly being filled by the rivers that flow into it, but it remains deep and unchanging. Similarly, one who recognizes that sensual desires are constantly flowing into him will attain peace, and not the person who attempts to satisfy them all.

11. THE MOTH

The *avadhuta* took this lesson from the moth: sense objects attract us by their beauty, but to our destruction, like a moth drawn by the firelight to its death.

In his description of the universal form, Arjuna also uses the example of the moth to describe how all creatures are drawn into the fire of death:

yathā pradīptaṁ jvalanaṁ pataṅgā
viśanti nāśāya samṛddha-vegāḥ
tathaiva nāśāya viśanti lokās
tavāpi vaktrāṇi samṛddha-vegāḥ

> Just as moths rush into the bright flames of the fire, meeting their destruction, so too do all these worlds rush into the mouths of Your universal form with great speed, there meeting their death. (Bhagavad Gita 11.29)

The world is also a form of the Lord, known as His universal form. However, one who sees it as the object of enjoyment instead of an object of service is like the moth, which mindlessly follows the light and falls to his death. As an object of enjoyment, the phenomenal world is a creation of Krishna's illusory power.

12. THE HONEYBEE

From the honeybee, the mendicant learned several lessons. The bee goes from flower to flower, taking just a sample of what each has to offer. *Śrīmad-Bhāgavatam* (11.8.9) states:

stokaṁ stokaṁ grased grāsaṁ
deho varteta yāvatā
gṛhān ahiṁsann ātiṣṭhed
vṛttiṁ mādhu-karīṁ muniḥ

> One should take only small mouthfuls when one eats, taking only enough to maintain the body. One should not stay as a guest in anyone's home to the extent that it disturbs them. This is called the honey bee's way of life.

The bee that becomes greedy and continues to long drink the nectar from a flower risks being trapped after the sun sets and the flower's petals close.

Of course, in this example, as in others, the mendicant was speaking of someone who has taken the hermit's way of life and who depends on charity to maintain body and soul. There are still some people who live like this. The Six Goswamis, Sri Chaitanya Mahaprabhu's beloved companions, for example, lived in this way. Describing Raghunatha Das Goswami's renunciation, Krishna Das Kaviraj writes in the *Caitanya-caritāmṛta* (2.6.220):

mahāprabhura bhakta jata vairāgya pradhāna
jāhā dekhi tuṣṭa han gaura bhagavān

> Renunciation was the predominating characteristic of every one of Mahaprabhu's devotees. When Lord Gauranga saw this, he was very pleased.

However, even though these standards of renunciation are not possible for the great majority of people in today's world, the basic principles of simple living and high thinking are still basic to our culture of spiritual life. Rupa Goswami summarizes this point in the *Bhakti-rasāmṛta-sindhu* (1.2.108):

yāvatā syāt svanirvāhaḥ
svīkuryāt tāvad arthavit
ādhikye nyūnatāyāṁ ca
cyavate paramārthataḥ

> One who knows his purpose should accept only as much as he needs to maintain his existence. If he accepts more or less than that, he will fall away from the supreme objective.

13. THE ELEPHANT

Like the moth, the elephant is led to destruction by desire. In India, wild elephants were typically captured by using a domesticated she-elephant to attract them to a pit into which a lusty bull would fall. Again, the lesson is that a renunciant should not allow himself to be attracted to the opposite sex.

For the householder, of course, the lesson is the same. One should remain satisfied with one's spouse, as long as he or she is a true partner in the cultivation of spiritual life. The wife or husband who helps the other partner cultivate his or her relationship with Krishna becomes *sat-saṅga*, beneficial association. On the other hand, if one quits one's husband or wife because he or she interferes with one's sense pleasure, this will not lead to auspiciousness. In *Śrīmad Bhāgavatam* (5.1.17) Lord Brahma says:

bhayaṁ pramattasya vaneṣv api syād
yataḥ sa āste saha-ṣaṭ-sapatnaḥ
jitendriyasyātma-rater budhasya
gṛhāśramaḥ kiṁ nu karoty avadyam

> Fear follows one who has no control over the mind, even in the forest far from temptation, because his six enemies (lust, anger, greed, envy, intoxication, and illusion) accompany him wherever he goes. But what harm can living with one's wife and children do to one who has conquered his senses, and who is self-satisfied and awake to the spiritual purpose of life?

14. THE HONEY GATHERER

In ancient Indian society, some people specialized in gathering wild honey from hollow trees and other places where bees made their hives. The *avadhuta* told King Yadu, "Some miserly people are like bees who gather honey and store it. They neither enjoy the honey nor share it.

Eventually, someone else comes along and steals the miser's wealth, just as a honey-gatherer takes all the bees' honey." The holy mendicants who come to householders and ask for charity give those householders the chance to engage their wealth in productive ways that will bring them eternal benefit.

15. THE DEER

A monk should never listen to mundane songs or gossip, for these will enchant him into forgetting his spiritual goal. In ancient India, hunters used a flute or other musical instrument to attract deer, which they then killed.

16. THE FISH

Similarly, the lesson the *avadhuta* learned from fish was not to be too attracted to nice food. The fish sees the bait but not the hook. Of all the senses, says the *avadhuta*, the tongue is the most difficult to control. Someone who has been able to overcome the desire to please all the other senses will still be tempted by the tongue: *Śrīmad-Bhāgavatam* (11.8.20–21) states:

indriyāṇi jayanty āśu nirāhārā manīṣiṇaḥ
varjayitvā tu rasanaṁ tan nirannasya vardhate
tāvaj jitendriyo na syād vijitānyendriyaḥ pumān
na jayed rasanaṁ yāvaj jitaṁ sarvaṁ jite rase

> One can quickly conquer the other senses simply by disengaging them from their objects. The only exception is the tongue, whose desires simply increase when one does not have tasty food to eat. But until one conquers over the tongue, one cannot be said to have controlled the senses. Only one who has conquered the tongue has conquered all the senses.

All yoga practices ultimately rest on the strength of gaining a higher taste. The pleasure that an advanced yogi experiences, whatever path he or she follows, is greater than the pleasure that comes from the various delights afforded by the material world. The Bhagavad Gita (2.59) teaches:

viṣayā vinivartante
nirāhārasya dehinaḥ
rasa-varjaṁ raso'py asya
paraṁ dṛṣṭvā nivartante

> Although the spiritual aspirant may externally avoid sense objects, he will not so easily be able to give up his inbred taste for them. This taste for sense gratification can only be overcome when one has direct experience of the Supreme.

The path of devotion is somewhat different from that of yoga, gnosis, or other paths of renunciation. Though the adherents of all the yogic paths claim to experience this higher taste, this can only be truly said of those who engage in devotion to the personal God, for on the devotional path one actually uses and spiritualizes the mind and senses themselves through hearing and chanting, and even through eating *prasāda*.

Devotees control the tongue by taking Krishna's remnants. Bhaktivinoda Thakur sings:

śarīra avidyā jāla jaḍendriya tāhe kāla
jīva phele viṣaya sāgare
tāra madhye jihvā ati lobhamaya sudurmati
tāhe jetā kaṭhina saṁsāre

> This material body is the net of ignorance. The material senses are death. They fling the conditioned soul into the ocean of sensual existence. Of the senses, the tongue is the greediest and the most resistent to control.

kṛṣṇa boro dayāmaya karibāra jihvā jaya
sva-prasāda anna dila bhāi
sei annāmṛta khāo rādhā kṛṣṇa guṇa gāo
preme ḍāko caitanya-nitāi

Being most merciful, Krishna has given us the gift of His *prasāda* to help us conquer the tongue. So take this nectarean food, sing the glories of Radha and Krishna, and lovingly call out the names of Sri Chaitanya and Sri Nityananda.

17. THE PROSTITUTE PINGALA

The *avadhuta* then told the story of the prostitute Pingala, his seventeenth guru. Pingala lived in the ancient city of Videha. She would stand in front of her house on the street, watching the men as they walked by, sizing them up and speculating whether or not they were prospective clients. "Does this fellow have money? This fellow looks rich. Will he pay me well?" One night went by without a single customer, and she anxiously went in and out of her doorway, gradually losing hope that anyone would come. After she had lost hope completely, she said:

"How foolish I have been. I have abandoned God, my true beloved, who is nearer to me than anyone and who alone can give me love. Instead I looked for happiness in insignificant men who are unable to satisfy my innermost desires but indeed who bring me unhappiness, fear, anxiety, lamentation, and illusion. How much suffering I have brought on myself through my despicable profession, selling my body to lusty, greedy men who are themselves objects of pity, all from a desire for money and the hope of finding love. But how can anyone hope to find love in this temporary body, which only houses the soul? The Soul of all embodied beings is my true friend, my true lover and husband. I will give myself to Him and enjoy with Him on the spiritual platform, just as Lakshmi does."

Feeling great detachment from her old way of life, Pingala thought that she must have done something to gain the Lord's mercy. With full faith, she took shelter of Him and vowed, "Henceforth I will maintain myself with whatever comes of its own accord and only take pleasure with my true beloved, the Lord, who is the Soul of my soul."

The *avadhuta* concluded his tale: "And so Pingala cut off all her sinful desires to enjoy with worldly lovers and became situated in perfect peace. Truly, desire for material enjoyment is the source of all unhappiness, and freedom from such desires brings happiness. Freed at last from her desire to enjoy any lover other than the Lord, she happily went to sleep.

18. THE KURARI BIRD

The *avadhuta* then said, "Accumulation of things leads to misery. One who knows this becomes an *akiñcana*—someone who knows that nothing is truly his." To support this, he told the story of the *kurarī*, an osprey. One day, this osprey had a successful hunt and had caught a mouse. The other ospreys had not caught anything, however, so they ganged up on the first, who immediately dropped his prey in order to save his life, thus attaining peace of mind. One who accumulates things becomes an object of envy, leading to so many unwanted troubles.

19. THE INNOCENT CHILD

The *avadhuta* then said, "I am indifferent to praise and insult. I have no worries for wife or children. I take pleasure and joy in my own being. In this way, I go through life like an innocent child. There are two kinds of persons who are free of worry—the fool, who is bewildered and ignorant, and the sage, who is beyond the entanglements of material nature."

20. THE VIRGIN

The *avadhuta's* twentieth lesson came from a young girl whose parents were looking to get her married. One day, when she was alone at home, several suitors came to seek her hand. Since no one else was there, she greeted them. While she was preparing a meal for them, the bangles on her wrists made a great deal of noise. Afraid the sound would disturb her guests, she broke her bangles one by one, leaving only one pair on each wrist. When she returned to cutting vegetables, however, the bangles again clinked, so she slipped another one off each wrist. The *avadhuta* concluded:

vāse bahūnāṁ kalaho
bhaved vārtā dvayor api
eka eva vaset tasmāt
kumāryā iva kaṅkaṇaḥ

> When many people live together in a single dwelling, there is a lot of noise. Even when there are two people living together, there is still conversation. One should therefore live alone, just like the virgin's bangle. (ŚB 11.9.10)

In his commentary on this verse, Vishwanatha Chakravarti reminds us of the difference between the *jñāna-yoga* followed by the *avadhuta* and the path of devotion. He writes, "*Jñāna-yoga* requires its followers to avoid all company, just like this poor girl, who had neither lover nor husband, got rid of her bangles. *Bhakti Devi*, however, is like a princess with a husband. When she goes to meet her husband, she puts on her most colorful bangles so that the sounds they make will accompany their embraces. In the same way, *Bhakti Devi* brings the devotees who have taken shelter together so that they can make the beautiful sweet sounds of *harināma-saṅkīrtana*. Devotees do not avoid the company of others at all costs. The *Bhāgavatam* (3.25.34) states:

naikātmatāṁ me spṛhayanti kecin
mat-pāda-sevābhiratā mad-īhāḥ
ye'nyonyato bhāgavatāḥ prasajya
sabhājayante mama pauruṣāṇi

> Devotees who are addicted to My service never seek becoming one with Me in all respects. All

> their activities are dedicated to Me and so they are attached to each other's company, where they can enjoy glorifying My pastimes.

This verse shows specifically that devotees have no interest in attaining oneness with Brahman, which is the goal of the *jñānīs*, because in this form of liberation there is still no joy of service to the Lord's lotus feet. *Jñānīs* do not relish the Lord's beauty and sweetness, or the happiness of hearing and glorifying His nectarean pastimes. So although it may consider their level of realization happiness, the devotees find their type of liberation a kind of hell.

In the Bhagavad Gita (9.13–14) Krishna speaks of the joy His devotees take in one another's company:

mahātmānas tu māṁ pārtha
daivīṁ prakṛtim āśritāḥ
bhajanty ananyamanaso
jñātvā bhūtādim avyayam

satataṁ kīrtayanto māṁ
yatantaś ca dṛḍha-vratāḥ
namasyantaś ca māṁ bhaktyā
nitya-yuktā upāsate

> O Arjuna, son of Pritha, the great souls take shelter of My divine nature, worship Me with undivided attention because they know My unlimited opulences. They are constantly chanting My glories. Firm in their vows, they bow down to Me with devotion and worship Me in permanent union with Me.

By taking shelter of the Lord's divine nature, devotees have no reason to fear the activities of the senses. Prabodhananda Saraswati says that for those who have taken shelter of Sri Chaitanya Mahaprabhu and received His mercy, the senses are like poisonous serpents with their fangs removed. Such senses can no longer cause harm because they have been transformed through devotional service.

So even though devotees avoid the company of those who are opposed to devotional service, they do not generally favor a life of absolute solitude.

21. THE ARROW-MAKER

There once was an arrow-maker who was so absorbed in sharpening arrows that he did not notice the king passing by in great pomp just outside his workshop. Similarly, the yogi becomes so absorbed in the self that he does not even notice what is going on around him.

22. THE SNAKE

From the example of the snake, the *avadhuta* said, he learned that a renunciant should live alone, without a fixed home, with invisible movements, without depending on anyone, and speaking little. He says:

gṛhārambho hi duḥkhāya
viphalaś cādhruvātmanaḥ
sarpaḥ para-kṛtaṁ veśma
praviśya sukham edhate

> Building one's own home is a source of distress. Ultimately, it is a failure, because no one lives forever. The snake sets the example of living in a home made by someone else. He enters that home and lives there happily. (ŚB 11.9.15)

Srila Bhaktisiddhanta Saraswati Thakur comments: "There have always been people in this world who carry the burden of material life yet who nevertheless are ready to give the fruits of their labor to the Vaishnavas by providing them with modern amenities like electric light, fans, cars, and other comforts. The devotees are on the path to transcendence and so are fixed on the essence; they are *saragrahis* (essence seekers) and not *bhāravāhis* (those bearing the burden of collected knowledge). However, they do not find the discomforts of the premodern way of life particularly favorable to the cultivation of transcendence. At the same time, although they may live in a palace built by someone else, they do so with detachment. It is not the transcendentalist's purpose to restore ancient monuments or preserve memories of the past: these are sentimental goals on the mundane plane."

23. THE SPIDER

The spider emits its thread from its own body, creating a complex web, and when its work is finished, draws the thread back into itself. Similarly, the Supreme Lord creates the universe out of Himself, and when the work of the creation is complete, draws it back into Himself. This teaching is also found in the (*Muṇḍaka Upaniṣad* 3.2.7):

> *yathorṇa-nābhiḥ sṛjate gṛhṇate ca*
> *yathā pṛthivyām oṣadhayaḥ sambhavanti*
> *yathā sataḥ puruṣāt keśa-lomāni*
> *tathā'kṣarāt sambhavatīha viśvam*

> Just as the spider emits and draws up its thread, just as the plants and trees grow out of the earth, and just as hairs grow out of a human body, so does this world grow out of the imperishable Supreme Truth.

24. THE WASP

It is seen that certain kinds of wasp make a nest of mud in which they place a caterpillar that has been paralyzed by its sting and their its eggs. Then the wasp closes the mouth of the nest with mud and leaves it alone for a few weeks. After the gestation period, the eggs hatch and the larvae eat the caterpillar. When they are grown enough, the young wasps break through the mud shell of the nest and fly away.

In ancient times, observers thought that the caterpillar had become so frightened by the wasp that it froze. Then, once trapped inside the nest, it remained so afraid that the wasp could return that it would be transformed by its fear and turn into a wasp.

Although empirical observation has shown many of the examples from ancient texts to be factually incorrect, there is nevertheless a truth with which modern psychology has come to agree: whenever we are absorbed in something, whether favorably or unfavorably, that absorption changes our character. Sometimes we even become the thing we are trying to avoid.

The lesson the *avadhuta* drew from the wasp was this: the *sādhaka* is transformed by meditation on the Supreme Lord, eventually becoming qualitatively one with the Lord. Thus even the most sinful person changes by practicing devotion. The Bhagavad Gita (9.30–31) says:

api cet sudurācāro
bhajate mām ananya-bhāk
sādhur eva sa mantavyaḥ
samyag vyavasito hi saḥ

> Even if a person of very bad behavior worships Me with undivided devotion, he is to be thought of as saintly, for he has the proper resolution.

kṣipraṁ bhavati dharmātmā
śaśvac-chāntiṁ nigacchati
kaunteya pratijānīhi
na me bhaktaḥ praṇaśyati

> He quickly becomes righteous and attains everlasting peace. O son of Kunti, let it be known that My devotee never perishes.

25. THE HUMAN BODY

After discussing his twenty-four gurus, the *avadhuta* stated that he had a twenty-fifth guru: his own body. What exactly do we learn from the human body? *Śrīmad Bhāgavatam* (11.9.28–29) states:

> *sṛṣṭvā purāṇi vividhāny ajayātma-śaktyā*
> *vṛkṣān sarīsṛpa-paśūn khaga-dandaśūkān*
> *tais tair atuṣṭa-hṛdayaḥ puruṣaṁ vidhāya*
> *brahmāvaloka-dhiṣaṇaṁ mudam āpa devaḥ*

> With the help of His maya potency, the Supreme Lord created this visible world with its trees, serpents, animals, birds, and other creatures, but His heart remained dissatisfied. Then He created man, who alone possesses the intelligence to see Brahman, and was delighted.

> *labdhvā sudurlabham idaṁ bahu-sambhavānte*
> *mānuṣyam arthadam anityam apīha dhīraḥ*
> *tūrṇaṁ yateta na pated anumṛtyu yāvat*
> *niḥśreyasāya viṣayaḥ khalu sarvataḥ syāt*

> After many, many births, one finally is born in this most rare and valuable human body, which, though temporary, provides an opportunity to attain the supreme goal. Therefore, the wise individual should immediately take up the effort to find the source of the supreme good in all times and circumstances, and not give up that effort to the very moment of his death.

Thus, the *avadhuta* recognized that the power of intelligence that is present in the human form of life is a rare gift that made it possible for him to learn about his true spiritual nature.

TAKING MANY GURUS

When Jiva Goswami discusses the topic of guru in the *Bhakti-sandarbha*, he refers to the concluding verses of the *avadhuta's* teachings to justify his idea that devotees who need a rational confirmation of their faith (*vicāra-pradhāna* devotees) may approach a number of gurus in order to understand the path of devotion. *Śrīmad Bhāgavatam* (11.9.31) states:

na hy ekasmād guror jñānam
susthiram syad apuṣkalam
brahmaikam advitīyaṁ vai
gīyate bahudharṣibhiḥ

> An understanding that is entirely dependable and clear cannot come from a single teacher. The Supreme Truth is One without a second, but is glorified by the seers in many different ways.

This statement should not be misunderstood as approval for mental speculation and going from one person to another to accumulate a large amount of knowledge for its own sake. The *Mahābhārata* says, "One is not considered a seer unless one has a different opinion from everybody else. But in spiritual life, one should take the path that has been followed by great souls."

Srila Jiva Goswami takes it that, although the Supreme Truth is one without a second, the various different opinions put forth by the atheist and agnostic philosophical schools will only disturb one's faith. When one has become fixed on the path of devotion, one should use intelligence or approach other *śikṣā-gurus* in order to understand the position taken by one's principal guru and to refute opposing opinions. One should not take shelter of Kapila or Gautama and others who preach ideas that are diametrically opposed to devotional service.

Conclusion

Others, who are followers of an undisciplined, disorderly, and confused path, resist following the scriptures or taking shelter of a spiritual master. Nevertheless, they become the leaders of many innocent souls and drag them down. They exemplify a verse from the *Kaṭha Upaniṣad* (1.2.5):

> *avidyāyām antare vartamānāḥ*
> *svayaṁ dhīrāḥ paṇḍitaṁ-manyamānāḥ*
> *dandramyamānāḥ pariyanti mūḍhaḥ*
> *andhenaiva nīyamānā yathāndhāḥ*

> Abiding in the midst of ignorance, thinking themselves wise and learned, fools go aimlessly hither and thither, like the blind being led by the blind.

Although they themselves have fallen into a blind well of ignorance, they consider themselves clear-thinking and wise. Puffed up with the idea that they are learned scholars, they take a position of leadership among the ignorant, and with their clever speech manage to drag the unlettered in the villages and countryside, or in the city's markets and streets, into iniquity. These fools deceive other fools by calling the pleasures of this world *nityānanda*, "eternal joy."

The *Taittirīya Upaniṣad* (2.7) says:

raso vai saḥ rasaṁ hy evāyaṁ labdhvānandī bhavati

> The Supreme Truth is the juice of life. Anyone who attains Him tastes true joy.

Krishna is the transcendental lover and enjoyer; He is permeated through and through by the joy of loving relationships, which He shares with His infinite devotees in an unlimited variety of delectable ways. Just as a poor man becomes rich by attaining wealth, so does the suffering soul of this temporary world become joyful on attaining Krishna, the embodiment of transcendent bliss.

govindānandinī rādhā govinda-mohinī
govinda-sarvasvā sarva-kāntā-śiromaṇiḥ

> Only Govinda's beloved Radha, the daughter of King Vrishabhanu, teacher of the fourteen worlds, can, through Her infinite compassion, bestow the greatest good fortune of love for Krishna on the lost souls of this creation. Therefore, Krishna, the son of Nanda Maharaja, the king of the cowherds in Vraja, has borrowed Her bodily effulgence and loving mood in order to engage in His most munificent pastimes as Gauranga Mahaprabhu, distributing love of God to the entire world. In order to be able to receive this gift, it is necessary to take shelter of Nityananda Prabhu, the spiritual master of the universe. And in order to take shelter of Nityananda Prabhu, it is first necessary to take shelter of his present-day manifestation in the form of the *sad-guru.*

śrī-guru-caraṇe rati
ei se uttama gati
je prasāde pūre sarva āśa

> Affection for the guru's lotus feet is the ultimate goal, for by his mercy all of one's aspirations are realized. (*Prema-bhakti-candrikā*)

Narottama Das says in his *Prārthanā*:

> *nitāyer karuṇā hobe*
> *vraje rādhā-kṛṣṇa pābe*

> When Nityananda gives his blessing, one can attain Radha and Krishna in Vrindavan.

Those who reject the guru and disregard the injunctions and teachings of the scriptures can never get Nityananda Prabhu's blessings, nor attain the supreme prize of divine love, *prema*. Nityananda Prabhu's blessings show us the joys of this world for the insignificant trivialities they are. With this realization, it becomes easy to leave them and to purify the heart. In the pure heart, one gets the vision of the eternal spiritual abode of Vrindavan-dhama, and one's eagerness to find a place at the lotus feet of Rupa and Raghunatha increases. This makes it possible to become truly fortunate and get an understanding of the Divine Couple, Radha and Krishna. This is the highest qualification, whereby one attains the wealth given by Lord Chaitanya, who is Himself unlimitedly wealthy with the riches of divine love.

Lord Nityananda and Sri Chaitanya Mahaprabhu are the sole progenitors of the *saṅkīrtana* movement (*saṅkīrtanaika-pitarau*). To attain their mercy, we must first take shelter of the saintly spiritual master and chant the *mahā-mantra* that they themselves chanted. Through the Holy Name, all perfections are achieved. *Harer nāmaiva kevalam.* Those who are bereft of *prema* are truly poverty-stricken. Just as a poor man who wants to become rich in this world must take a loan from a bank and then work to pay it back with interest, so must we who wish to attain the wealth of *prema* first receive the mercy of the *sad-guru* and then serve him, in body, mind, and word.

Glossary

Note: Throughout this book, for Sanskrit, Bengali, and Hindi terms that appear in *Merriam-Webster Online Dictionary* or *Merriam-Webster Unabridged Dictionary*, we have adopted the spelling given in those sources. Diacritics and italics have also been dropped for Sanskrit names and their honorifics, locations, and eras.

A

abhidheya: The stage of performing regulated activities to revive one's relationship with the Lord.

abhiṣeka: Method of worship, often expressed in puja, or purifying ritual practice.

abhyāsa: Practice; determination.

ācamana: A ritual of purification, in which one sips water and simultaneously chants names of the Supreme Lord.

ācāra: Conduct.

ācārya: The spiritual master, guru.

acintya-bhedābheda-tattva: Lord Chaitanya's "simultaneously one and different" teaching, which establishes the inconceivable, simultaneous oneness and difference of the Lord and His expansions.

acyuta-gotra: Divine family of Vaishnavas.

adhikāra: Qualification; capacity to understand.

Āgamas: Scriptures delineating the path of tantra.

ahaitukī: Without fraudulent motivation.

ahantā; Without violence; nonviolent.

aikāntikī: Exclusive.

aiśvarya: Wealth; power; opulence.

ājñā gurūṇām avicāraṇīyā: Obeying the spiritual master's order without argument.

ajño paṇḍita-mānī: The pride of thinking oneself learned, despite the fact that one is ignorant.

akiñcana: One who possesses nothing in this world, but Krishna.

akrodha paramānanda: One who is free of anger and full of supreme joy.

alasa: Laziness; being indifferent to the effort needed to make progress in spiritual life.

amānī: Without desire for prestige.

āmnāya: Revealed truth.

amogha-vāk: Disciplined in speech and completely free from engaging in conversation on trivial matters; one who speaks only about Krishna.

anantavat: Possessing no end, being unlimited.

anasūyaḥ: Nonenvious.

anubhāvas: External symptoms of ecstatic love for Krishna.

anuddhata-matiḥ: Steadiness of will.

anumāna: Inference.

anumṛtyu: Always subject to death.

antaryāmī: The Supersoul within.

anvaya: Directly; family.

anyāya: Unethical, dishonest, or improper activities.

anyāyopārjita-dhana: Earning money by illegal or immoral means.

apratihatā: Uninterrupted.

Apsaras: Heavenly courtesans.

āpyāyaana: A purifying procedure.

arcana: A set of procedures followed in Deity worship.

arcana-mārga: The path of regulated Deity worship.

arcāsu kṛta-dhīḥ: Expert and faithful in worship.

arghya: Water mixed with auspicious substances and offered to an honored guest, either sprinkled on their head or offered into their hands.

artha: Economic development, one of the four standard goals of human life.

arthāḥ: Meaning; purport.

ārūḍha-cyuta: One who has fallen after climbing a mountain.

ashram: A temple or dwelling for spiritual practice. The term *four ashrams* refers to four stages of one's spiritual life: ***brahmacharya*** (student), ***grihastha*** (householder), ***vanaprastha*** (retired person), and ***sannyasa*** (renunciate).

āśrami: Renunciant.

āśraya: Shelter; one who is the source and support of all.

āśraya-vigraha: The manifestation of the Lord of whom one must take shelter.

Aṣṭottara-śata-śrī: "One who possesses 108 kinds of opulence"; in other words, one who possesses unlimited glory and good fortune; honorary title for Vaishnava ***ācārya.***

asūyā: Seeing fault where there is virtue; enmity, anger, jealousy.

asūya-grasta: Vengefulness.

avadāta: Spotless; pure.

avadātānvayah: Born into a spotless (without scandal) family.

avadhūta: A spiritually advanced person whose activities are not restricted by social convention; one who is above all rules and regulations.

avāg-vādī: Someone who likes to talk about others' sinful activities.

avatāra: A partially or fully empowered incarnation of the Lord who descends from the spiritual sky to the material universe with a particular mission described in scriptures.

avatāri: The original Supreme Lord, from whom all ***avatāras*** expand.

āyatana: Place, home, or refuge.

āyatanavat: Having a refuge or place.

B

bahirvāsa: Outer garment.

bahv-āśī: Gluttony.

bhaga: Opulence.

Bhagavan: The Supreme Personality of Godhead, who possesses in full the six opulences (***bhagas***), namely, wealth, strength, fame, beauty, knowledge, and renunciation.

bhāgavata-dharma: The principles of devotional service to the Supreme Lord.

bhāgavata paramparā: Disciplic succession.

bhāgya: Good fortune; accumulated piety that comes from activities that lead to or awaken devotion.

bhajana: Loving devotional service to the Supreme Lord, performed favorably and free from the selfish motives of profit and liberation; a devotional hymn.

bhakta: A devotee; a worshipper; a practitioner of bhakti.

bhakti: Loving devotional service to the Supreme Lord; bhakti in practice is considered to be the prime means of spiritual success, and perfected bhakti, pure love of God, the ultimate goal of life.

bhakti yoga: The spiritual discipline of linking to the Supreme Lord through pure devotional service.

Bharata or **Bharatavarsha:** The planet Earth, named after Bharata the son of Rsabhadeva; in a more restricted sense, greater India.

bhāravāhi: The carrier of a heavy load; specifically, those bearing the burden of collected scriptural knowledge that has no connection to the Lord.

bhāva: Emotion; sentiment; particularly, ecstasy in love of God.

bheda: Difference.

bhedābheda-prakāśa: A simultaneously different and yet nondifferent manifestation.

bheda-vāda: Dualism.

bhoga-lālasa: Greed for material sense gratification.

bhraṣṭa-vrata: Being incapable of keeping one's word or maintaining the principles that are favorable to devotional life.

bīja: Seed.

bīja-mantra: The seed sound or essential sound of a mantra.

Brahma: The first finite living being in the material creation. He was born from the lotus growing from the navel of ***Garbhodaka-śāyī Viṣṇu***. At the beginning of creation, and again at the start of each day of his life, Brahma engineers the appearance of all the species and the planets on which they reside. He is the first teacher of the Vedas and the final material authority to whom the demigods resort when belabored by their opponents.

brahmacārī: Celibate student.

brahma-jñāna: Knowledge of the Absolute.

Brahmaloka: Realm of Lord Brahma.

Brahman: The impersonal, all-pervasive aspect of the Supreme Truth; the transcendental sound of the Vedas.

brāhmaṇa: A member of the class of educators, law makers, scholars, and preachers of dharma, the first of the four occupational classes in the ***varṇāśrama*** social system.

brahmaṇi: The wife of a brāhmana.

brahma-vidyā: Knowledge of the Absolute.

C

caraṇāmṛta: The water that has been used to bathe the feet of the Supreme Lord or His devotee. Normally collected after the daily worship of the Deity, one honors ***caraṇāmṛta*** by sipping it and sprinkling it on one's head.

chaitya-guru: The Supersoul, the expansion of Krishna who is seated as the spiritual master within the heart of the living being.

cid-rūpa-prakṛti: Spiritual nature.

cintamaṇi: A spiritual mystically potent gemstone ("touchstone") found in the transcendental realm. It fulfills all the desires of one who possesses it. When applied to a metal, it transforms it into gold.

D

dakṣiṇā: Alms, particularly offered to a guru or a holy person.

dāmbhika: Hypocrisy or advertising oneself as religious when in fact one is not.

dānta: Sense-controlled.

daridra: Poverty; real poverty is expressed when one does not make the effort to earn the wealth of love for God.

demigods: Empowered beings with vast intelligence and influence for administration of the material universe on behalf of the Supreme Lord.

dharma: Religious principles; individual duty. In another sense, dharma is the inseparable nature of a thing that distinguishes it, like the heat of fire or the sweetness of sugar.

dharma-śāstras: Twenty great law books written by seers such as Yajnavalkya.

dhīmān: Intelligent.

digvijayi: One who has conquered everyone, particularly by his erudition.

dīkṣā: Spiritual initiation.

dīkṣā-guru: Initiating guru.

dīkṣā-mantra: The mantra given by the guru at the time of spiritual initiation.

dīna-dayārdra-nātha: The Lord, who is merciful to the destitute and distressed.

dīpana: Purifying procedure.

dīrgha-sūtrī: One who puts off to tomorrow what can be done today.

divya-jñāna: Transcendental knowledge .

doṣa-dṛṣṭi: Fault-finding.

durātmā: A wicked person.

duṣṭa: Wicked; bad; vengeful.

Dvapara Yuga: The third of four eons (yuga) that form the cycle of universal time. The latest Dvapara Yuga, which ended about five thousand years ago, witnessed the descent of Krishna.

E

eka-daṇḍi: Single-staff, symbol of the Sankarite sannyasis.

G

gandha-vāha: Carrier of fragrances; one of the names for the wind.

garimā-nidhiḥ: As deep as the ocean.

Gaudiya Vaishnava: One who is a follower of Sri Krishna Chaitanya Mahaprabhu and worships, through the practice of bhakti and the recitation of the Holy Name, the divine couple Sri Sri Radha and Krishna.

ghara-pāgalā: Householder madmen.

Goloka Vrindavan: The highest spiritual planet in the kingdom of the Supreme Lord, Lord Krishna's personal abode.

Gopāla: A name for Krishna, which refers to His form as a young cowherd.

Gopāla mantra: A confidential ten-syllables hymn to ***Gopāla.***

gopana: A purification ritual.

gopī: A cowherd girl.

gopīcandan: Type of clay used to mark the body ***(tilaka)***.

Goswami or ***gosāi:*** One who has mastered the senses.

gotra: Family lineage.

gṛhastha: Householder.

gṛhī: House.

guhyatama: Confidential.

guṇa-nindakaḥ: Someone who out of envy finds fault even in another's virtues.

guṇas: The three modes of material nature, or controlling principles, ***sattva-guṇa*** (goodness), ***raja-guṇa*** (passion), and ***tama-guṇa*** (ignorance).

guru: Literally: ***gu*** "darkness," ***ru*** "that which counteracts"; spiritual master.

guru-daivatātmā: The process of making the spiritual master one's personal Deity.

guru-pādāśrayaḥ: Taking shelter of a spiritual master.

guru-paramparā: Disciplic succession.

gurūpasatti: Approaching the spiritual master.

guru-pūjā: Worship of the spiritual master.

guru-tattva: The principles defining a spiritual master.

gurv-ātma-daivataḥ: The spiritual master as one's personal worshipable Deity.

gurv-avajñā: Insubordination to the spiritual master .

H

haṁsa: Swan.

hari-kathā: Topics of Lord Hari, Krishna.

harināma-saṅkīrtana: Congregational chanting of the Holy Names of the Supreme Lord.

hetu-vāda-rataḥ: One who engages in useless speculation or argumentation.

hetu-vādin: Dry speculator.

homa: Fire sacrifice.

homa-mantra-parāyaṇaḥ: Devoted to the performance of sacrifice and the recitation of mantras.

I

iṣṭa-devatā: The form of the Lord one desires to attain.

J

jāgrata: Awakened state.

japa: Repeated chanting of a mantra; particularly in a soft voice, quietly to oneself.

jāti goswāmī: The claim of hereditary guru privilege.

jīva: Living entity.

jñāna: Knowledge.

jñāna-yoga: The spiritual discipline of cultivating transcendental knowledge.

jñānī: One who is engaged in the cultivation of knowledge (especially by philosophical speculation).

jyotiṣmat: Luminous.

K

kaitava: Fraudulent.

Kali: The predominating personality of Kali Yuga.

Kali Yuga: The last of four eons (yuga) that form the cycle of universal time. It is also known as the "age of quarrel and hypocrisy."

kalpa: Ritual.

kāma: Lust; the desire to gratify one's own senses.

kaniṣṭhā: Literally: "one who is not fully fixed in devotional services"; beginner.

karma: Action or, more specifically, any material action that brings a reaction binding us to the material world. According to the law of karma, if we cause pain and suffering to other living beings, we must endure pain and suffering in return.

karmī: One whose aim in life is to achieve material elevation by acting dutifully, especially by performing Vedic sacrifices.

kartals: Hand cymbals used in devotional singing.

kaṣṭa-vṛtti: Having great difficulty making a living; those who make little or no effort to advance in material life sometimes take shelter of a spiritual master in order to extract some benefit for themselves and their family.

kathā: Tale; discussion.

kavayaḥ: Knowledgeable persons.

kavi-karṇapūra: The name given by Lord Sri Krishna Chaitanya Mahaprabhu to the youngest son of Sivananda Sena; literally: "the poet who has described the ornament on the ears of the ***gopīs*** (Krishna)."

kevala: Only.

khala: Giving pain to others, like a poisonous snake that is by nature dangerous to everyone.

kirtan: The primary devotional practice of chanting the Supreme Lord's glories.

kliṣṭa: The need to burden oneself with unnecessary tasks.

krodha-rahita: Free from anger.

kṛpālayaḥ: A reservoir of compassion.

kṛpaṇa: Miserliness; refers to someone who is reluctant to spend money.

kṛṣṇa-bhakti: Devotion to Krishna.

kṛṣṇa-līlā: Krishna's transcendental pastimes.

kṛṣṇa-mantra: The hymn dedicated to Lord Krishna.

kṛṣṇa-prema: Pure ecstatic love for Krishna.

kṛṣṇa-tattva-vit: Knower of Krishna.

kṛtajñaḥ: Showing gratitude toward others, especially one's guru and the Vaishnavas.

krūra-ceṣṭa: Engaging in cruel activities, like murder.

kṣaṇa: A very short period of time.

kṣatriya: A warrior who is inclined to fight and lead others, the second of the four occupational classes in the ***varṇāśrama*** social system.

kula: Guru system.

kulādhidaivata: The family's worshipable Deity.

L

laghu: Light.

Lakh or ***lakṣa:*** One hundred thousand.

līlā: A transcendental pastime or activity performed by the Lord or his devotee.

M

mad-abhijña: "One who knows My nature well"; characteristic of the guru; the qualified guru has personal and direct experience of Krishna's glories.

mad-ātmaka: "One who has made Me the center of his life"; characteristic of the guru; the qualified guru has given his soul, or his entire inner life, over to Krishna.

mahad-atikrama: A breach of etiquette toward an elevated person.

madhyama: Intermediate.

madhyama-adhikārī: A devotee whose advancement in spiritual life is midway between the neophyte (***kaniṣṭha***) and advanced (***uttama***) levels.

madya: Alcoholic beverages.

mahā-bhāgavata: A devotee in the highest stage of devotional life.

mahā-mantra: The greatest mantra for deliverance:

Hare Krishna Hare Krishna
Krishna Krishna Hare Hare
Hare Rama Hare Rama
Rama Rama Hare Hare

mahānta: The great devotee.

***Mahārāja* (Maharaja):** "Great king"; the spiritual master is the greatest of kings, in the sense that he is the lord of the transcendental realm.

maithuna: Sexual relationships.

mālā: Garland; a string of 108 beads use for chanting.

malina: Unclean.

māṁsa: Meat.

mānasika: Mental.

mānasika-japa: Mantra recitation within the mind.

mantra: A mystical formula of invocation or incantation.

mantra-guru: The spiritual teacher who imparts the mantra to the disciple; one who gives initiation.

mantra-sāra: The essence of all mantras.

maṭha: Temple; ashram.

mati: Determination.

matsara-grasta: Envy.

matsya: Fish.

maya: Illusion.

Mayavadis: Impersonalists.

mokṣa or ***mukti:*** Liberation from the cycle of birth and death.

monism: A view that there is only one kind of ultimate substance; the view that reality is one unitary organic whole with no independent parts.

mṛdaṅga: Two-headed clay drum.

mudra: Fried grain.

mūla-mantra: Root mantra; a short incantation uttered before one offers an item of worship to the Lord.

N

nāma-bhajana: Congregational chanting of the Holy Names of the Supreme Personality of Godhead, usually accompanied by hand cymbals (***karatālas***) and clay drums (*mṛdaṅgas*).

nāmābhāsa: Offense to the Holy Name.

nāmācārya: The authority on the chanting of the Holy Names of Lord Krishna; a title conveyed upon Srila Haridas Thakura by Sri Caitanya Mahaprabhu.

namaḥ: Word of respect denoting the act of offering or sacrificing to the Lord.

nāmāparādha: Offensive chanting of the Holy Name.

nibodhata: Become aware of.

nigama: Another name for Veda.

nindita: Engaging in activities that make one universally despised or criticized .

ninditāśrama-sevaka: One does not compromise with people who are engaged in sinful activities to make a living in order to gain personal benefit.

nirapekṣā: Independent.

niṣṇāta: Immersed.

niṣṇātam: Fully conversant.

niṣṇāyāt: Expertise characterized by devotion to Krishna.

nityānanda: Eternal joy; the name of Sri Chaitanya Mahaprabhu's counterpart and chief associate.

nṛṇām: Of human beings.

nyāsa: A purification ritual.

P

Pañcarātra: Vedic literatures describing the process of Deity worship.

parā bhakti: Highest devotion.

para-dāra-rata: Attachment to the wives of other men.

para-duḥkha-duḥkhī: Title for a Vaishnava; one who has no personal troubles but has compassion for those that are unhappy or in trouble.

paramahaṁsa: "Supreme swan"; one who is able to seek the essence; a title given to anyone who is in the highest stage of the renounced order.

pāramārthika: Real, essential, true, related to the highest spiritual truth.

paramarthika-guru: True spiritual teacher.

Param-brahma: The Supreme Brahman, the Personality of Godhead, Lord Krishna.

para-tattva: Transcendental truth.

paribabhrima: Wander aimlessly.

paripraśna: The act of appropriate inquiry.

paripraśnena: Asking submissive questions; spiritual inquiry.

parivrājakācārya: Used to designate a stage of the ***sannyāsa-āśrama***, referring to one who travels in order to teach the conditioned souls about devotional service to Krishna.

paruṣa-vādī: The speaking of harsh words.

phālgu-vairāgya: False renunciation.

piśuna: Backbiting; slanderous, calumnious, treacherous behavior.

Prabhupada: Literally: "one who has taken shelter at the lotus feet of the Lord"; honorary title used before or after the name of a revered Vaishnava ***ācārya.***

prakāśavān: Self-manifest and self-luminous.

prakāśavat: Endowed with splendor.

prakāśa-vigraha: The Lord's manifestation.

prakṛṣṭā-janma: The second "birth" of ***brāhmaṇa*** initiation.

prakṛti: Material nature.

prameya: Principal point; that which is provable.

praṇa: Life air.

pranayama: Vital force; life air.

praṇipāt: The act of surrendering.

praṇipāta: Offering of obeisance before the spiritual master.

praṇipātena: Surrender with humility.

prāpya varān: Blessings that can be attained.

prasāda: Food presented to a Deity (Krishna); mercy.

prasthāna-traya: Three reliable sources of scriptures namely ***śruti***, ***śmṛti***, and ***sūtras***.

pratyakṣa: Direct perception.

prayojana: Pure ecstatic love of God, the highest and perfected stage of life.

prema: Pure ecstatic love of God.

prema-bhakti: The highest and perfected stage in the progressive development of devotional service.

preṣṭha: Most dear.

priya-darśanaḥ: One who has a pleasing appearance.

priya-vāk: One who speaks pleasingly.

puja: Formal worship of the Supreme Lord or some demigod or respected person.

Purāṇas: The histories of the universe, supplements to the Vedas. There are eighteen major ***Purāṇas*** and many secondary ones. The major ***Purāṇas*** are divided into three groups of six, meant for readers in each of the three modes of material nature.

pūrṇa: Full.

puraścaraṇa-vrata: A traditional ritual performance for purification.

puruṣādhama: The lowest of men; morally destitute person.

puruṣārthāḥ: Objectives of human life.

puruṣottama: Literally: "the most exalted person"; name for Lord Krishna, the Supreme Person.

R

rāgānuga-bhakti (anurāga-patha): Spontaneous devotional service; spontaneous devotion characteristic of the inhabitants of Vrindavan.

rāgī: Attachment to material sense objects.

rahasya: Esoteric meaning or significance of rituals.

raja: King.

rasa: "Transcendental taste or mellow"; the five primary spiritual ***rasas*** are moods in relationship with the Supreme Lord: reverence, servitude, friendship, parental affection, and conjugal love; rasa also indicates the boundless pleasure enjoyed in such reciprocations.

rati: Love; affection.

rogī: A sickly person.

ṛṣi: A sage who performs austerities.

ruṣṭa: Anger.

S

śabda: Sound; revealed knowledge through hearing.

śabda brahma: The revealed knowledge of the Vedic scriptures.

sad-ācāra: Correct or proper behavior.

sad-guru: Bona fide spiritual master.

sādhaka: Practitioner.

sādhana: Regulated practice.

sadhu: A saintly person.

sa-guṇaḥ: Characteristic of the guru; one who is virtuous.

sahajiyā: Literally: "natural"; refers also to a practitioner of a form of tantric Vaishnavism.

śālagrāma-śilā: Sacred black stone, revered and worshipped as a Deity of Lord Krishna or Shiva.

śama: Tranquility; control of the mind.

samāmnāya: Complete knowledge.

sambandha-jñāna: Knowledge of one's original relationship with Lord Krishna.

sāmīpya: The liberation of becoming a personal associate of the Supreme Lord.

samit-pāṇiḥ: Carrying fuel for the sacrifice; an attitude one needs to develop when approaching the spiritual master.

sammohana: Enchanting; the name of a mantra that reveals the Lord Krishna's sweet Vrindavan form.

sampradāya: Tradition; lineage.

samskāra: Mental impression; purification ceremony.

sanātana-dharma: "Eternal activity of the soul"; the eternal duty of the living being—to render service to the Supreme Lord, which in this age is executed mainly by chanting the ***mahā-mantra*** or Holy Name.

sandhya: Religious practices.

saṅkalpa: Determination to perform any ritual observance.

saṅkīrtana: Congregational chanting of the Holy Name.

saṅkīrtana-yajña: The congregational chanting of the Holy Name viewed as the topmost Vedic sacrifice.

sannyasi: One in the renounced order of life, the final stage of spiritual progress in the ***varṇāśrama*** system; sannyasis take a vow of lifetime celibacy.

śānta: Peaceful.

sarāgrāhi: Essence seekers.

śaraṇāgati or śaraṇāpatti: The process of surrender to the Lord; seeking refuge.

sarva-bhūta-hite rata: Characteristic of the guru; one who is engaged in serving the welfare of all living beings by extensively glorifying Krishna's names, forms, qualities, and pastimes, for their benefit.

sarva-śāstravit: Characteristic of the guru; one knows all the scriptures.

shastra: Scripture.

śaṭha: Treachery; refers to someone who is two-faced, a cheater, or someone who acts sweetly but who has a nefarious purpose.

sat-saṅga: Good association; association of devotees.

sattva: One of the three modes of material nature; goodness.

satya-dhṛti: So determined to find the truth that one is able to resist all distractions.

Satya Yuga: The first of four eons (yuga) that form the cycle of universal time; the golden age in which humanity is righteous and devoid of wickedness—the age of truth, virtue, and righteousness.

sāyujyā: The liberation of merging into the spiritual effulgence of the Supreme Lord.

sevā: Devotional service.

sevayā: Render service.

siddhānta: The perfect conclusion drawn from the Vedic scriptures.

śikṣā-guru: The instructing spiritual master.

śiṣya-vatsalaḥ: Characteristic of the guru; one who is as affectionate to his disciples as he would be to a son or daughter and does everything to further their advancement in devotional life.

śiva-saṁstuta: Praised by Lord Shiva, or auspiciously praised.

Six Goswamis: A group of devotional teachers (gurus) from the Gaudiya Vaishnava tradition who lived in India during the fifteenth and sixteenth centuries. They are closely associated with the land of Vrindavan where they spent much time in service of Chaitanya Mahaprabhu.

smriti: "What is remembered," the secondary Vedic literatures, which need not be passed down verbatim but may be reworded by the sages who transmit them in each age. The ***Purāṇas*** and ***Dharma-śāstras*** are among the smṛtis.

snigdha: Affectionate.

śraddhā: Faith.

śraddhāvān: Characteristic of the guru; one who possesses strong faith.

śrauta-paramparā: The disciplic succession based on hearing.

śravaṇa: Hearing.

Sri/Srila: These two honorifics are given to spiritual teachers out of respect. Of the two, the latter is particularly reserved for saints.

śṛṅgāra-rasa: Amorous love.

śrutis: "That what has been heard," the original Vedas, meant to be passed on orally from generation to generation without change. They are considered coexistent with the Supreme Lord Himself.

śuciḥ: Characteristic of the guru; pure within and without.

śuddha: Pure goodness.

śuddha-bhakti: Pure devotion.

śuddhādvaita: Pure non-dualism, the philosophy propagated by Srila Visnuswami.

śuddhātmā: Characteristic of the guru; one whose heart is pure, for he is always thinking of Krishna.

śūdra: A member of the laborer class, the last of the four occupational classes in the ***varṇāśrama*** social system.

sujñāna: Proper knowledge.

śuśrūṣā: Desire to hear; performing personal service to the spiritual master, such as bathing him or massaging his feet.

suveśaḥ: The guru wears the appropriate dress for someone who is worshiping the Lord.

svābhāvikī: Spontaneous.

svāhā: Word denoting the act of offering or sacrificing to the Lord.

sva-tattva: The true nature of the self as worshiper of the Lord.

svayaṁ-bhagavān: The undifferentiated, nondual Supreme Truth and the son of the king of Vraja.

svocitācāra-tat-paraḥ: The guru should be faithful to the religious duties his own spiritual master has ordained for him.

T

tadīya: Servant; everything belonging to the Lord.

tad-vijñāna: Knowing fully the Supreme Lord, through the process of devotional service; transcendental knowledge.

tantra: One of the later Hindu or Buddhist scriptures dealing especially with techniques and rituals including meditative and sexual practices.

tapas: Penance.

tapasā: By austerity.

tarpaṇa: Oblations.

taruṇaḥ: Characteristics of the guru; one who is youthful; one whose enthusiasm to serve the Lord is as vigorous as that of a youth.

***Ṭhākura* (Thakur):** Deity or divinity.

tilaka: Auspicious mark of sacred clay, applied daily on the forehead and the body to mark one's identity as a servant of the Lord.

tīrtha: Holy place.

Treta Yuga: The second of four eons (yuga) that form the cycle of universal time.

tridaṇḍa: Triple-staff order.

tulasi: Holy basil plant.

tyāgīs: Renunciants.

U

upādhi: Identification with bodily designations; deceit.

ūhāpoha-prakāra-jñaḥ: Characteristic of the guru; one who is expert in the art of debate.

upāṁśu-japa: Mantra recitation in a low voice.

upanayana: A boy's investiture with the sacred thread, a ceremony that marks the beginning of his Vedic education.

upaśama: Supremely peaceful .

upaśamāśrayam: One whose desires for the temporal have been quieted and who is thus free from the control of lust and greed, as having taken shelter of ***bhakti-yoga***.

V

vācika: Audible; verbal.

vācika-japa: Audible mantra recitation.

vaidhi-bhakti: The regulative practice of devotional service to the Lord.

vairāgya: Detachment; renunciation.

Vaishnava: Literally: "one who belongs to Lord Vishnu." One who is initiated into a Vishnu mantra and who is devoted to worshipping Lord Vishnu, is a Vaishnava.

vaiśya: A member of the mercantile or agricultural class, the third of the four occupational classes in the ***varṇāśrama*** social system.

vāmācāra: Follower of left-handed tantra.

vānaprastha: Retired person; one of the four stages in one's spiritual life.

vartma-pradarśaka-guru: Guru who indicates the path of spiritual life and practice.

varṇāśrama: The Vedic social system, consisting of four occupational divisions (***varṇas***) and four stages of spiritual development ***(āśramas).***

varṇāśrama-dharma: Religious principles or duty associated with the Vedic social system. See ***varṇāśrama.***

vāsanā: Latent desires or deep longings that are in our subconscious.

Vasudeva: The father of Krishna.

Vedanta: The conclusion of Vedic philosophy.

Vedas: Revealed scriptures eternal like the Supreme Lord; large body of text composed in Vedic Sanskrit.

veda-vit: Characteristic of the guru; one who knows the Vedas.

vibhinnāṁśa: Separated part; refers to the individual soul.

vidhi-marga (maryādā patha): Path of scriptural injunctions.

viduṣāṁ vairī: Envy; refers to one who is inimical to those who know more than him.

vijñāna: Practical realization of spiritual knowledge.

vimarśakaḥ: Characteristic of the guru; one who has good judgment.

virodhi-tattva: The things that are inimical to attaining spiritual perfection.

viṣaya: The object of worship; an object of material sense gratification.

viṣaya-vigraha: Object of devotion or love.

viṣayādiṣu lolupaḥ: One who is excessively attached to his wife and children or to the sense objects related to taste, touch, sight, smell, and sound.

viśeṣa: Special attribute.

Vishnu: An expansion of Lord Krishna, the Supreme Personality of Godhead.

viśiṣṭa: The one possessing the special attribute .

Viṣṇupāda: One who sits at the feet of Lord Vishnu.

viśrambha: Firm faith based on intimate understanding.

viśrambheṇa guroḥ sevā: Serving the guru with deep faith and affection.

Vraja: Another name for Vrindavan, the transcendental abode of Lord Krishna.

Vraja gopīs: Cowherd girls of Vrindavan, worshipped for their unconditional, pure, and spontaneous devotion to Krishna.

vyavahārika: Conventional, functional, relative.

vyavaharika-guru: Relative teacher.

Y

Yadus: Members of the Yadu dynasty. Lord Krishna appeared as a member of this dynasty.

yantra: A geometrical diagram revered and usually used like an icon.

yoga: The path or practice of linking oneself to the Supreme.

yogi: One who practices one of the many authorized forms of yoga, or processes of spiritual purification.

yuga: Eon; era.

yukta-vairāgya: Engaged detachment; renunciation in connection to the Lord.

About the Author

"He has love for his guru; and let it be known
that his life is one with his words."

—Srila Bhaktisiddhanta Saraswati Thakur Prabhupada on Srila B.P. Puri Goswami Thakur

Srila Bhakti Pramode Puri Goswami Thakur, born in Ganganandapur in Jessore district (present-day Bangladesh) on October 19, 1898, dedicated his life, spanning over a century, to the service of his guru, the Vaishnavas, and his Deities. He taught and exemplified the spiritual concepts of pure devotion, or *Kṛṣṇa-bhakti*, as expressed within the Gaudiya Vaisnava tradition.

In 1915, Srila Puri Maharaj first met his guru, Srila Bhaktisiddhanta Saraswati Thakur Prabhupada in Sri Mayapur and Srila Puri Maharaja would often recount that upon seeing Srila Prabhupada for the first time, he knew in his heart that he had met his spiritual master. Following his guru's directives, Srila Puri Maharaj would, over the course of more than eighty years, edit, write for, publish, and help distribute countless spiritual publications on Vaishnava philosophy and theology. His writings reflect the disciplined eye of a scholar who expresses with grace and directness profound scriptural conclusions.

In 1989, at the age of ninety-one, Srila Puri Maharaja established the Sri Gopinath Gaudiya Math in Ishodyan, Sri Mayapur, which is now in the care of his successor Srila B.B. Bodhayan Maharaja. At that time, he began accepting disciples, and now his mission has temples and followers all across India and other parts of the globe.

Most of Srila Puri Maharaj's articles were published over the years in various magazines, including the *Gaudiya* and *Chaitanya Vani*, a monthly magazine of the Chaitanya Gaudiya Math where he was president of the editorial board from its founding in 1961 until his disappearance in 1999. These articles are now being collected, translated into English, and presented in beautifully designed and illustrated publications. To date, Mandala Publishing has released numerous magazines and several volumes based on these articles, including *The Heart of Krishna* (1995), *Art of Sadhana* (1999), *Of Love and Separation* (2001), *Samadhi* (2004), and *The Heart of a Vaishnava* (2004).